Interpreting the CMMI®

A Process Improvement Approach

OTHER AUERBACH PUBLICATIONS

The ABCs of IP Addressing
Gilbert Held
ISBN: 0-8493-1144-6

The ABCs of TCP/IP
Gilbert Held
ISBN: 0-8493-1463-1

**Building an Information Security
Awareness Program**
Mark B. Desman
ISBN: 0-8493-0116-5

The Complete Book of Middleware
Judith Myerson
ISBN: 0-8493-1272-8

**Computer Telephony Integration,
2nd Edition**
William A. Yarberry, Jr.
ISBN: 0-8493-1438-0

**Global Information Warfare:
How Businesses, Governments, and
Others Achieve Objectives and Attain
Competitive Advantages**
Andy Jones, Gerald L. Kovacich,
and Perry G. Luzwick
ISBN: 0-8493-1114-4

Information Security Architecture
Jan Killmeyer Tudor
ISBN: 0-8493-9988-2

**Information Security Management
Handbook, 4th Edition, Volume 1**
Harold F. Tipton and Micki Krause, Editors
ISBN: 0-8493-9829-0

**Information Security Management
Handbook, 4th Edition, Volume 2**
Harold F. Tipton and Micki Krause, Editors
ISBN: 0-8493-0800-3

**Information Security Management
Handbook, 4th Edition, Volume 3**
Harold F. Tipton and Micki Krause, Editors
ISBN: 0-8493-1127-6

**Information Security Management
Handbook, 4th Edition, Volume 4**
Harold F. Tipton and Micki Krause, Editors
ISBN: 0-8493-1518-2

**Information Security Policies,
Procedures, and Standards:
Guidelines for Effective Information
Security Management**
Thomas R. Peltier
ISBN: 0-8493-1137-3

Information Security Risk Analysis
Thomas R. Peltier
ISBN: 0-8493-0880-1

**A Practical Guide to Security Engineering
and Information Assurance**
Debra Herrmann
ISBN: 0-8493-1163-2

**The Privacy Papers:
Managing Technology and Consumers,
Employee, and Legislative Action**
Rebecca Herold
ISBN: 0-8493-1248-5

Securing and Controlling Cisco Routers
Peter T. Davis
ISBN: 0-8493-1290-6

**Securing E-Business Applications and
Communications**
Jonathan S. Held and John R. Bowers
ISBN: 0-8493-0963-8

**Securing Windows NT/2000:
From Policies to Firewalls**
Michael A. Simonyi
ISBN: 0-8493-1261-2

Six Sigma Software Development
Christine B. Tayntor
ISBN: 0-8493-1193-4

**A Technical Guide to IPSec Virtual Private
Networks**
James S. Tiller
ISBN: 0-8493-0876-3

Telecommunications Cost Management
Brian DiMarsico, Thomas Phelps IV,
and William A. Yarberry, Jr.
ISBN: 0-8493-1101-2

AUERBACH PUBLICATIONS

www.auerbach-publications.com
To Order Call: 1-800-272-7737 • Fax: 1-800-374-3401
E-mail: orders@crcpress.com

Interpreting the CMMI®

A Process Improvement Approach

MARGARET K. KULPA
KENT A. JOHNSON

AUERBACH PUBLICATIONS

A CRC Press Company

Boca Raton   London   New York   Washington, D.C.

Special permission to reproduce and adapt portions of CMMI^SM for Systems Engineering/Software Engineering/Integrated Product and Process Development/Supplier Sourcing, Version 1.1, Staged Representation (CMMI-SE/SW/IPPD/SS, V1.1, Staged), CMU/SEI-2002-TR-012© 2002; CMMI^SM for Systems Engineering/Software Engineering/Integrated Product and Process Development/Supplier Sourcing, Version 1.1, Continuous Representation (CMMI-SE/SW/IPPD/SS, V1.1, Continuous), CMU/SEI-2002-TR-011© 2002; Appraisal Requirements for CMMI^SM, Version 1.1 (ARC, V1.1), CMU/SEI-2001-TR-034© 2001; and Standard CMMI^SM Appraisal Method for Process Improvement (SCAMPI^SM), Version 1.1: Method Definition Document, CMU/SEI-2001-HB-001© 2001 by Carnegie Mellon University, is granted by the Software Engineering Institute.

Library of Congress Cataloging-in-Publication Data

Kulpa, Margaret K.
    Interpreting the CMMI® : a process improvement approach / Margaret K. Kulpa, Kent A. Johnson.
        p. cm.
    Includes bibliographical references and index.
    ISBN 0-8493-1654-5 (alk. paper)
    1. Capability maturity model (Computer software) 2. comptuer software--Development.
I. Johnson, Kent A. II. Title.

    QA76.758.K85 2003
    005.1'0685--dc21

                                                                                        2002043910

Visit the CRC Press Web site at www.crcpress.com

Contents

About the Authors

Margaret Kulpa is the Chief Operating Officer of AgileDigm, Incorporated. As such, she provides senior-level management support for SEI initiatives and software process improvement. Her work includes writing materials and providing training for Software Capability Evaluations (SCEs), Capability Maturity Model training, and process improvement training, as well as performing these evaluations and improvement activities. Ms. Kulpa has over 30 years of consulting experience. She has experience in all phases of the system development life cycle, focusing on management, coding, quality assurance and testing, training, database design and analysis, technical writing and editing, business process reengineering (BPR), and electronic data processing (EDP) auditing (twenty years total, including ten years of management experience in large-scale mainframe and client/server applications). Her most recent assignments have involved software process improvement (eleven years) and software performance engineering (three years). These services have been provided to federal government (U.S.) clients, as well as to the private sector. She is an SEI-authorized SCE Lead Evaluator and is also authorized by the SEI to teach both the Introduction to the CMM® and the SCE Team training course. She is an SCE Lead Evaluator for not only the Software CMM, but also for the Software Acquisition CMM and has performed over 60 SCEs. Ms. Kulpa was a featured speaker in the cutting-edge category at the 2002 Software Engineering Process Group (SEPG) annual conference in Phoenix, Arizona. Her presentation, entitled "CMMI — Not for the Little Guy?" discussed the advantages and disadvantages of small organizations thinking about transitioning to the CMMI from the CMM.

Ms. Kulpa was a member of the CMM version2 Author and Reviewer Team. She has worked with clients in five countries to improve their processes.

Kent A. Johnson is the Director of Systems Engineering for TeraQuest and an SEI-authorized CBA IPI[1] Lead Assessor, an authorized SCAMPI[2] Lead Assessor, and an authorized CMMI Instructor. Mr. Johnson's background includes over 25 years of experience in the development of complex software-intensive systems. He provides training, consulting, and assessments for clients working to improve their systems and software development capabilities. He works with clients in a variety of industries, and has successfully helped organizations go from Level 1 to Level 5. He has conducted over 20 formal assessments, including systems engineering assessments and several high-maturity software assessments. Internationally, he has helped clients in nine countries improve their systems and software processes.

Mr. Johnson is a former project manager of the Process and Methods Program at the Software Productivity Consortium (SPC). While at the SPC, he co-authored and led the team that created the software and system development method used by over 800 engineers in a dozen companies for the development of the F-22 Advanced Tactical Fighter. He is also a co-author of the book *Ada 95 Quality and Style* published by Springer. Prior to joining the SPC, he was a Senior Engineering Scientist at the Electronics and Space Division of Emerson Electric Company, where he successfully managed the development and integration of several complex software-intensive systems.

Mr. Johnson presents tutorials on systems and software engineering, process improvement, and development methodologies at international conferences. He is a past Chairman, International Council on Systems Engineering (INCOSE), Systems Architecture Working Group.

Notes

1. CMM®-Based Appraisals for Internal Process Improvement.
2. SCAMPI and SCAMPI Lead Assessor are service marks of Carnegie Mellon University, Pittsburgh, PA.

Chapter 1

Introduction

What Is the CMMI®?[1]

CMMI is an acronym (it is not a four-letter word); it stands for Capability Maturity Model Integration. Some people would say that the CMMI is a model with multiple representation while others would describe it as a set of models. But most will agree that the CMMI is a merger of process improvement models for systems engineering, software engineering, integrated product development, and software acquisition.

Some of the goals of the CMMI are to provide a common vocabulary across the set of models and to provide clarification on how these areas interrelate. The integrated model has both a continuous and staged architecture.

Why Did We Write This Book?

In this book we hope to show you some possible benefits of using the CMMI and some possible problems to be overcome when using the CMMI. We try to present a balanced viewpoint.

After using the CMMI with organizations in different parts of the world, we found that the new model is difficult for most people to pick up and use right away. Two of the problems in the CMMI include interpretation and organizational decisions. The model itself was written to cover many different organizational and project situations. An ambiguous style was intentionally chosen by the authors of the CMMI to fit these many situations. This ambiguity results in the need for a lot of interpretation and decision making by the model's users. We hope to help identify these decisions for you and provide a positive influence in your decision making.

How to Read This Book

We have tried to write this book for the widest audience possible — that is, for the experienced process improvement practitioner, the inexperienced practitioner, the CMMI expert, and the CMMI novice. This book is divided into three sections. Section I includes this chapter, up to and including Chapter 8. Chapter 1 introduces the reader to the purpose of this book and answers some questions in very general terms as to why to use the CMMI and how to use it. Chapters 2 through 8 discuss the structure of the CMMI and its process areas. Section II includes Chapters 9 through 20. Chapters 9 through 20 go more into the process improvement area and offer some of our suggestions and hints on how to apply the concepts proposed in the CMMI to your organization. These chapters often display tables, templates, and charts that may prove applicable in your improvement efforts. Section III of the book comprises the appendices. These appendices contain interesting bits of information and brief, summarized discussion points that were further explained in the preceding chapters. So, readers new to the CMMI should first concentrate on Chapters 2 through 8. The CMMI "expert" may wish to skip Chapters 2 through 8. The reader seeking help in process improvement techniques (whether using the CMMI or not) should focus on Chapters 9 through 20. And those of you who only want to skim through this book may find that the appendices are all you wish to read. However, we do caution those of you who skip to the appendices; most of the information contained in the appendices is only really understood after reading the entire book. Of course, everyone should read Chapter 1. If you have gotten this far, you are doing great. Give yourself a star. We thank you for buying this book. If you did not buy the book, but just borrowed it, we are happy about that too. At least you are reading something we sweated over. We hope you like it.

Why Use the CMMI?

Many readers will already know why they want to start using the CMMI in their organizations to drive their process improvement programs; some of the reasons we have heard include:

- You want to be on the cutting edge of process improvement.
- CMMI must be better than CMM because it is newer.
- You have a customer that is making you use CMMI.
- The "owner" of the CMM is telling you that it is a good thing to do and that they (the SEI[2]) will be sunsetting the model.

Some readers are looking for other reasons to invest in this model, such as:

- This model includes help, direction, and ideas about software engineering, systems engineering, supplier sourcing and integrated team development.
- One of the primary goals of the CMMI is to allow organizations to reduce the cost and confusion incurred from multiple assessments and multiple process improvement programs to cover both their systems and software engineering activities.

Family of CMMs

Most readers will come to this book with knowledge of the Capability Maturity Model (CMM), also known as the CMM for Software. So, to describe concepts within the CMMI, we will often compare the approaches taken in the CMMI to a similar topic in the CMM for Software. In some cases, we may describe the concept within the CMMI as it relates to other models, such as the Systems Engineering CMM (SE-CMM) or Systems Engineering Capability Model Electronic Industries Association (EIA) 731. But for the most part, we will stay within what some call the Family of CMMs. Some readers would, of course, want us to consider other models and evaluation approaches in our discussions, including, to name a few, the Software Development Capability Evaluation (SDCE), International Organization for Standardization (ISO) 9000, Six Sigma, etc.; however, that is not what this book is about.

Terminology

This book uses the language that has become a part of the process improvement community. This community has grown up around the family of CMMs. It includes process practitioners, process improvement specialists, evaluators, assessors, appraisers, project managers, and executives who have invested significant effort to implement, evaluate, and improve processes in a wide variety of domains. Unfortunately, not all the sources that make up the overall process improvement body of knowledge are consistent in their use of terms. For that reason, we define a number of terms throughout this book. In some cases, these definitions will come from a specific reference and we will note that reference in the text. In other cases, we will just give you our definition.

People first coming to model-based process improvement can misunderstand the term "model." These models are not intended to be architectural-type plans for your organization's processes. You do not just follow these steps and obtain a good process. Models are more a yardstick or guideline to determine what might be missing from your processes.

The term "organization" is used in a general sense throughout the book to mean the group that the process improvement initiative covers. In some cases, an organization is an entire company; in some cases, a division or department within a company; and in some cases, the group responsible for developing a specific product.

One more thing… "Data" are plural. Although most folks generally say, "the data is not yet available," proper grammar is to say, "the data are not yet available." So it may sound a little funny when you read it.

History of the CMMI

Here is a very short history of the CMMI — short because most readers of this book will already know this and because other sources can give you much more detail.

People were successfully using the Capability Maturity Model (CMM), which was designed for improving software processes and measuring the maturity of software processes in an organization. This success brought more and more attention to model-based process improvement in other areas and resulted in a number of other models being developed, including the:

- Systems Engineering CMM (SE-CMM)
- Software Acquisition Capability Maturity Model (SA-CMM)
- Integrated Product Development Team Model (IPD-CMM)
- System Engineering Capability Assessment Model (SECAM)
- Systems Engineering Capability Model (SECM)

Exhibit 1 shows the relative timeline for the primary models directly influencing the CMMI. It may be of interest to note that, as shown, the SECM is actually an integrated model in its own right; that is, an integration of two systems engineering models (the SE-CMM and SECAM) as shown

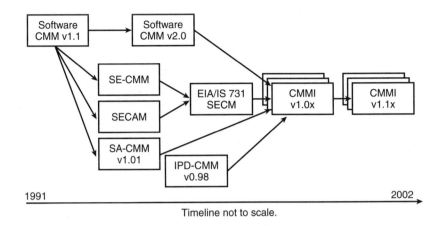

Exhibit 1. **Models Directly Influencing CMMI.**

by the two arrows coming into SECM. CMMI was most directly influenced by CMM v2.0c for software, SECM for systems engineering, SA-CMM for acquisition, and supplier sourcing and IPD-CMM for integrated teaming.

Some organizations that wanted to use this collection of models were confused because each model was slightly different. The new model — CMMI — is designed to integrate the plethora of models created throughout the years by the SEI and other organizations. The idea of reconciling these models with other methodologies and standards — ISO 9001, 15504, among others — was advanced. Several adopters of the SEI's software process improvement mantra, including the Department of Defense (DoD), requested a halt to the generation of more models and, instead, recommended that the SEI integrate the concepts expressed in these disparate models into one model. Hence, the journey toward CMMI began.

Some readers will take us to task for starting our history with the CMM for Software. They will be right to say that the CMM is based on years and years of quality and process improvement performed by many great and wonderful people. Because we do not think that merely mentioning Walter Shewart, W. Edwards Deming, Joseph Juran, and Philip Crosby helps the reader understand the CMMI, we have left them out of our history, but clearly the CMMI would not be here without their significant contributions in this area.

Assessment View versus Improvement View

It is often the case while working with organizations that we encounter two distinctly different views on how to use the CMMI. We call these views:

1. The assessment view
2. The process improvement view

The assessment view is more focused on what is the minimum required to satisfy the model and what is needed to pass the test (assessment or evaluation or SCAMPI). The process improvement view is more focused on what is best for your organization and what is needed to improve the organization.

An example of how these different views would address a CMMI practice can be seen in the area of how an organization would *objectively evaluate adherence* to the plans, processes, procedures, and methods within a process area.

Taking an assessment view, an organization might decide to have developers and engineers perform a review of each other's work. This approach looks like a quick way to get independent verification until you realize that these developers and engineers will still need to be trained in evaluation and will need additional budget and schedule to perform the evaluations. A dysfunctional assessment view might go as far as having one person reviewing all of a large program or project (clearly an overwhelming job for just one person) to get the checkmark during an assessment.

Taking a process improvement view, an organization would realize the need for clear responsibility defined for quality-related activities. Establishing an independent quality group staffed with trained and experienced professionals would go a long way toward ensuring that the organization continues to perform the processes as written. This group would need to be staffed at a sufficient level to be effective. In many cases, this means three to five percent of the technical staff, or more.

We have worked with many organizations, and our experience tells us that organizations that focus only on an assessment view will fail. They fail to truly satisfy the model, primarily because of the lack of institutionalization, but will also fail to provide any real business value to their organization in return for the expense.

Those organizations taking the process improvement view will succeed in providing business value and will also do much better in an assessment — yes, sometimes this requires hard work but this is the only truly successful path that we have seen. Therefore, this book will most often take the process improvement view.

Summary

The CMMI builds on a history of process improvement. The CMMI by its nature can impact a large part of your organization because it combines models from systems engineering, software engineering, acquisition, and integrated teaming.

Two of the problems in the CMMI include interpretation and organizational decisions. The model itself was written to cover many different organizational and project situations. An ambiguous style was intentionally chosen by the authors of the CMMI to fit these many situations. This ambiguity results in the need for a lot of interpretation and decision making by the model users. We hope to help identify these decisions for you and provide a positive influence in your decision making.

Notes

1. CMMI and CMM are registered in the U.S. Patent and Trademark office by Carnegie Mellon University.
2. The Software Engineering Institute (SEI; which is run under the guidance of Carnegie Mellon University in Pittsburgh, Pennsylvania) considers itself the steward of the CMM and the CMMI and related products.

Chapter 2

Beginning the Journey

This chapter is for those individuals who are just beginning a process improvement program. This chapter focuses on defining what a process is and why it is important; gives a brief comparison of improvement models; offers suggestions of where and how to start your program; and discusses some of the problems you can expect to encounter. This chapter should be considered introductory only. For more information, read subsequent chapters that delve into how to write processes and procedures, and how to set up a process improvement program.

What Is a Process?

A process is a series of steps that help to solve a problem. The steps must be defined in such a way as to be unambiguous — that is, readily understood and capable of being followed in a consistent manner by anyone using the process. Why do we want to do things consistently? Are we promoting turning the workers into robots? No. What focusing on process does for your organization is to reduce redundant work. Why recreate the wheel every time you begin a new project? If you are required to submit a project plan, why not have a procedure that tells you how to write one, plus an example of one that you can copy and paste from? Is that not easier than just wringing your hands and worrying about it, and sweating blood devising a new project plan for your new project? OK — you may not be a project manager, so you do not like the example about the project plan. Suppose you are a programmer. Does your manager ever ask you how difficult a particular program might be? Does he ever ask you how long it will take you to code each program? Or does he just give you a list of programs assigned to you and tell you when they are due? Do you ever have heartburn over his estimates? Do you ever say anything, or do you just work unpaid overtime because of his unrealistic schedule? Having a process for estimating schedules into which you have input will create a more realistic schedule and help relieve some of the burden on you of having to adhere to something that just does not make sense. Does this scheduling process always work perfectly? Can you just say, "No, this schedule stinks, so my manager must change it?" Of course not! But it does give you some room for negotiation.

Processes are like recipes. A recipe tells you the ingredients, how to mix the ingredients, what temperature to use, and how long to cook those ingredients. However, it does not teach you the techniques of slicing and dicing, mixing, beating, whipping, blanching, grilling, poaching, etc. And recipes also leave room for some experimentation and modification. Some recipes even give you suggestions on how to make changes to the dish.

A process as used in process improvement is usually defined at a somewhat higher level, with associated procedures supporting the process. The procedures are written in much more detail than the process. Examples follow.

Suppose your organization is focusing on creating a risk management process. This risk process is being developed because the project managers in your organization have been unable to proactively predict troubling issues that end up affecting the delivery of their products to the customer. Perhaps they have delivered late because of high staff turnover and being unable to get enough people with the proper skills on their projects; or the people they get are pulled onto other projects when those projects run into trouble. Another risk may be that the budgets for the projects are usually overrun. So all of the project managers get together and determine a risk management process that they feel will cover all (or at least most) of the risks they encounter. The risk management *process* they come up with is to:

- Identify the risk
- Analyze the risk
- Categorize the seriousness and probability of the risk
- Mitigate the risk

We can be sure that these managers feel they have done a brilliant job, but what is the problem with this process? It is too general. If I had handed out this process for all of my managers to follow, each manager would have interpreted *how* to do this process differently. We are trying to find a way to document how we do work in the organization in a consistent way so that everyone will do things somewhat similarly, and so that people can benefit from the good work being done by others.

So now we go back to the managers and say, "Great — you have a process. How do we do the steps in your process?" Well, that is a different problem. The managers are tasked with devising *procedures* for *how* to do *what* they have written as the steps in the process.

Using our process example, the first item says "Identify the risk." The managers would need to come up with how they identify risks. One of the ways they might do this identification is to start tracking the problems they have in delivering products and then find trends. From the list of trends, they would create a list of the ten most frequently occurring problems on the projects. The procedures would then discuss how to use the information in the list to estimate risks that might occur on another project. The third item in the list of steps in the risk management process says, "Categorize the seriousness and probability of the risk." Maybe your organization defines risks as 1 — most critical and most likely to occur; 2 — critical but work may continue; and 3 — not critical, work may continue, fix this problem during the next phase or release. The managers would need to come up with procedures for how to determine what would put a risk into category 1, 2, or 3.

These scenarios are just simplistic examples used to illustrate process versus procedures.

So why is focusing on process important? Why not focus on the product, or the people, or the technology used? Let me explain.

Writing standards for what a *Requirements Specification* should look like is a product focus. You are focusing on the template itself. For example, you might want your Requirements Specification to list all of the requirements for the system and categorize them as to whether they are system-level requirements, software requirements, hardware require-ments, safety requirements, performance requirements, etc. Great — this is a good thing to do; but how does anyone know which categories they fit in? This is where a requirements process comes in. It will tell you not only what the Requirements Specification should look like, but also *how* to write it — how to fill in the blanks for each paragraph in the specifications. The requirements process would also tell you how to elicit requirements from your stakeholders (e.g., customers, end users, require-ments analysts) and how to manage the changes to the requirements. The *product* focus would then continue on to what a *Design Specification* should look like, what coding standards should be followed, what test cases should consist of, etc. The *process* focus would then give guidelines to the people responsible for doing this work on *how* to do it.

Why not focus on the people? Puhleeeeez! Whenever anything goes wrong on a project, is not the first, visceral reaction to blame the people doing the work? Well, that is highly motivating (not!). We do not want you to think that people are not important — they are the most important part of any project or any work undertaken. But not everyone can be as brilliant as everyone needs to be every day. It is not like we wake up one day out of 300 days and say, "Yesterday I was just OK. Today I will be brilliant." Focusing on process puts the emphasis on having good processes to follow, not on hiring only brilliant people. Rather than having people work harder, have them work smarter. That is what process does for you.

Why not focus on technology? Have you ever heard the saying "garbage in, garbage out"? Well, that is what just plastering new technology onto an old problem does for you. This author has been paid big bucks for converting existing systems from one language or database to another. There are even tools now that will do that for you (with a lot of work). What do you get? The same system you always had with both the old problems and the new ones. Technology does not provide a quick fix, but it is the one answer that executives are most likely to choose because technology is easily quantifiable and easily budgeted. Look at the dot.com bust. Most of those companies sold quick-fix technologies without any underlying analysis of the problems organizations faced. Most of the dot.coms that operated without this sort of planning are out of business. Technology is our friend — but it is not the only answer to our problems.

Why focus on process? What personal benefit can you gain from all this work? What is in it for you? Well, the following examples are drawn from personal experience in some of the organizations we have helped along this path.

- *Configuration management.* One individual had spent hours trying to find the correct version of source code to make a simple change. He was never sure before whether he had the latest copy of the source code. Now, after following procedures for change control, he is reasonably sure that the code he is using to make updates is actually the code used in production. No more searching for hours to find the right program.
- *Testing.* Prior to this effort, developers handed the system to the testers and told them, "Here — write a test plan and test this. These are the changes I made." The test people were never quite sure how thorough their testing was, and they spent hours trying to figure out what the actual requirements for the system were. (You test to ensure that the requirements have been met.) Now, with a process for the Requirements Traceability Matrix and the

Requirements Specification, the testers spend less time figuring out what to do, and more time actually testing. It has greatly simplified their jobs and greatly improved the testing of the resulting products.

■ *Planning*. Prior to this effort, the organization could not predict the number of projects that needed to be scheduled ahead of time. Now, with the use of the process for devising a Statement of Work and the focus on the Project Planning process area, the organization is aware of the number of projects requested, what their initial requirements are, the approximate number of staff needed, the approximate size and complexity of the project, and how to prioritize the projects. Requests for support have actually been deferred, based on these measures. Time is not wasted on developing systems that will not be used or fixing problems that go away by themselves.

■ *Communication*. There is more communication up and down the chain of command as well as across the organization. For example, the Director of Software Engineering is talking to developers, and in some cases the developers are talking back. This is good. Quality Assurance (QA) is reviewing products and processes across several projects, and seeing the results of these processes and the problems, as well as the differences between the ways project teams perform. QA is also talking to the EPG (the process improvement team) and, in some cases, swaying them to change some decisions made, based on how things are actually working (or not working).

So, is process the only answer? No. Process is part of the answer. Process, when supported by training, enough money, enough skilled people, proper tools, and management commitment, can help your organization.

Models

What is a model and why do I have to use one? A *model* is considered a guideline of best practices found by studying other, highly functioning and successful organizations. A model does not contain the steps needed or the sequence of steps needed to implement a process improvement program. The model used simply says, "this is a good thing to do." For example, the Project Planning process area suggests that you write a project plan. The Requirements Management process area recommends that you track changes to requirements.

There are many models to choose from, depending on the problems in your organization that you want to solve. Why use a model? Well, we have worked in many organizations that just decided to "improve." Without using a model as your basis of reference, you have nothing around which to plan your improvement, and nothing against which to measure your results. Some organizations have decided they did not like the guidelines in the models used for process improvement in the industry, so they created their own. Most of these organizations failed. It is not easy to write a model. It takes a long time and it costs a lot of money. And remember that the models are summaries of the best practices of effective, successful organizations. So, it would behoove someone to follow most of the practices documented in these models. Most models allow an organization to substitute alternative practices for those practices in the chosen model that do not fit the organization. But beware — the more alternatives you select, the more you deviate from best practices in a model, the less likely you are of improving the problems in your organization.

A brief overview of some of the more frequently used models follows. Do not consider this overview exhaustive, as we simply summarize the basic thrust of each model. We do not purport to be experts in all of these models. Those of you who are experts in any of the models may take exception to some of our statements. These statements are offered, once again, only as high-level summarizations.

"In the beginning," there were ISO and the CMM®. ISO stands for International Standards Organization. The ISO 9000/9001 series generates a fundamental quality management framework. The ISO 9000 series is a set of documents that discusses quality systems to use when instituting quality assurance in an organization or enterprise. ISO 9000 itself is a guideline that directs the user as to which set of documents to use and the interrelationship of quality concepts. ISO 9001, 9002, and 9003 deal with external quality assurance pursuits while ISO 9004 deals with internal quality assurance. ISO 9001 is used to ensure that quality systems are delivered by the supplier during several stages of creation (which may include design, development, production, installation, and servicing). This document is the most pertinent to software development and maintenance. ISO 9000-3 is used when applying ISO 9001 to the development, supply, and maintenance of software. ISO 9001 requires that a documented quality system be implemented, with procedures and instructions. ISO 9000-3 further specifies that this quality system be integrated throughout the entire life cycle.

The CMM stands for the Capability Maturity Model. Most people call it the CMM for Software. The reason for this appellation is that after the CMM was developed, several more CMMs relating to different areas were generated (e.g., Systems Engineering, Acquisition). The CMM was created to help manage organizations that develop software. The CMM was created by analyzing the activities of highly functioning software organizations;

that is, those organizations that consistently delivered software systems to their customers on time, within budget, and that actually worked. These activities became the 316 key practices in the CMM, and the practices themselves were grouped into categories called Key Process Areas. There are 18 Key Process Areas that focus on the best practices found among the organizations reviewed. The Key Process Areas concentrate on such things as managing requirements, managing changes, creating project plans, tracking estimates against actuals, implementing quality assurance activities, instituting peer reviews, and training personnel in processes related to their job duties.

What is the difference between the CMM and ISO? Well, both were developed to improve the quality of systems. ISO was developed in Brussels, Belgium, and related originally to the manufacturing arena. The CMM was developed in the United States for managing the development of software systems. Over the years, the CMM made its journey across the ocean and is now used almost as much internationally as within the United States alone. ISO also "crossed the pond," that is, made inroads into the United States in manufacturing businesses, concentrating most often in the Midwest.

ISO focuses primarily on broader issues of quality within an entire enterprise or company. Executives of these organizations are often inter-viewed. The main product of ISO is the creation of a quality manual that discusses quality initiatives to be implemented throughout the enterprise. The CMM takes a much more limited view; it focuses only on software-intensive projects. It does not look at an entire enterprise or company. It describes an organization (admittedly, ambiguously) as several projects managed under one director (an example). Interviews in assessments may include an executive manager or two, but mostly focus on project man-agers and their team members.

If your organization is ISO certified, does that mean you are automat-ically CMM Level 3? No — it is like comparing apples and oranges. If you are CMM Level 3, does that mean you are ISO certified? No. Once again, while the two methods have similar goals, they are very different in implementation and scope. Chapter 4 in ISO 9001 is about five pages in length, while Sections 5, 6, and 7 of ISO 9000-3 are about 11 pages long. The CMM is over 400 pages long. So, clearly, the two models are different.

The models we are most familiar with are the Capability Maturity Model (CMM) for Software and the CMMI®. CMM and CMMI implement processes that reflect best practices found in industry. The CMM focuses on the software domain of organizations. However, because the problems with software organizations were deemed to fall mostly in the management area, this book can be, and has been, used not only in software organi-zations, but broadened to include most management situations.

The model that inspired this book is the Capability Maturity Model Integration (CMMI). The CMMI officially expanded the scope of the CMM from software to the entire enterprise. That expansion includes systems engineering as well as software engineering, integrated product and process development (specialized teams that design and develop systems), and acquisition (procuring systems, and monitoring the procurement and management of contracts awarded).

Other models in use include the Federal Aviation Administration's (FAA's) Integrated CMM, which builds upon the original CMM and other models as they relate to FAA issues. However, parts of this model can also be extracted and used in other business endeavors (not just aviation).

Six Sigma is also being used more and more frequently. Six Sigma attempts to reduce the variation in processes to a very small number. It focuses on improvements and measures that will lower the cost of doing business. Six Sigma consists of defining project goals and objectives; measuring narrow ranges of potential causes and establishing a baseline; analyzing data to identify trends and causes of the deviations; improving the processes at the identified cause level; and controlling the problem.

Some organizations are now merging Six Sigma and CMM/CMMI activities into one process improvement effort. Six Sigma focuses heavily on selecting a limited number of issues, measuring the problem (e.g., number of defects in a product line, excessive time to build a product), and then measuring the results (e.g., the effectiveness) of the fix. CMM/CMMI focuses on implementing best practices found in the industry and changing the infrastructure and culture of an organization. The two can complement one another. However, we feel that Six Sigma is better performed on only those organizations that have already been rated at a strong CMM/CMMI Maturity Level 3 or higher. Six Sigma requires a high degree of sophistication in aligning business objectives with Six Sigma techniques, as well as a high degree of sophistication in other areas of management (e.g., business, quality, process, and change).

Business Goals and Objectives

Much is made about aligning your process improvement effort to the business goals that the organization is trying to achieve. This alignment is easier said than done. Most organizations just beginning process improvement do not really have clearly defined business objectives. In fact, what we most often hear from executives when we ask them what they are trying to accomplish by doing process improvement is to reduce the number of people they need to staff projects, and have the people who survive the cut become more productive — that is, have the people do more work in less time. Of course, that does not include the executive doing the talking. Well, process improvement will not allow you to significantly reduce your task force. In fact, especially over the short term, you may have to actually hire more people in order to structure process improvement efforts and staff them adequately. So this "goal" is simply wrong.

Another often-heard response to "What are your business goals as they relate to process improvement?" is to get Maturity Level 3 for contract awards. If these organizations could buy Level 3 (and there is some discussion as to the ability to buy a level rating), these organizations would be most willing to go that route.

The other problem we run into is, when we ask, "What are your business objectives?", we repeatedly hear one answer — an incredulous, "Why, to make money of course!" The point of this discussion is that most organizations beginning process improvement are simply not sophisticated enough to have clear goals.

There is a technique that can be used to help define business goals and process improvement focus areas. It is called the Goal-Question-Metric technique. In this method, a workshop is held. It should actually be called the Problem-Goal-Question-Metric approach. During the workshop, a list of the most common problems found in the organization is presented. Questions are then asked relating to the problems, and the areas of the CMMI are used to help focus ensuing process improvement efforts. The approach starts with a business goal and works backward to identify improvement actions to achieve that goal. Here is a basic example:

- *Problem:* We cannot keep up with the number of requirements changes.
- *Goal:* To improve our requirements change process.
- *Question:* How can we improve our requirements change process?
- *Metric:* Number of requirements changes submitted, approved, implemented, or cancelled versus the number of original requirements documented. Time it takes to implement a change in requirements.
- *Associated process areas:* Requirements Management (Level 2), Project Planning (Level 2), Product and Process Quality Assurance (Level 2), Requirements Development (Level 3).

The main difference between this approach and addressing the seven process areas in Level 2 of the CMMI staged representation simultaneously is that structuring your process improvement program to focus on key problems in your organization helps define the scope of initial efforts and their sequence. Some members of your process improvement team and of your organization will find this approach more relevant to their everyday work, and will therefore be more enthusiastic about the program.

Although we have discussed this Goal-Question-Metric approach, we do not strongly recommend it for low-maturity organizations. Why not? Because most beginning organizations do not have a clear understanding of business objectives and business goals. They also will not readily admit that there are problems in the organization. The example we used was pertinent to requirements problems in systems. However, most true business objectives are at a much higher level. For example, an organization that clearly understands business objectives would state that one of its business objectives would be to improve customer satisfaction by 10 percent by reducing the number of defects embedded in their systems and delivered to their customers by 15 percent. To truly be effective, this type of business objective, backed by this metric, requires a sophisticated approach to identifying problems in organizations; fully defining the problem; relating the problem to existing, documented business goals; measuring the current process and its results; and measuring the expected versus realized outcome. This approach is way beyond most low-maturity organizations.

So, what to do? Because the approach above is used to structure your improvement efforts, why not use an officially approved assessment method? We suggest that if you are using the CMMI, that a SCAMPI be used. The SCAMPI is a method whereby a team is formed that examines any processes (both formal and, in low-maturity organizations, informal) that exist in an organization and rates their strengths and weaknesses as they relate to the CMMI. The organization will then decide which process areas to focus on first. Guidelines for beginning and assessing your process improvement trek are given in subsequent chapters in this book.

Problems

The process focus is not without its challenges. That is a nice way of saying that "it ain't perfect." If you look at the last line of one of the preceding paragraphs, it says, "Process, when supported by training, enough money, enough skilled people, proper tools, and management commitment, can help your organization." Most people do not understand process until they have been struggling with it for at least a year. "Training" is considered a dirty word in some organizations — "If they don't have the skills, we don't hire them," or "We only hire skilled people." And as most of you know, if you are really good at something, your organization is going to place you on one project full-time, and then pull you off that project and place you on one in trouble (full-time), and then have you "help out" on another project in your "spare" time. And when you do a wonderful job on the project in crisis and bring it in on time, your reward is to get your butt kicked on the other two projects because you are late delivering them. This is an example of a dysfunctional, low-maturity, yet commonly found organization.

The same problems occur in process improvement. You seldom get the "right" people. You get a lot of people just waiting to retire, or out of rehab, or summer interns, or "burnouts," or people who just cannot code well. You staff up with five or six full-time process improvement team members, only to find them pulled off when their former projects run into trouble. Training for process improvement is absolutely mandatory; but once the people get the training and start to do the work, they become overwhelmed and decide to go back to their old jobs, or leave the company for greener pastures. Or, the organization decides to give a "condensed" version of the training because it is too expensive — both in dollars spent and in time spent not doing "real work." Or the organization buys a process improvement tool guaranteed to get you your level rating in one year, only to discover that you cannot just plug it in — you have to actually write procedures and do work.

The answer? Well, just like anything else, there is no one answer, except maybe the following: tell your boss (or whoever's idea this whole process improvement thing was), in a tactful way, to put his money where his mouth is. If he wants it, it will cost him — in dollars, people, and time, including his time. Do not commit to "Level 2 in 2 years," or any other such slogan. Commit to trying to improve your organization. And mention to the boss that most improvement models focus improvement activities on *management* — not worker bees and practitioners. See if he then wants to continue. Educating your boss, as well as the rest of the organization, is key to a smooth transition to the process improvement path.

Process improvement is really about *change*. No one really likes to change, unless the current way of doing things is so onerous and repulsive that they just cannot stand it anymore. Most people do not get to this state when working for an organization — they simply go elsewhere. Thus, no one in your organization will be really excited to adopt a program that makes him change the way he does his job. Most people have developed, over the years, their own system or process for doing their job. And if you are the process improvement specialist, you will be responsible for making them change. And guess what? You will also have to change the way you do your job. One way to get people to buy into this whole change/process thing is to have them write the procedures. If they cannot or will not write, then get them to at least participate in meetings where they can voice their issues and contribute to creating the process for doing their work.

Summary

This chapter attempted to introduce the novice process improvement individual to some terms and concepts commonly used and why process improvement is important. This chapter should be considered a high-level overview. More information is contained in the following chapters of this book. The power of the CMMI lies in that it lets you define your job — how you do it and what gets produced from it. But with power comes responsibility. If you want to control how you do your job, you need to fully participate in the process improvement program.

Mistakes are a good thing. They show that you are trying. They show that you are improving after your mistakes go down. However, the predominant mantra in the industry is that mistakes are bad. If you make a mistake, you get hammered for it. There is no middle ground — no shades of gray. You are either 100 percent right or 100 percent wrong. With process improvement, if no mistakes are made, then the processes are probably not being used. Processes are generally not written "right" or perfectly the first time around, nor are they initially implemented and practiced correctly.

Also remember that although we say that process improvement involves skilled professionals with an objective, unbiased, professional attitude toward their work, everyone on the process improvement team has a large amount of personal investment in this effort. So things do tend to get *personal*. Try to see the big picture and try to be flexible.

Chapter 3

Structure of the CMMI®

To explain the structure of the CMMI®, we first use the staged representation of the model as our example and then follow up with a brief discussion of the continuous representation. The reader is directed to read Chapter 4 concerning CMMI representations along with this chapter.

Terms and Definitions

Before we begin, there are two very important concepts that need to be discussed:

1. Implementation
2. Institutionalization

Implementation is simply performing a task within the process area. (A process area is an area defined by the CMMI as an area that organizations should focus on — such as Project Planning or Configuration Management. It is a set of related tasks that address an area of concern.) The task is performed according to a process, but the action performed or the process followed may not be totally ingrained as part of the organization's culture.

Institutionalization is the result of implementing the process again and again. The process has become totally integrated into the organization. The process will continue after those who created it have left the organization. An infrastructure to support this way of doing business exists and provides support for the process and the individuals following it.

Other definitions that might prove helpful include:

- *Development:* the Construction phase of a life cycle, including Maintenance.
- *Project:* activities and resources necessary to deliver a product to the customer. A project is not just a software project. A project can also consist of many projects. The term "program" is not used. A project is also expected to have a start and end date, with a formal project manager assigned.
- *Product:* a service or system or tangible output delivered to the customer.

Another term that is frequently used, extremely important, yet very difficult to define is *organization*. What is an organization? Well, normally an organization is a series of projects currently underway within a department. The term "organization" also implies people, the structure of the departments, and the physical plant and equipment. So, if you are a developer, you might be working on coding five programs to maintain an automobile insurance system, developing a small Web site to track customer complaints about medical reimbursement, and beginning to design a document management system to document work hours performed for payroll purposes. That sounds like three projects to me. However, depending on how your place of business is set up, you could be working in three different organizations — the auto insurance department, the medical insurance department, and the payroll department. Or, you could be working in just one organization — the Technical Information Systems department. An organization can also consist of one individual! So, the definition of an organization *depends*.

Our advice to the scenario above is to develop improvement programs (and resultant assessments) based on the three different organizations mentioned in the first scenario (automobile insurance, medical insurance, and payroll as three separate organizations). Why? Because each organization has different rules it must follow. For example, automobile insurance may have state department of transportation regulations to follow, medical insurance may have federal medical regulations to follow, and payroll may have federal IRS and state tax regulations to follow. Therefore, the processes will be different. For example, do you think a customer service department of a utility company answering billing complaints from customers should be run the same way as a nuclear power plant? The nuclear power plant has environmental regulations, nuclear regulations, and other federal, state, and local policies it must implement in its processes. The customer service organization probably has fewer. The margin of error allowed in the safety factor is also significantly different.

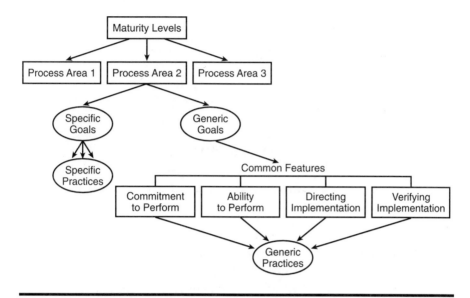

Exhibit 1. CMMI Model Components as Shown in the Staged Representation

With the CMMI, the definition of organization becomes even less clear. An organization can be one department headed by one director, or it can be expanded to include the entire company or enterprise. Our advice? De-scope. Do not bite off more than you can chew when beginning process improvement efforts. They tend to mushroom anyway. Start small — such as with the project in the above example doing Web-based medical insurance design and coding, and increase your efforts as necessary.

Model Structure for the Staged Representation

The CMMI is structured as follows:

- Maturity Levels (staged representation) or Capability Levels (continuous representation)
- Process Areas
- Goals: Generic and Specific
- Common Features
- Practices: Generic and Specific

Exhibit 1 is taken from the CMMI staged representation that states that "maturity levels organize the process areas. Within the process areas are generic and specific goals, as well as generic and specific practices. Common features organize generic practices."

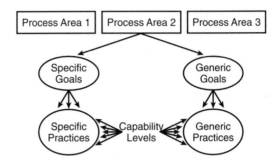

Exhibit 2. CMMI Model Components as Shown in the Continuous Representation

Exhibit 2 is taken from the CMMI continuous representation that states that "the specific goals organize specific practices and the generic goals organize generic practices. Each specific and generic practice corresponds to a capability level. Specific goals and specific practices apply to individual process areas."

Maturity Levels

A Maturity Level signifies the level of performance that can be expected from an organization. For example, Maturity Level 1 organizations have ad hoc processes, and Maturity Level 2 organizations have a basic project management system in place. There are five Maturity Levels.

Process Areas (PAs)

Each Maturity Level consists of several Process Areas. A Process Area is a group of practices or activities performed collectively to achieve a specific objective. Examples include Requirements Management at Maturity Level 2, Requirements Development at Maturity Level 3, and Quantitative Project Management at Maturity Level 4.

Relationship between Goals and Practices

Every Process Area has several goals that must be satisfied. Because goals are at a high level, each goal has practices associated with it. Practices are specific tasks that should be performed within the Process Area to achieve the goal. There are both generic and specific goals, as well as both generic and specific practices.

Goals

Each Process Area has several goals that need to be satisfied to satisfy the objectives of the PA. There are two types of goals:

1. *Specific goals (SG):* activities that relate to the specific PA under study
2. *Generic goals (GG):* goals that are common to multiple PAs throughout the model; they help determine whether the PA has been institutionalized

Practices

Practices are activities that must be performed to satisfy the goals for each PA. Each practice relates to only one goal. There are two types of practices:

1. *Specific practices (SP):* relate to specific goals
2. *Generic practices (GP):* are associated with the generic goals for institutionalization

For example, in the Project Planning PA, one of the practices is to write a Project Plan. Another is to estimate the number of people needed and to derive a schedule. Subpractices and examples are provided in the model to help explain the practices in more detail.

Common Features

Common Features simply group together the generic practices within a PA, according to the function that the practices fulfill. There are four Common Features:

1. Commitment to Perform (CO)
2. Ability to Perform (AB)
3. Directing Implementation (DI)
4. Verifying Implementation (VE)

Commitment to Perform (CO) is shown through senior management commitment and written policies. Ability to Perform (AB) is shown through training personnel in their duties, providing adequate resources and funding, assigning responsibility, planning the process, and establishing a tailored and defined process. Directing Implementation (DI) is demonstrated by managing configurations, identifying and involving relevant stakeholders, monitoring and controlling the process, and collecting improvement information. Verifying Implementation (VE) is demonstrated via objectively evaluating adherence (both process and product adherence to organizational policies, procedures, and standards) and by reviewing status with higher-level management. The continuous representation does not provide a mapping of practices to common features.

Other terms discussed throughout the CMMI include:

- *Typical Work Products:* each process area gives examples of typical documents, deliverables, or other outputs produced within the process area.
- *Subpractices:* lower-level practices that provide more information about the practice. For example, the Practice may be to write a project plan. The subpractice would offer information as to what should go into the project plan itself.
- *Discipline Amplifications:* simple guidance offered to direct the user as to which discipline is more relevant for specific practices, or to offer some guidance in applying the PA to the discipline. The disciplines are Systems Engineering, Software Engineering, Supplier Sourcing, and Integrated Product and Process Development (IPPD).
- *Elaborations:* more information and examples concerning generic practices.
- *References:* refer the reader to related portions of the CMMI for more information.
- *Labels:* each practice has a full name but is often documented and referred to by its shortened name or label. An example is in the continuous representation, Generic Practice 4.2. The label of this practice is Stabilize Subprocess Performance. The entire name of the practice is "Stabilize the performance of one or more subprocesses of the process to determine its ability to achieve the established quantitative quality and process performance objectives."
- *Resources:* in the previous CMM for Software, resources generally referred to only people (e.g., staff, individuals, personnel). In the CMMI, resources can mean not only people, but also equipment, funds, facilities, and technology.

So, what do you really have to do? Are all of these elements as important as the next? No. The CMMI gives us some guidance as to what is a required component, an expected component, and simply informative.

Required, Expected, and Informative Components

- *Goals* are *required* to be achieved.

- *Practices* are *expected* to be followed. Alternative practices that achieve the same concept can be substituted when the practice listed does not meet business objectives or fit the organization. Alternatives must be justified, documented, planned, implemented, and measured. The alternative substituted must be equal to the intent of the original practice. Do not try to substitute another practice because your organization is having trouble instituting the original practice.
- *Subpractices, elaborations, typical work products, and notes* are *informative* and are used to help the reader understand the intent of the goals and practices, as well as how they can be achieved. Do not discount the subpractices. Sometimes, they are much more helpful and specific in understanding the activity than their associated practice.

Model Structure for the Continuous Representation

The continuous representation uses the same basic structure as the staged representation, with a few extra wrinkles. Once again, specific practices relate to specific goals; generic practices relate to generic goals; but there are both *base* practices and *advanced* practices.

Base practices are those practices that are at Capability Level 1. Base practices essentially involve identifying the scope of work and performing the process informally without following a documented process description or plan. The degree to which the practices are performed can vary from individual to individual. A Capability Level is not a Maturity level. Capability Level 1 simply means that the base practices are performed in some way in your organization. So, base practices are very simple building blocks in the stratification of attaining capability levels. Advanced practices are those practices that show more sophistication and rigor in a process area. Advanced practices may or may not build on base practices.

Goals and Practices

Specific goals and practices relate to specific process areas and to tasks that make sense for that process area only. For example, Project Planning requires a project plan. Quantitative Project Management requires a process performance baseline. Generic goals and practices relate to multiple process areas. So, Requirements Management, if desiring a Capability Level 2, would have to establish an organizational policy, plan the process, and train the people. To attain Capability Level 3, Requirements Management must do the aforementioned actions, as well as define the process and collect improvement information relating to the process. Project Planning and Organizational Process Focus would have to do the same as well. Thus, the generic goals and practices can be applied to all process areas. Both specific goals and practices and generic goals and practices must be satisfied to achieve the Capability Level. Alternatives that clearly and unequivocally accomplish a result that meets the goal can be substituted. Again — required, expected, and informative components.

Generic Goals and Practices

Each Capability Level has only one generic goal associated with it. Each generic practice maps to only one generic goal.

Target Profile

A target profile is a list of process areas and their corresponding capability levels that represent an objective for process performance. One example is when comparing Maturity Levels to Capability Levels. Capability Level 3 can only be determined as equivalent to Maturity Level 3 in the staged representation when all of the goals for all of the process areas at Maturity Levels 2 and 3 in the staged representation have been met. So, the target profile 3 would include satisfying seven process areas at Maturity Level 2 plus 14 process areas at Maturity Level 3. An organization may decide on its own unique target profile. For example, a contracting company specializing in providing third-party Independent Verification and Validation services may select a target profile of Capability Level 2 for Project Planning and Project Monitoring and Control, and Capability Level 3 for Verification and Validation.

Target Staging

Target staging is a sequence of target profiles that describe the path of process improvement that the organization will take. Care should be taken to ensure that dependencies between the generic practices and process areas are implemented. This is where the organization documents the process areas (PAs) it will focus on, justifies this approach, and tracks the PAs back to business objectives.

The CMMI focuses on institutionalization. Goals cannot be achieved without proving institutionalization of the process. Generic goals and generic practices support institutionalization and increasing sophistication of the process. Specific goals and specific practices support implementation of the process area. Process maturity and capability evolve. Process improvement and increased capability are built in stages, as some processes are ineffective when others are not stable.

Summary

No matter which representation of the CMMI is used, each has levels. Within each level are generic goals pertaining to all of the process areas in that level and specific goals pertaining only to a specific process area. Goals have practices associated with them. Common Features group the practices together into categories. Practices are associated with only one goal.

Chapter 4

CMMI® Representations

There are two different representations of the CMMI®: the staged representation and the continuous representation.

The following discussion contains a lot of "CMMI-ese." There is just no way around it. When using the CMMI, you must use the terminology associated with it. However, the words are sometimes confusing. A trick we use is to look at the words as separate entities and then just "turn them around." For example, the next paragraph contains the words *process capability*. Well, what is that? Look at the words. *Process capability* is how *capable* is a *process* of actually providing the results we are looking for. And so on. Good luck.

The Staged Representation

The staged representation focuses improvement on the process capability an organization can expect to attain; however, this expected capability (or ability to function in a mature manner) is contained within maturity levels or stages. There are five maturity levels, with each level providing the foundation for further improvements. This structure mirrors that of the previous CMM for Software.

Maturity Level 1: Initial

Organizations have no structured process in place. Development is chaotic and ad hoc. Budgets and schedules are often exceeded. Product quality cannot be predicted. Maturity Level 1 is considered ad hoc — meaning you make it up as you go along, which is something we want to avoid — so this level has no real structure associated with it. That is, this level represents a chaotic approach toward developing products. If chaos were structured, it would not be chaotic. So, there is nothing structured in Maturity Level 1, and being Level 1 is a bad thing.

Maturity Level 2: Managed

Basic project management processes are in place and are followed. Institutionalization is achieved by:

- Adhering to organizational policies
- Following a documented plan and process description
- Applying adequate funding and resources
- Maintaining appropriate assignment of responsibility and authority
- Training people in their appropriate processes
- Placing work products under appropriate configuration management
- Monitoring and controlling process performance, and taking corrective action
- Objectively reviewing the process, work products, and services, and addressing noncompliance
- Reviewing the activities, status, and results of the process with appropriate levels of management, and taking corrective action
- Identifying and interacting with relevant stakeholders

Maturity Level 2 begins with basic management practices and continues with increasingly sophisticated focus areas that belong within a specific level.

Maturity Level 3: Defined

The organization has achieved all of the goals of Maturity Level 2. There is an organizational way of doing business, with tailoring of this organizational method allowed under predefined conditions. The organization has an organization's set of standard processes. The following characteristics of the process are clearly stated:

- Purpose
- Inputs
- Entry criteria
- Activities

- Roles
- Measures
- Verification steps
- Outputs
- Exit criteria

Institutionalization is achieved by:

- Satisfying the institutionalization factors for Maturity Level 2
- Establishing the description of the defined process
- Establishing a plan based on the description of the defined process
- Performing the process according to the planned defined process
- Collecting work products, measures, and improvement information derived from performing the process
- Performing the process to support future use and improvement of the organization's process assets

Maturity Level 3 continues with defining a strong, meaningful, organizationwide approach to developing products. An important distinction between Maturity Levels 2 and 3 is that at Level 3, processes are described in more detail and more rigorously than at Level 2. Processes are managed more proactively, based on a more sophisticated understanding of the interrelationships and measurements of the processes and parts of the processes. Level 3 is more sophisticated, more organized, and has developed an organizational identity — a way of doing business particular to this organization.

Maturity Level 4: Quantitatively Managed

The organization has achieved all of the goals of Maturity Levels 2 and 3. The organization controls its processes by statistical and other quantitative techniques. Product quality, process performance, and service quality are understood in statistical terms and are managed throughout the life of the processes. Institutionalization occurs via:

- Satisfying the factors for institutionalization at Levels 2 and 3
- Establishing and maintaining quantitative objectives for product quality, service quality, and process performance
- Establishing and maintaining a statistically stable and predictable process performance
- Establishing and maintaining a statistical understanding to determine whether the process is capable of achieving these goals

Maturity Level 4 focuses on using metrics to make decisions and to truly measure whether progress is occurring and the product is improving. Distinctions between Levels 3 and 4 are that at Level 3, processes are *qualitatively* predictable. At Level 4, processes are *quantitatively* predictable. Level 4 addresses *special* causes of process variation and takes corrective action.

Maturity Level 5: Optimizing

The organization has achieved all of the goals of Maturity Levels 2, 3, and 4. Processes are continually improved, based on an understanding of *common* causes of variation within the processes. Institutionalization is accomplished by:

■ Satisfying the items for institutionalization for Levels 2, 3, and 4
■ Establishing and maintaining quantitative process improvement objectives
■ Identifying and preventing common causes of defects
■ Identifying and deploying both incremental and innovative technological improvements that continually improve process performance

Maturity Level 5 is Nirvana. Everyone is a productive member of the team, defects are reduced, and the product is delivered on time and within the estimated budget.

In the staged model, the Maturity Levels serve as process boundaries — meaning that the efforts documented in that Maturity Level relate *only* to that Maturity Level. For example, Requirements Management is a Level 2 Process Area. The next Process Area in Level 2 is Project Planning. Then there is Project Monitoring and Control, Supplier Agreement Management, Measurement and Analysis, Process and Product Quality Assurance, and Configuration Management. So, to be considered a Maturity Level 2 organization, the projects undergoing process improvement need to satisfy the goals for all of the process areas for Maturity Level 2.

In Maturity Level 3, there are the following process areas:

■ Requirements Development
■ Technical Solution
■ Product Integration
■ Verification
■ Validation
■ Organizational Process Focus

- Organizational Process Definition
- Organizational Training
- Integrated Project Management (for Integrated Product and Process Development — IPPD)
- Risk Management
- Integrated Teaming
- Integrated Supplier Management
- Decision Analysis and Resolution
- Organizational Environment for Integration

Thus, an organization seeking to be Maturity Level 3 would need to structure its process improvement program to satisfy the goals for *both* Levels 2 and 3. The point to note is that the process areas listed in Level 2 are not listed in Level 3, and vice versa. The same holds true for Maturity Levels 4 and 5. You must satisfy all of the goals in the previous levels, plus the goals for the current level, to attain that Maturity Level rating. Each Maturity Level consists of process areas. Each process area contains goals that must be satisfied. Each goal has certain practices or actions associated with it.

The Continuous Representation

The continuous representation has the same basic information as the staged representation, just arranged differently. The continuous representation focuses process improvement on actions to be completed within process areas, yet the processes and their actions can span different levels. More sophistication in implementing the practices is expected at the different levels. These levels are called Capability Levels. There are six Capability Levels:

Level 0: Incomplete
Level 1: Performed
Level 2: Managed
Level 3: Defined
Level 4: Quantitatively Managed
Level 5: Optimizing

What is a Capability Level? Capability Levels focus on maturing the organization's ability to perform, control, and improve its performance in a process area. This ability allows the organization to focus on specific areas to improve the performance of that area. A brief explanation of each Capability Level follows.

Capability Level 0: Incomplete

An incomplete process does not implement all of the Capability Level 1 specific and generic practices. This is tantamount to Maturity Level 1 in the staged representation.

Capability Level 1: Performed

A Capability Level 1 process is a process that is expected to perform all of the Capability Level 1 specific and generic practices. Performance may not be stable and may not meet specific objectives such as quality, cost, and schedule, but useful work can be done. This is only a start, or baby-step, in process improvement. It means that you are doing something but you cannot *prove* that it is really working for you.

Capability Level 2: Managed

A managed process is planned, performed, monitored, and controlled for individual projects, groups, or stand-alone processes to achieve a given purpose. Managing the process achieves both the model objectives for the process as well as other objectives, such as cost, schedule, and quality. As the title of this level indicates, you are actively managing the way things are done in your organization. You have some metrics that are consistently collected and applied to your management approach.

Remember: metrics are collected *and used* at all levels of the CMMI, in both the staged and continuous representations. It is a bitter fallacy to think that an organization can wait until Capability Level 4 to use the metrics.

Capability Level 3: Defined

A defined process is a managed process that is tailored from the organization's set of standard processes. Deviations beyond those allowed by the tailoring guidelines are documented, justified, reviewed, and approved. The organization's set of standard processes is just a fancy way of saying that your organization has an identity. That is, there is an organizational way of doing work that differs from the way another organization within your company may do it. So, suppose there are two companies developing anvils. Those two companies are Roadrunner Software Enterprises and Wily Coyote Industries. The people at Roadrunner Software Enterprises consistently beat the pants off Wily Coyote Industries when developing anvils. Why? Because Roadrunner Software Enterprises has a special way, specific to them, of developing anvils. It is documented and measured, people are trained in it, and the results are tracked.

Capability Level 4: Quantitatively Managed

A quantitatively managed process is a defined process that is controlled using statistical and other quantitative techniques. Product quality, service quality, process performance, and other business objectives are understood in statistical terms and are controlled throughout the life cycle. Yes, this is where such ideals as statistical process control come into being. However, the point to be made here is to *keep it simple*. Metrics do not have to be difficult to be useful. In fact, the opposite holds true. I do not want to have to grit my teeth and get a tension headache every time I think about collecting and analyzing the metrics collected in my organization. Make them meaningful and associate them with some problem you would like to conquer. For example, assume that your company makes personal computers (PCs) and ships them to customers. One day, you are sitting at your desk and receive a call from an irate customer. How did that call get to you? Who knows — but it did. (This could be an opportunity in disguise.) The customer describes his tale of woe and ends by stating that the PC arrived at his house with the box intact and unopened, but the monitor was smashed to bits. Well, if this is your first phone call about it, you are busy, and this is not your job, you might ignore it. But if you start receiving five such calls every day, you might want to start counting the number of calls, analyzing where the problem was injected into the shipping process, instituting a new process for fixing this defect, and tracking the effectiveness of your process. Then, by analyzing the number of defects expected in prior months versus the actual number of defects this month, you can come up with a standard number of expected defects. When this number is exceeded, the process is broken and must be fixed. Also, you can work on reducing this number. That is "Quantitatively Managing."

Capability Level 5: Optimizing

An optimizing process is a quantitatively managed process that is improved, based on an understanding of the common causes of process variation inherent in the process. It focuses on continually improving process performance through both incremental and innovative improvements. Both the defined processes and the organization's set of standard processes are targets of improvement activities. Capability Level 4 focuses on establishing baselines, models, and measurements for process performance. Capability Level 5 focuses on studying performance results across the organization or entire enterprise, finding common causes of problems in how the work is done (the process[es] used), and fixing the problems in the process. The fix would include updating the process documentation and training involved where the errors were injected. Thus, the process may only be broken at the project level; or, it could be entirely broken and the process at the organizational level and all resultant levels may need to be repaired.

The continuous representation contains the same basic information as the staged model — the information is just arranged differently. The information (process areas, goals, practices) is arranged in what we can call functional categories; that is, each process area is grouped by the functionality it performs. There are four types of process categories:

1. Process Management Processes
2. Project Management Processes
3. Engineering Processes
4. Support Processes

So, for example, in the continuous representation, the "Project Management Processes" category contains the following process areas in the following order:

- Project Planning
- Project Monitoring and Control
- Supplier Agreement Management
- Integrated Project Management
- Risk Management
- Integrated Teaming
- Integrated Supplier Management
- Quantitative Project Management

These process areas are all related in some way. They are categorized as Project Management Processes. Although an organization may select which processes to focus improvement efforts on when using the continuous representation, this representation seems to suggest that, if your organization needs help in improving its project management approach to product development, start with these process areas in this order.

The continuous representation does not overtly suggest a sequence to use for process improvement; however, a sequence is implied. In the list of Project Management Processes above, it would be ludicrous for an organization to attempt to institute Quantitative Project Management before successfully achieving the goals of the Project Planning Process area (as Quantitative Project Management is more sophisticated and more complex than Project Planning). If you review the order of the process areas in the list, you will surmise that the less sophisticated process areas are listed first, with the more sophisticated process areas following. For example, before you can focus on Project Monitoring and Control, Project Planning should be in place. It seems that the continuous representation is saying that Project Planning should be attempted first, followed much later by Risk Management, because Risk Management is more sophisticated (and probably more complicated to institute) than Project Planning. Also, without the basis of Project Planning, Risk Management could not be performed effectively.

A more subtle, less obvious subject that bears discussing is that of Generic Practices and how they relate to Process Areas, Maturity Levels, and Capability Levels. Process Areas at Maturity Level 2 in the staged representation include entire Process Areas for planning, managing changes, ensuring quality, and tracking progress. The Generic Practices for Capability Level 2 in the continuous representation also include statements for the same things — planning, managing changes, ensuring quality, and tracking progress. Generic Practices are used to determine whether generic goals have been satisfied. Generic goals must be satisfied to achieve a level — either a Capability Level or a Maturity Level. What this means is that, because an organization is expected to implement the Generic Practices, an organization using the continuous representation and selecting separate process areas to focus on, must in reality also satisfy the basic concepts of Maturity Level 2 in the staged representation. An example follows.

An organization may decide to use the continuous representation. This organization selects the Process Area of Technical Solution, and is seeking a Capability Level 2 for it. To achieve this Capability Level, all of the specific practices for Technical Solution are expected to be implemented, and all of the Generic Practices for this level are expected to be instituted. That means that activities surrounding planning, managing changes, ensuring quality, and tracking progress for Technical Solution must be addressed. To address these issues and institute the Generic Practices, the organization discovers that it must actually back up a bit and also focus on the Process Areas of Project Planning, Project Monitoring and Control, and Configuration Management. So, although it may appear that an organization can skip process areas when using the continuous representation, the actions of those process areas must be met.

Which One Should I Use?

It depends...

The staged representation is like most of the currently accepted models, such as the CMM for Software. It is very useful for assessments; most recent procurements have mandated contract awards based on Maturity Level ratings. Following the staged representation produces a Maturity Level rating.

The continuous representation was designed to tailor the model and process improvement approaches, focusing on specific categories that might match those areas in your organizations where problems exist. For example, suppose your organization does only Independent Verification and Validation. You do not write software. You produce no product. You simply review, as an independent third party, those products produced by some other party and you write your report. This type of organization might want to focus on the Verification, Validation, and Product Integration process areas. The continuous representation allows this approach to take place.

One approach to take in selecting which representation to use is to consider the following two questions.

How Much Experience Does Your Organization Have with Process Improvement?

Why? Because we believe that the continuous representation requires a higher level of process improvement understanding than the staged representation. The staged representation embeds Process Area decisions that an inexperienced organization might not be prepared to make. For example, an organization just beginning process improvement usually has little idea as to where to start. The staged representation tells you to begin at the beginning — Maturity Level 2 — and after attaining that level, continue to the next — Maturity Level 3. And so on. Within those levels are the process areas to include in your process improvement strategy. So, when just beginning, an organization might state that "We will begin with Maturity Level 2, which means satisfying the goals for all of the process areas in Maturity Level 2." The organization would then prioritize which process areas to focus their efforts on first (see subsequent chapters of this book for how to set up and structure your process improvement initiative). Our experience has also shown that organizations inexperienced in process improvement often put too much focus on technological solutions and not enough focus on management issues. Therefore, an inexperienced organization using the continuous representation might focus its efforts on the Engineering Processes, as opposed to those emphasizing project and process management. While improving engineering is, of course, important, without the foundation of strong project and process management, it is likely that engineering improvements would not be sustained, if accomplished at all. Those organizations that are more experienced with process improvement, and more experienced with identifying and mapping their organizational weaknesses to areas where the CMMI can offer help, would probably be able to use the continuous representation more successfully. Remember: the continuous representation allows an organization to select (that means "pick and choose") which process areas to focus on by determining which of the process areas match the organization's business needs and objectives.

What Model(s) Is Your Current Process Program Based On?

Our experience shows that an organization should build on the positive experiences it has had with other models used in that organization. The CMMI requires enough changes without introducing unnecessary confusion. So, if you have been happy with the staged structure, continue to use it. If you have been happy with the continuous structure, continue to use it. If you want to try something new, then be our guest. Just remember that whenever you introduce something new, you introduce new problems and new headaches; but you also may stimulate and revive your organization's process improvement effort.

Exhibit 1 shows the impact of process improvement experience and current model experience on the representation decision. Four approaches are shown, as represented by the leftmost column. The four other columns represent model experience and process improvement experience. An entry with a plus (+) sign indicates a positive impact and a minus (–) sign indicates a negative impact on the approach.

The two representations are not mutually exclusive. Each representation contains the same basic information — it is just structured differently. Each representation promotes process improvement and can be used in assessments. The continuous representation allows the organization to choose which process areas to focus on, as well as which discipline to focus on (e.g., software engineering, systems engineering, IPPD, supplier management). The CMMI also suggests that tailoring of the model can be done, *but...*

> **Caveat:** The more tailoring of the model done, the less likely an organization is to achieve its improvement goals. The CMMI contains best practices of organizations. If you deviate from a best practice, you must strongly justify why and substitute another practice that satisfies the *intent* of the CMMI practice originally listed. Intent is like beauty — different in the eye of every beholder. It is also difficult to define intent. Most organizations try to justify their not doing something in the model. What they really would like to write, but cannot for obvious reasons, is "It was too hard for us to do. We didn't have the money. We didn't have the people. We didn't have the time before the assessment team came in." These are *not good* justifications for not doing something described in the model.

Exhibit 1. Representation Selection Matrix

Approaches	Based on CMM for Software	Based on SECM or Related Model	Current Process Improvement Program	
			High Process Improvement Experience	Low Process Improvement Experience
Staged Representation	+ Builds on current experience – May overlook interpretation issues	– Learning curve for new paradigm + Defined sequence of improvements		+ Easier to understand + Helps maintain focus
Continuous Representation	– Learning curve for new paradigm + Allows focus on significant area	+ Builds on current experience + Can continue with current plans	+ Supports informed decisions	– Bad focus decisions likely
Start with Continuous, move to Staged	– Major short-term impact + Allows focus on significant area	– Minor short-term impact + Longer-term easier comparison	+ Able to make informed focus decision	+ Harder to build experience
Start with Staged, move to Continuous	– Minor short-term impact + Longer-term focus on significant areas	– Major short-term impact		+ Easier to build experience

There is also the concept of Equivalent Staging. What is Equivalent Staging? It is an attempt to match Maturity Levels in the staged representation to Capability Levels in the continuous representation. The levels compared are called "Target Staging." Target Staging is a sequence of targeted process areas that describe the path of process improvement the organization will take. Care should be taken to ensure that dependencies between the generic practices and process areas are implemented. This is where the organization documents the process areas (PAs) it will focus on, justifies this approach, and tracks the PAs back to business objectives (see Exhibit 2).

The reader should be advised that to be Target Profile 4 or 5, you do not need to achieve the Generic Goals for Capability Levels 4 and 5. That means that you need to satisfy the *specific goals and practices* for the process areas (Organization Process Performance — OPP — and Quantitative Project Management — QPM — for Target Profile 4, and Organizational Innovation and Deployment — OID — and Causal Analysis and Resolution — CAR — for Target Profile 5); plus, you need to satisfy the *generic goals and practices* for Capability Levels 1, 2, and 3 — not 4 or 5. Careful reading of the table should lead the reader to conclude that to achieve Target Profile 3, an organization needs to satisfy the goals for all of the process areas in Maturity Levels 2 and 3 — even if using the continuous representation. Remember that not all of the process areas contained within Maturity Level 3 in the staged representation are also contained within the process categories for Capability Level 3 in the continuous representation. Proceed along this path with caution.

As of this writing, the authors of this book know of no procurement agency that has allowed the substitution of a Capability Level for a Maturity Level for contract award.

The interesting point to make here is that the staged representation is really continuous; and the continuous representation is really staged. That is, because of all the interdependencies among the process areas and relationships that must be met among the generic goals and practices, everything is related to everything else. For example, in the staged representation, you cannot really plan your project in Project Planning (Level 2) if you have not already begun to manage your requirements in Requirements Management (Level 2). So Requirements Management feeds into Project Planning. How can you manage requirements (Requirements Management Level 2) if you have not defined them in some way, shape, or form yet (Requirements Development Level 3)? How can you effectively start a process improvement program if you have not set up a group of people and follow the guidelines in Organizational Process Focus (Maturity Level 3)? Yet that is Level 3 and the organization is just starting its process improvement program, and so is at Level 1. How can you have Verification,

Exhibit 2. Equivalent Staging

Name	ML	CL1	CL2	CL3	CL4	CL5
Requirements Management	2					
Measurement and Analysis	2					
Project Monitoring and Control	2					
Project Planning	2	Target Profile 2				
Process and Product Quality Assurance	2					
Supplier Agreement Management	2					
Configuration Management	2					
Decision Analysis and Resolution	3					
Product Integration	3					
Requirements Development	3					
Technical Solution	3					
Validation	3					
Verification	3				N/A	N/A
Organizational Process Definition	3	Target Profile 3				
Organizational Process Focus	3					
Integrated Project Management	3					
Risk Management	3					
Organizational Training	3					
Integrated Teaming	3					
Integrated Supplier Management	3					
Organizational Environment for Integration	3					
Organizational Process Performance	4	Target Profile 4				
Quantitative Project Management	4					
Organizational Innovation and Deployment	5	Target Profile 5				
Causal Analysis and Resolution	5					

Validation, and Product Integration as separate entities? Generally, in most organizations, if you do one, you must do the others. The CMMI states that using the continuous representation, and focusing on Capability Levels, allow an organization to select process areas within process categories on which to focus their process improvement efforts. In the continuous representation, how can you attempt Validation, or Verification, or practically any other process area without also tackling (to some extent) Project Planning, Project Monitoring and Control, and Product and Process Quality Assurance? So, those of you thinking of selecting the continuous representation so that you can select only a few process areas for improvement will find that you are sadly mistaken. Everything is related. The different representations used are simply to help the reader understand the basic tenets of the model.

Summary

Although the CMMI is promoted as having two very different representations, the representations are really more similar than dissimilar. Instituting the practices and subpractices is where the real benefits can be found. There are no new generic goals for Maturity Levels 4 and 5 in the staged representation because the process areas in both levels include the basic tenets of those maturity levels. The continuous representation *does* have new generic goals because the continuous representation allows the selection of various process areas. Thus, your organization may decide not to select the process areas in Maturity Level 4. If you do that, then the generic goals of the continuous representation have been added to ensure that the basic concepts of statistical control and its application will be met.

Chapter 5

Understanding Maturity Level 2: Managed

This chapter is designed to help the reader understand the basic tenets of Maturity Level 2 in the staged representation of the CMMI®. However, because this chapter consists of summaries of the process areas, anyone wishing to get a better idea of the model — no matter which representation is to be used — can benefit from this chapter. Once again, this is not an attempt to teach the CMMI; we simply offer a condensed version of the various areas and key points to consider.

New concepts are introduced in Level 2 in CMMI. They include:

- Integrated Product and Process Development (IPPD)
- Supplier Management

One Concept — Measurement and Analysis — has a greatly expanded role and is discussed later in this chapter.

IPPD, while introduced in Supplier Agreement Management at Maturity Level 2, is more rigorously addressed in Level 3, and will be explained in Chapter 6. Suffice it to say that IPPD is about forming teams that include subject matter experts from all areas needed to produce the product for the customer.

Supplier Agreement Management (SAM) has to do with ensuring that any organization or business external to the actual project is selected and monitored appropriately. This external source (supplier) may be responsible for delivering either a product or a service, and may be involved in the design, development, maintenance, manufacture, modification, upgrade, or supply of any of the items required to produce the product. This supplier has an agreement (contract) with the acquiring body, and it is this agreement that is used to effectively manage the effort provided by the suppler. This agreement must be properly defined, documented, used, monitored, and measured. Supplier Agreement Management replaced Software Subcontract Management (SSM) in the CMM for Software. SSM was the key process area most often tailored out of assessments and software process improvement activities because if there were no subcontractors used, then this area did not apply. SAM has been broadened somewhat, and probably will apply much more often, as almost everyone building an entire system/product using the CMMI will have some sort of outside assistance requiring contracts. Including SAM in the CMMI also makes a correlation to the Software Acquisition Capability Maturity Model (SA-CMM) more plausible. Although both SAM and the Software Acquisition Model discuss suppliers, vendors, procurements, and acquisition roles, more information from a different perspective may be found in the Acquisition Model.

When comparing the CMM for Software to the CMMI, what has been left out? There are no longer Project Management/Manager reviews as part of the Verifying Implementation Common Feature. The reviews focus on senior management. Few groups are included (e.g., no mention of the Software Quality Assurance group). Also as part of Verifying Implementation, there are no specific references or requirements for a Quality Assurance review.

Moving from Maturity Level 1 to Level 2

The biggest hurdle that most organizations face when embarking on the journey from an immature organization to a more mature one is the jump from Maturity Level 1 to Maturity Level 2. Maturity Level 1 is characterized by ad hoc processes; that is, processes that the people doing the work have created themselves in order to accomplish their tasks. The problem with this method is that redundant work is often done, people do not share their methods across the organization, and some approaches are in opposition to actually making the organization run more effectively. While some individual approaches may work for that individual, that person's approach may actually conflict with work being done downstream. The results are more rework, delays, and frustration. Turf wars are common, and the organization functions due to the heroics of its people. When these people move on (or burn out), the organization suffers.

Maturity Level 2 is characterized by individuals sharing their lessons learned and best practices; and devising preliminary processes that will function at the project level and, in some cases, across the organization as a whole. Maturity Level 2 focuses on management issues that affect normal, day-to-day work routines. Maturity Level 2 consists of seven process areas (PAs) that contribute to project management efficiencies.

1. Requirements Management
2. Project Planning
3. Project Monitoring and Control
4. Supplier Agreement Management
5. Measurement and Analysis
6. Process and Product Quality Assurance
7. Configuration Management

Each PA has specific goals (specific to that process area) and generic goals that are applied to every PA in that Maturity Level. Generic goals for Maturity Level 2 are listed below. These goals lead to institutionalizing the PA; that is, when an organization ensures that these goals are practiced consistently across the organization, the PA associated with these goals will continue to be applied appropriately in the organization even after those who created the procedures for this area have left. The generic goals and their corresponding generic practices and Common Features for Maturity Level 2 are:

- ■ Generic Goal 2: Institutionalize a Managed Process
    - − Generic Practice 2.1 (Commitment 1): Establish an organizational policy
    - − Generic Practice 2.2 (Ability 1): Plan the process
    - − Generic Practice 2.3 (Ability 2): Provide resources
    - − Generic Practice 2.4 (Ability 3): Assign responsibility
    - − Generic Practice 2.5 (Ability 4): Train people
    - − Generic Practice 2.6 (Directing Implementation 1): Manage configurations
    - − Generic Practice 2.7 (Directing Implementation 2): Identify and involve relevant stakeholders
    - − Generic Practice 2.8 (Directing Implementation 3): Monitor and control the process
    - − Generic Practice 2.9 (Verifying Implementation 1): Objectively evaluate adherence
    - − Generic Practice 2.10 (Verifying Implementation 2): Review status with higher-level management

Each process area has specific and generic goals. Both types of goals must be satisfied to successfully achieve the benefits of process improvement for that PA. Each PA is described below. We begin by describing the purpose of the PA (directly from the CMMI), listing specific goals for the PA by goal label, discussing anything interesting or unusual about the PA, and then summarizing the PA.

The Process Areas for Maturity Level 2: Managed

Requirements Management

The purpose of Requirements Management is to manage the requirements of the project's products and product components, and to identify inconsistencies between those requirements and the project's plans and work products. Specific Goals (SGs) and Specific Practices (SPs) for this PA include:

- SG1: Managed Requirements
  - SP1.1: Obtain an understanding of requirements
  - SP1.2: Obtain commitment to requirements
  - SP1.3: Manage requirements changes
  - SP1.4: Maintain bi-directional traceability of requirements
  - SP1.5: Identify inconsistencies between project work and requirements

Why is Requirements Management at Maturity Level 2? Why is there another PA called Requirements Development at Level 3? What is the difference? Requirements Management for Maturity Level 2 is all about managing already existing requirements; that is, those requirements that have been elicited from the customer are documented and are ready to be worked or are in the process of being worked. This PA refers to capturing and managing the requirements that set the scope of the project. It is at this level because if you do not set the scope, you cannot control how much work will need to be done by the project. So, at this level, requirements already exist, and we are basically just managing the changes to them. Requirements Development at Maturity Level 3 is all about identifying requirements at a high level and decomposing them down to more detailed, testable levels. Because you need to have requirements in existence before you can manage changes to them, why is Requirements Development not at Maturity Level 2? Because eliciting requirements, developing them, and ensuring that they are "good" requirements is a much more difficult and sophisticated a concept. Because Level 2 is the first level in the CMMI with process areas, and Level 2 is about building a foundation for further process improvement, it sort of makes sense that managing requirements resides at this level, and creating requirements is at the next level. Another way of looking at it is to consider that the CMMI is not really a model for *improvement* (although it does lead to improvement), but is really a model for *assessing* or evaluating an organization's improvement effort. If you look at the model as an assessment model, then the first level assessed should be easier than the next, and the next, and the next.

The counterpoint is that we really do have an improvement model. The reason Requirements Development is at Maturity Level 3 is that technical organizations first have to do something to define and refine requirements before they can begin to manage them. Sometimes, this same technical organization will then forget that it has to manage the requirements it has defined, in addition to just defining requirements.

Another point to remember is that most organizations develop requirements first; so if it makes sense in your organization to form one team to improve processes for both gathering requirements and managing changes to them, fine — do it. Most organizations handle process improvement this way. But assessment teams must remember that they cannot fault an organization during an appraisal for failing to attack requirements' development at Maturity Level 2 when the concept is not concentrated on until Level 3.

Items to note in this process area are that bi-directional traceability is listed as a practice, which means that it is an expected component. In the CMM for Software, requirements traceability was not mentioned until Level 3 in the Software Product Engineering Key Process Area. However, most organizations realized that they could not adequately manage changes to requirements without tracing those requirements in some way. Traceability tools are mentioned as part of the elaboration for GP 2.3: Provide Resources, and are examples of work products reviewed (Requirements Traceability Matrix — RTM) for GP 2.9: Objectively Evaluate Adherence. Most organizations had actually constructed RTMs to manage their requirements, but now it is an *expected* practice in the CMMI. Constructing and using an RTM is not a trivial exercise. So this practice in this process area is an example of considerable growth beyond the CMM for software.

Organizations have asked how far forward and backward must they trace requirements. Our answer is: as far forward and backward as you can. It is not enough to trace one high-level requirement from the Requirements phase straight to the Test phase. Why? Because when problems occur in test (and they will), the fix for the problem may be found back in the Requirements phase, or the Design phase, or the Development phase. That is the purpose of tracing requirements — to assist in finding where the problem occurred so it can be fixed more quickly.

This process area does not seem to address corrective actions that may be needed once inconsistencies are found. The model seems to assume that perhaps these problems will be addressed as part of Project Monitoring and Control (a later process area).

Requirements Management includes understanding the requirements for all parts and components of the system (not just software); obtaining customer, management, and developer commitment to the requirements; managing changes to the requirements; maintaining traceability from the requirements forward in the development cycle, as well as backward to discover where changes may have introduced problems; and identifying inconsistencies between the requirements, ensuing work products, and ensuing activities. Requirements Management feeds into Project Planning, Project Monitoring and Control, Technical Solution (Level 3), etc. This Process Area forms the basis of project development, so it touches just about every Process Area in the model. Remember: the scope of the model has greatly expanded; you are devising and managing requirements not only for software, but for all parts of the product.

Project Planning

The purpose of Project Planning is to establish and maintain plans that define project activities. Specific Goals and Practices for this Process Area include:

- ■ SG1: Establish estimates
  - – SP1.1: Estimate the scope of the project
  - – SP1.2: Establish estimates of work product and task attributes
  - – SP1.3: Define project life cycle
  - – SP1.4: Determine estimates of effort and cost
- ■ SG2: Develop a project plan
  - – SP2.1: Establish the budget and schedule
  - – SP2.2: Identify project risks
  - – SP2.3: Plan for data management
  - – SP2.4: Plan for project resources
  - – SP2.5: Plan for needed knowledge and skills
  - – SP2.6: Plan stakeholder involvement
  - – SP2.7: Establish the project plan
- ■ SG3: Obtain commitment to the plan
  - – SP3.1: Review plans that affect the project
  - – SP3.2: Reconcile work and resource levels
  - – SP3.3: Obtain plan commitment

Although we have used the labels of the practices (the shortened names of the practices), the actual practice itself uses the term "establish and maintain," not just "establish." Let us talk about that phrase "establish and maintain." Sometimes in the CMMI, a word is just a word. Other times, the words have special meanings. That is the case here. "Establish and maintain" does not just mean to create and control; it means that you must *define* the plans, *document* the plans, *use* the plans, *monitor* what happens when using the plans, and *measure* the results of the plans. This phrase should be applied to all documentation created for process improvement. We say, "Just because you have crates of documentation, if you don't use it, you ain't got it." So use the plan; do not just stick it up on your shelf and show it to the auditors when they come to town.

SP1.1 discusses Estimating the Scope of the Project, but in actuality is expecting a Work Breakdown Structure (WBS). The CMM for Software did not expect a WBS, although this instance is probably an inclusion of a best practice from other organizations.

A Data Management Plan is now expected (SP2.3). That plan covers how to manage all the data and documentation your project will create, acquire, or require. Listed as work products are privacy and security requirements, security procedures, schedule for collection of project data, format descriptions, and mechanisms for reproduction and distribution. It sounds like a lot of work.

Project Planning includes identifying and documenting the scope of the project in order to define and maintain work boundaries; estimating the size and complexity of work products; estimating tasks, effort, and cost; defining the project life cycle or selecting a preexisting life cycle that matches the project; determining preliminary and follow-on budgets and schedules; identifying and documenting project risks; planning the extent to which stakeholders should become involved to ensure success; planning for managing information, staff, computer resources, and hardware; and planning for the training needs of project team members. The scope of work here has greatly expanded from just planning the software portion of a project to planning the design, development, and delivery of the entire product. This work will include systems engineering.

Project Monitoring and Control

The purpose of Project Monitoring and Control is to provide an understanding of the project's progress so that appropriate corrective actions can be taken when the project's performance deviates significantly from the plan. Specific Goals and Practices for this Process Area include:

- ■ SG1: Monitor project against plan
  - − SP1.1: Monitor project planning parameters
  - − SP1.2: Monitor commitments
  - − SP1.3: Monitor project risks
  - − SP1.4: Monitor data management
  - − SP1.5: Monitor stakeholder involvement
  - − SP1.6: Conduct progress reviews
  - − SP1.7: Conduct milestone reviews
- ■ SG2: Manage corrective action to closure
  - − SP2.1: Analyze issues
  - − SP2.2: Take correction action
  - − SP2.3: Manage corrective action

SP1.1 talks about Monitoring Project Planning Parameters. In this case, parameters is just a big word for project planning "stuff," things like cost, size, effort, actuals, estimates. Some of the subpractices for this practice suggest that this monitoring effort may be done simultaneously with Project Planning, not after. For example, most of the subpractices discuss reviewing the project plan (which comes out of the previous Project Planning Process Area). However, subpractices 5 and 6 specifically describe monitoring project personnel skill levels and documenting "significant" deviations in project planning parameters. So perhaps this Process Area has some linkage back to what is occurring in the Planning area.

Reviews are held "regularly," rather than event-driven. While we encourage regular reviews of project activities, we also encourage event-driven reviews. Event-driven reviews may be held when an "event" occurs, which usually means when something bad has happened or might happen — like missing a due date, or funding being temporarily suspended. One simple method to determine whether you are holding your meetings regularly enough, is to measure the number of issues or action items coming out of each review meeting. If the number of issues increases, you may need to hold your meetings a bit more regularly — that means more meetings. Also make sure that any Steering Committees that exist are actively playing a role, and the role they play is appropriate. While some Steering Committees take too hands-on an approach, most just want to know "How's it going?". And of course, the answer they expect to hear, and want to hear, is "fine." Keep your Steering Committee informed. Also, are your process improvement leaders getting feedback and comments back from the project members? No news is *not* good news.

How many reviews should be held? Who knows? It depends on your organization, the size of the project, the complexity, the visibility, etc. If your project is a six-month project with only three or four people, you probably hold informal meetings every day. The Project Manager is probably another programmer, and everyone basically knows what everyone else is doing, what is working, and what is not working. You probably share the same cubicle. In larger projects that take up to six years with 600 people, this is not the case. In this case, formal meetings must be coordinated and held on a regular basis, with minutes taken, and issues formally entered into an action item database for tracking. In this case, we would normally expect to see a weekly meeting held within every organizational unit (software, systems engineering, hardware, etc.) between the manager of the unit and his supervisors and workers, and then another meeting held weekly that includes the managers of the units and senior-level management. Meetings held twice a week or once a month with the customer would probably work, unless the project is in the early stages of requirements gathering, in the test phase, or in trouble. In such cases, we would expect meetings to be held either once a week, or even every day.

Reviews should be scheduled in the project plan. If the reviews are documented in the schedule, they will probably occur. Meetings should produce meeting minutes, action items should be tracked, and people who attend should also be monitored. Informal meetings may occur, but do not substitute informal meetings when formal ones are needed.

Project Monitoring and Control includes monitoring the attributes of the project specified in the project plan; monitoring the staff availability and stakeholder involvement; monitoring and revising project risks; monitoring information handling; conducting reviews to ensure progress is being made (usually conducted at least at major milestone completion); bringing to light potential problems and issues, and analyzing those issues; and taking corrective action to ameliorate project issues.

Supplier Agreement Management

The purpose of Supplier Agreement Management is to manage the acquisition of products and services from suppliers for which there exists a formal agreement. Specific Goals and Practices for this Process Area are:

- ■ SG1: Establish supplier agreements
  - – SP1.1: Determine acquisition type
  - – SP1.2: Select suppliers
  - – SP1.3: Establish supplier agreements
- ■ SG2: Satisfy supplier agreements
  - – SP2.1: Review COTS products
  - – SP2.2: Execute the supplier agreement
  - – SP2.3: Accept the acquired product
  - – SP2.4: Transition products

As discussed previously, this book uses the practice labels, and not the entire practice. However, please review SP1.2: select suppliers. The entire practice is much different from the label. The entire practice reads: "Select suppliers based on an evaluation of their ability to meet the specified requirements and established criteria." SP1.3: Establish Supplier Agreements is really about that phrase "establish and maintain" formal agreements with the supplier. Commercial-off-the-shelf (COTS) products are specifically covered in SP2.1, not just buried as an example, as in the CMM for Software.

If your organization does not have external suppliers (including contractors providing services), this Process Area may be "Not Applicable" (N/A) for your organization. However, considering the expanded nature of the model, this N/A seems less and less likely. Your organization probably will have formal agreements for delivery or development or installation of hardware, tools, COTS products, simulators, etc. This area is not just about subcontracting, as in the CMM for Software.

While Release Management is not covered extensively in the CMMI, some guidance for releasing the product built by suppliers is described here. Evaluating project risks that might occur, and Acceptance Testing, are also discussed in this process area.

Supplier Agreement Management includes determining the type of acquisition the project requires; determining the type of products or product components to be acquired; selecting appropriate suppliers; deciding to purchase COTS products when appropriate; defining and executing agreements with the chosen suppliers; and accepting and deploying products developed by suppliers into the project.

Measurement and Analysis

The purpose of Measurement and Analysis is to develop and sustain a measurement capability that is used to support management information needs. Specific Goals and Practices for this Process Area include:

■ SG1: Align measurement and analysis activities
  – SP1.1: Establish measurement objectives
  – SP1.2: Specify measures
  – SP1.3: Specify data collection and storage procedures
  – SP1.4: Specify analysis procedures
■ SG2: Provide measurement results
  – SP2.1: Collect measurement data
  – SP2.2: Analyze measurement data
  – SP2.3: Store data and results
  – SP2.4: Communicate results

This Process Area describes what to do when instituting a measurement process in your organization, not just which measurements to collect. This Process Area should be considered global because all processes should be measured, and most work products also produce meaningful metrics.

Measurement and Analysis (M&A) appeared throughout the CMM for Software as a Common Feature. M&A is now its own Process Area at Maturity Level 2. Why? Because high-maturity organizations have stated quite clearly that the key to success in process improvement is measurement and actually using those measurements to make decisions and monitor the process improvement effort. The authors of this book agree that measurement is key, but also feel that this one process area, while well-written and certainly necessary, is too sophisticated to reside at Maturity Level 2. We feel that most organizations will find this area very difficult to implement when operating at the degree of sophistication required for a Maturity Level 2 organization; that is, Level 2 is usually referred to as "the baby steps" of process improvement. That is not to say that it is easy to get to Level 2 (watch any toddler learning to walk — and watch how they learn to stop). The M&A Process Area expects that measurements are aligned with business goals. This expectation may be too much for low-maturity organizations. With little or no experience in measurement, it is easy for organizations to go either too far and measure everything, or not far enough and only measure things that they "already know" are important.

The Common Feature Directing Implementation has replaced the previous Measurement and Analysis Common Feature. Directing Implementation seems quite weak, with few meaningful examples. The Directing Implementation Common Feature does not actually state that measures are taken and used. Measures are the only examples given in the common feature, but a dysfunctional organization or a dysfunctional appraisal team might not use the "informative" examples correctly.

The other reason for breaking out measurement into its own process area was that organizations were good at *collecting* measurements, but not in actually *using* the measurements. It seems that just creating a process area will not handle that problem. Anyone can make a case for ignoring something, or just paying superficial compliance to the process area and its practices.

Measurement and Analysis includes defining measurement objectives; defining measures and procedures for collecting, storing, and analyzing metrics; executing the procedures to collect and analyze measurement data; storing the data and results in a manner fostering their usage by appropriate parties; and reporting measurement information to individuals and groups requiring the information.

A basic step-by-step approach to measurement is:

1. Select the process to measure.
2. Select the measures.
3. Determine when to collect data.
4. Determine how to collect data.
5. Record and store the information.
6. Analyze data for consistency and accuracy.
7. Chart the results.
8. Review the chart.
9. Do something (corrective actions).

Process and Product Quality Assurance

The purpose of the Process and Product Quality Assurance Process Area is to provide staff and management with objective insight into processes and associated work products. Specific Goals and Practices for this process area include:

- SG1: Objectively evaluate processes and work products
  - SP1.1: Objectively evaluate processes
  - SP1.2: Objectively evaluate work products and services
- SG2: Provide objective insight
  - SP2.1: Communicate and ensure resolution of noncompliance issues
  - SP2.2: Establish records

The term used is to "objectively evaluate adherence." This term is defined in the Glossary as reviewing activities and work products against criteria that minimize subjectivity and bias by the reviewer. The reference to the term "audit" is further defined in the Glossary as "an independent examination of a work product or set of work products to determine whether requirements are being met." The concept of independence is addressed by the Generic Practice 2.4: Assign responsibility, and states that those people assigned to perform this role should have "sufficient" independence and objectivity. In the verbiage following the purpose statement (Introductory Notes) at the beginning of the process area itself, some discussion of objectivity and independence may be found. These paragraphs discuss embedded quality assurance and independent QA groups. It is stated that "Those performing quality assurance activities for a work product should be separated from those directly involved in developing or maintaining the work product. An independent reporting channel to the appropriate level of organizational management must be available so that noncompliance issues may be escalated as necessary." We remind the authors of the CMMI that *processes* are not *products*; and that Notes are simply informative and not normative — that is, these dicta may prove useful for understanding the intent of the area but are not mandatory for process improvement implementation or assessment. We also find that by burying the definition of objectivity and independence in these paragraphs, a less-than-stellar implementation of this process area will be promoted.

Notice that the CMMI specifically calls out quality assurance reviews and activities for both product and process. Under the CMM for Software, Verifying Implementation 3 involved Software Quality Assurance (SQA). SQA groups were directed to review both products and processes. However, organizations tended to either focus on SQA reviews for products (reviewing documentation against formatting standards) or on reviewing process adherence (whether SQA reviews were held as documented in the process descriptions and the procedures). Few organizations realized that both types of reviews were necessary. So now the CMMI emphasizes that both must occur by including both in the name of the process area and in the specific practices.

To audit processes, simply review whether they were followed as documented, why or why not, where the problems are, and where improvements are needed. To audit products, use product standards and checklists to ensure compliance. Reviewing for content (as opposed to form or image) may best be left to the Peer Review process and the Technical Review process. It is often simply too difficult to get Quality Assurance personnel to review for "good" content, as this requires vast technical knowledge. Most techies prefer to stay techies, and getting superior technical experts into a QA role is difficult — not impossible, just difficult. If your organization would like to attempt this feat, we suggest rotating developers into QA, and QA personnel into the development arena. In some organizations, before someone can become a project manager, he or she must have served duty in both QA and technical development areas. Another way of trying to incorporate technical expertise into QA reviews is to perform audits with both technicians and QA individuals participating side-by-side.

SP2.1: Communicate and ensure resolution of noncompliance issues at first seems to indicate that all the QA people must do is report the problem and move on. But the full practice reads: "Communicate quality issues and ensure resolution of noncompliance issues with the staff and managers," with Subpractice 7 describing tracking issues to resolution.

Process and Product Quality Assurance includes providing a strategy and procedures for objectively evaluating processes and products; identifying personnel to fulfill this role objectively; reporting quality issues and noncompliance; and producing reports that provide verification that quality reviews were conducted and their results.

Configuration Management

The purpose of the Configuration Management process area is to establish and maintain the integrity of work products using configuration identification, configuration control, configuration status accounting, and configuration audits. Specific Goals and Practices for this process area include:

- SG1: Establish baselines
  - SP1.1: Identify configuration items
  - SP1.2: Establish a configuration management system
  - SP1.3: Create or release baselines
- SG2: Track and control changes
  - SP2.1: Track change requests
  - SP2.2: Control configuration items
- SG3: Establish integrity
  - SP3.1: Establish configuration management records
  - SP3.2: Perform configuration audits

Configuration Management is not just setting up libraries for files and then migrating files back and forth. It is also not about buying tools that will migrate files and tell you when they were moved, or that a change has been made. Configuration Management is about defining configuration items. "Configuration items" is a well-known term for DoD clients, but is not so well known outside that arena. We use the following example. When a software system is being designed, it can be broken up into several pieces. Those pieces can be the files, the data elements within those files, programs, reports, and integrated or called modules. Those pieces can be termed "configuration items." An organization can have both high-level configuration items and then lower-level configuration items that result from decomposing the high-level items into lower-level, more detailed, smaller pieces. Each piece (or configuration item) is assigned a label and a number to aid in tracking that all pieces of the desired system are included as part of the delivered product. It also helps in tracking changes, planning the effort, and auditing functionality satisfied.

Configuration Management is also about establishing baselines. Baselines are basically where you draw a line in the sand and say, "OK. Anything developed past this point, or any changes made past this point, must go through some sort of official review before being incorporated into the rest of the system." Factors such as impacts to already existing modules, costs, skillsets required, schedules and due dates, and technical feasibility are all analyzed before the modification or addition is made. The CMMI does not tell you when to establish a baseline; it just encourages you to do so. So when should baselines be established? Well, once again, we do not know your particular organization, but usually baselines are set after requirements have been approved and signed off, the design has been signed off, testing has finished, and the product has been delivered and is ready to enter the maintenance phase.

Configuration Management duties include verifying the contents of libraries and files. A tool may be used to track that changes were made, but a tool is usually not sophisticated enough to tell you what the change was, and how this change affects the rest of the system. So, a human being must be involved in reviewing and analyzing the effects of any changes. This type of review is called a configuration audit. Although both the CMMI and the CMM for Software discuss ensuring the "completeness and correctness" of the material in the libraries, the CMM for Software does not define what "completeness and correctness" means. Because of that, some organizations included physical configuration audits (where the physical structure of the system is reviewed against changes) and not functional configuration audits (where requirements are traced to confirm that they have been satisfied within elements of the system). Subpractice 4 of SP3.2: Perform configuration audits seems to imply that to ensure "completeness and correctness," both must occur.

Although throughout the CMMI, specific groups are generally not mentioned, in Configuration Management, subpractice 1 of SP1.3: Create or release baselines does specifically mention the Configuration Control Board (CCB). A "release" is the product that is released to the customer for use. A "build" is the work product that is passed onto other internal departments for further usage or work. Formal procedures for Release Management are not covered. This area also focuses on having a formal change request process in place.

Configuration Management includes defining configuration items; developing or implementing support tools, techniques, procedures, and storage media; generating and maintaining baselines; tracking change requests and controlling changes; documenting the results of the configuration management effort; and performing configuration audits.

Summary

Although at first glance it appears that Level 2 of the CMMI has not changed significantly from Level 2 of the CMM for Software, reality must set in. While the words in the CMMI and the layout of the Process Areas appear to be very similar, they are not. Remember: the CMMI includes

Systems Engineering, Software Engineering, Supplier Sourcing, and Integrated Product and Process Teams. So when planning and implementing these Process Areas, all levels and departments that will be necessary to create the final product (and any interim products) must be included.

There is also redundancy across the model. Examples at Maturity Level 2 are that the Measurement and Analysis and Product and Process Quality Assurance Process Areas must be performed at all levels and within all process areas, not just at Level 2. Further redundancy is shown within the Generic Practices. For example, GP2.2: Plan the Process can be traced back to the Project Planning Process Area. GP2.5: Train People is related to Organizational Training at Level 3. GP2.8: Monitor and Control the process is a reflection of the Project Monitoring and Control Process Area. GP2.6: Manage Configurations reflects Configuration Management. GP2.9 Objectively evaluate adherence is directly related to Product and Process Quality Assurance. While the argument has been made that these redundancies are included to aid the reader in how to implement the Generic Practices, we feel the hints provided are simply confusing. For example, when assessed, if GP2.6 is not followed in the Project Planning Process Area, does that mean that the organization is faulted in both Project Planning and in Configuration Management? Is this double jeopardy? To what degree is the organization in violation? Are these "showstoppers"? These supposed "hints and how-tos" just do not seem very helpful. They are either too generic or too prescriptive, depending on where the reader is referred.

Chapter 6

Understanding Maturity
Level 3: Defined

This chapter is designed to help the reader understand the basic tenets of Maturity Level 3 in the staged representation of the CMMI®. However, because this chapter consists of summaries of the process areas, anyone wishing to get a better idea of the model, no matter which representation is to be used, can benefit from this chapter. Once again, we are not attempting to teach the CMMI; we simply offer a condensed version of the various areas and key points to consider.

Moving from Level 2 to Level 3

Maturity Level 3 differs from Level 2 in that now an organizational way of doing business has been developed. What that means is that the best practices and lessons learned from the projects have bubbled up to the organizational level to create an organizational identity. There are common, shared approaches for performing daily tasks on each project. For example, estimating the size of a project may be done using the Delphi Technique (basically subject matter experts discussing a series of best-case and worst-case estimates), a standard metric may have been institutionalized (such as using function points instead of lines of code), and a standard tool may be in use to actually calculate the size.

This organizational way of doing business is documented in the Organization's Set of Standard Processes (OSSP). However, should a project need to tailor this OSSP to more adequately fit its needs, then that tailoring request is brought to a decision-making body (usually the Engineering Process Group — EPG), and if appropriate, the request is granted. An example may be a legacy system that calculates size by lines of code instead of by function point. Rather than reengineer the millions of lines of code in the system in order to use a tool to count function points, and rather than do it manually, the project is simply allowed to continue calculating size by lines of code. The Delphi Technique discussed above is still used, but lines of code is the measurement.

To perform at Maturity Level 3, an organization must have satisfied all the goals for all of the process areas in both Level 2 and Level 3. Sometimes, exceptions can be made. For example, if an organization has no outside agreements, then Supplier Agreement Management at Level 2 and Integrated Supplier Management at Level 3 may not apply. Therefore, those process areas are determined to be N/A. Caution should be exercised however. Entire *process areas* are generally not allowed to be tailored out of consideration. *Practices* can be tailored out if replaced by sufficient alternative practices. Remember: the more tailoring done, the less likely an organization is to achieve improvement, and the less likely the organization is to achieve a maturity level through an assessment.

The CMMI makes a point of stating that, at Level 3, the organization has more distinctly defined its processes. We feel that this statement leads the reader to many wrong conclusions. This statement does not mean to wait until Level 3 to define your processes. When defining processes, an organization should always try to define them so that they can be followed — even at Level 2. Processes are at a high level — it is their associated procedures that detail how to perform the processes. Review Chapter 16 of this book for more information.

The CMMI states that the following attributes of a process are necessary. We suggest that you follow this "mandate." However, we also suggest that you add what needs to be added. Some organizations have also combined the inputs and entry criteria into one attribute, and the outputs and exit criteria into another attribute. While purists will object to that, we have seen it work in organizations. And after all — the beef is in the procedures, not the processes.

The following items are to be included in process definitions:

- *Purpose:* Purpose of the process
- *Inputs:* Work products, plans, approval memoranda (usually nouns)
- *Entry criteria:* What must be triggered before this process can start? (Usually the exit criteria of the previous step or process. Usually stated as a verb.)

- *Activities:* Tasks that must be performed. These tasks are usually later broken down into the detailed procedures for *how* to perform the tasks.
- *Roles:* Who does what (usually by position)
- *Measures:* What measures does this process produce?
- *Verification steps:* What reviews are performed to determine that this process is followed and is producing the correct results? (Usually management and quality assurance reviews, but sometimes can include customer, peer, and project team reviews.)
- *Outputs:* Work products, plans, approved products. (Can be the completed inputs.)
- *Exit criteria:* How do we know when it is time to stop this process? (Usually expressed in verbs, and usually becomes the entry criteria for the next process step or next process.)

Another distinction is made concerning processes. A *managed* process is a process that tackles project management efforts, is planned and executed according to a policy, and is monitored and reviewed to ensure adherence to its process description. This is the type of process expected at Maturity Level 2. A *defined* process builds upon a managed process by creating an organizational process that is then tailored to fit the needs of a particular project, and involves gathering information related to improvement efforts undertaken by the organization, in order to improve both the organization-level process and the project-level process. This is the type of process expected at Maturity Level 3.

There are 14 process areas for Maturity Level 3:

1. Requirements Development
2. Technical Solution
3. Product Integration
4. Verification
5. Validation
6. Organizational Process Focus
7. Organizational Process Definition
8. Organizational Training
9. Integrated Project Management (including for IPPD)
10. Risk Management
11. Integrated Teaming
12. Integrated Supplier Management
13. Decision Analysis and Resolution
14. Organizational Environment for Integration

You will notice that Level 3 has expanded to include engineering process areas and Integrated Product and Process Development (IPPD).

IPPD is about forming teams that include subject matter experts from all areas needed to produce the product for the customer. An example might be when building a new jet fighter. This effort would require hundreds or thousands of individuals to work on developing all parts of the plane, including the sophisticated software systems for navigation, landing, communications, and attack; the actual construction of the hardware and fuselage of the plane; safety engineers to test safety-critical parts and functioning; mechanics to ensure that the plane would be easy and quick to repair under emergency and nonemergency conditions; pilots to ensure that the plane could actually be flown; documentation experts to ensure that all necessary documentation and manuals were written correctly; and others. In cases such as this one, rather than try to include comments and ideas from everyone working on the project (that is, to design and deliver a working jet fighter plane), representatives from each area would be assigned to an Integrated Product Team (IPT). This team would develop a shared vision of what the final product should look like and what its final functionality should include. They would also be responsible for ensuring that input from all areas was included in the requirements gathering, design, development, testing, and final delivery of the product.

The Generic Goals for Level 3 are somewhat different from Level 2. The generic goals are listed below. We use the abbreviations GG for Generic Goal and GP for Generic Practice. The Common Features (Commitment to Perform — CO, Ability to Perform — AB, Directing Implementation — DI, and Verifying Implementation — VE) are also abbreviated.

- GG3: Institutionalize a defined process
    - GP2.1 (CO1): Establish an organizational policy
    - GP3.1 (AB1): Establish a defined process
    - GP2.2 (AB2): Plan the process
    - GP2.3 (AB3): Provide resources
    - GP2.4 (AB4): Assign responsibility
    - GP2.5 (AB5): Train people
    - GP2.6 (DI1): Manage configurations
    - GP2.7 (DI2): Identify and involve relevant stakeholders
    - GP2.8 (DI3): Monitor and control the process
    - GP3.2 (DI4): Collect improvement information
    - GP2.9 (VE1): Objectively evaluate adherence
    - GP2.10 (VE2): Review status with higher-level management

To satisfy the goals for Level 3, the goals for Level 2 must be satisfied as well. This mandate holds true for both the specific goals and the generic goals listed above. So, reviewing the list of generic goals above reveals that the generic goals for Level 2 are still there, *plus* the addition of one more goal (actually replacing GG2 — or GG3 *subsuming* GG2 to use a CMMI phrase) and two more corresponding generic practices (GP3.1 and GP3.2). The Level 3 generic goal is Institutionalize a Defined Process; and the two generic practices that make that goal possible are Establish a Defined Process and Collect Improvement Information. So, the CMMI is asking us to implement these practices for each individual process area.

The following pages discuss each process area for Level 3. We use the abbreviations SG for Specific Goal and SP for corresponding Specific Practices.

Process Areas for the Maturity Level 3: Defined

Requirements Development

The purpose of Requirements Development is to produce and analyze customer, product, and product component requirements. Specific Goals and Practices for this process area include:

- SG1: Develop customer requirements
  - SP1.1: Elicit needs
  - SP1.2: Develop the customer requirements
- SG2: Develop product requirements
  - SP2.1: Establish product and product component requirements
  - SP2.2: Allocate product component requirements
  - SP2.3: Identify interface requirements
- SG3: Analyze and validate requirements
  - SP3.1: Establish operational concepts and scenarios
  - SP3.2: Establish a definition of required functionality
  - SP3.3: Analyze requirements
  - SP3.4: Analyze requirements to achieve balance
  - SP3.5: Validate requirements with comprehensive methods

SP1.1: Elicit Needs, when expanded to its full name, reads "Elicit stakeholders' needs, expectations, constraints, and interfaces for all phases of the product life cycle," and in the explanatory notes underneath it, states that this practice also includes identifying needs not explicitly stated by the customer.

Requirements Development is where requirements are initially defined and documented. Requirements Management at Level 2 is where changes are administered. Requirements Development gathers requirements and then must usually refine these requirements in some way — by stating them more clearly, determining whether they are redundant or inconsistent with other requirements, and breaking them down into more detailed and traceable requirements.

The CMMI uses the terms "Product, Product Component, and Component." Examples of these terms might be that a Product is the final deliverable, such as a jet fighter plane capable of flying and firing missiles. The Product Components might be the navigation system, the fire control system, the fuselage, the landing equipment, and the communications system. The Components might be software to determine the distance from the ground, the software to aim a missile, the control panel, the tires, and the headphones. The manufacture of a communications system may have a different mapping, starting with the communication systems product, radios and antennas as product components, and the receiver, transmitter, and tuner software as components.

This process area introduces the *Concept of Operations* or, using the CMMI term, *operations concept*. This document is usually the first document written when determining whether or not to pursue development of a product. It is usually a high-level statement of the desired functionality, and a preliminary plan and schedule for development. This document is then used as the basis for further requirements identification and refinement, as well as project planning. This concept works well in a DoD environment or when attempting to build a highly complex product with many people. However, in the commercial, non-DoD world, these documents are generally not used. This can be a problem when following the CMMI because this document is expected in several practices throughout the model.

Shaded, gray areas are included in the staged representation of the model. These areas document the differences between the staged and continuous representation. For example, SP1.1 in the staged is called "Elicit Needs." The subpractice under the practice describes gathering requirements from relevant stakeholders. The continuous representation has practice SP1.1–1. The "–1" signifies that this practice is a base practice ("–2" signifies that the practice is an advanced practice). SP1.1–1 of the continuous representation is called "Collect Stakeholder Needs." So, while the practices look somewhat different, they really contain the same information — they just state it a little differently and use a slightly different numbering system. Please see our discussion of the structure of the CMMI in Chapters 3 and 4.

Beta testing of requirements is mentioned here.

Requirements Development includes collecting and eliciting customer requirements from all involved parties at all levels; breaking down those high-level requirements into lower-level, more detailed requirements, and assigning them to categories for further development; defining interfaces among the requirements and any other areas necessary to fulfill the requirements; more adequately defining and documenting the operational need, concept, scenario, and functionality desired; ensuring that the requirements are complete, required, and consistent; negotiating needs versus wants versus constraints; and validating the requirements against risk in the early phases of the project.

Technical Solution

The purpose of the Technical Solution process area is to develop, design, and implement solutions to requirements. Solutions, designs, and implementations encompass products, product components, and product-related life-cycle processes, either singly or in combinations as appropriate. Specific Goals and Practices for this process area include:

- ■ SG1: Select product component solutions
  - − SP1.1: Develop detailed alternative solutions and selection criteria
  - − SP1.2: Evolve operational concepts and scenarios
  - − SP1.3: Select product-component solutions
- ■ SG2: Develop the design
  - − SP2.1: Design the product or product component
  - − SP2.2: Establish a complete technical data package
  - − SP2.3: Design interfaces using criteria
  - − SP2.4: Perform, make, buy, or reuse analyses
- ■ SG3: Implement the product design
  - − SP3.1: Implement the design
  - − SP3.2: Establish product support documentation

Technical Solution implies a complex product requiring a complicated approach. New items included tend to relate to the systems engineering side of the house. A complex system requires more groups and more people. The Technical Data Package is used to coordinate these group efforts, as well as to satisfy procurement interests. The package includes such items as product architecture description, allocated requirements, process descriptions as they relate to products, interface requirements, materials requirements, fabrication and manufacturing requirements, verification requirements, conditions of use, operating and usage scenarios, and decision rationale. That is a lot more than what was recommended by the CMM for Software. In our experience, some of this information can be found directly in the Request for Proposal and the Statement of Work from the customer. Some of it can be found in process documentation within the organization, some in the contract between the suppliers/servicers, some in the Requirements documentation, and some in the Design documentation. Maybe this package is just recommended as sort of a checklist to ensure that the supplier is delivering everything necessary to complete the product. However, if this documentation can be found elsewhere, is the CMMI requiring the project to collect this information and store it in one place? Is this redundant? Would it be better to include this practice in, perhaps, Product Integration?

Technical Solution also expects a formal approach to providing solutions — that is, to suggest alternatives and then study them. This approach is beneficial for large systems but probably overbearing for smaller ones. If an organization plans to undertake a new approach to an old problem, to use new technology, or to develop a totally new product, then this approach seems worthwhile. For example, I was once asked to do a feasibility study and alternatives analysis to determine whether using a specific programming language and database should be used to develop a warehouse system for a client. Because the client had already determined that this language would be used, as all of their software systems used this language and converting to something new would require a complete overhaul of all their code for lots of money, the expected outcome was a resounding "yes." This process area may promote a more balanced approach to deriving and evaluating alternatives, although there are always ways to get around the rules.

In this process area, when the model refers to processes, the model generally does not mean *process improvement*-type processes, but *design* processes. That is, the processes they are talking about in this process area focus on the technical steps necessary to produce the product. They do not focus on processes used to manage the project or manage the process for Technical Solution or the process used to improve processes in an organization. They are totally focused on engineering the product.

The continuous representation is referred to here by SP1.1–1, a base practice, which is named "Develop Alternative Solutions and Selection Criteria." While the subpractices, at first glance, look somewhat different, the information in them is contained in the staged representation practice SP1.1. Reading the practice documented in the continuous representation may simply give the reader a bit more understanding or information.

Peer reviews are mentioned in this process area. Technical Solution gives the reader some guidance on which products should be peer reviewed (SP3.1 and SP3.2 specifically discuss design and support documentation). The Organizational Process Definition Process Area also includes items and artifacts to be peer reviewed, including the Organization's Set of Standard Processes, life-cycle models, tailoring guidelines, measures, and the project's defined processes (also discussed in Integrated Project Management). We recommend that each process area be read for guidance on which products from each process area should be peer reviewed. For guidance on the steps to follow when planning and conducting a Peer Review, see the Verification Process Area.

Release baselines are presented here, as are unit testing and the operations concept.

Technical Solution includes determining how to satisfy the requirements via analysis of different alternatives and methods; creating operational scenarios; selecting solutions and follow-on designs; generating a technical data package that may include development methodologies, bills of material, life-cycle processes, product descriptions, requirements, conditions of use, rationale for decisions made, and verification criteria; defining and documenting detailed interface information; determining whether to make, buy, or reuse; and implementing the design and generating supporting documentation.

Product Integration

The purpose of Product Integration is to assemble the product from the product components; ensure that the product, as integrated, functions properly; and deliver the product. Specific Goals and Practices for this process area include:

- ■ SG1: Prepare for product integration
  - – SP1.1: Determine integration sequence
  - – SP1.2: Establish the product integration environment
  - – SP1.3: Establish product integration procedures and criteria
- ■ SG2: Ensure interface compatibility
  - – SP2.1: Review interface descriptions for completeness
  - – SP2.2: Manage interfaces
- ■ SG3: Assemble product components and deliver the product
  - – SP3.1: Confirm readiness of product components for integration
  - – SP3.2: Assemble product components
  - – SP3.3: Evaluate assembled product components
  - – SP3.4: Package and deliver the product or product component

SP3.1: Confirm Readiness of Product Components for Integration is expanded to "Confirm, prior to assembly, that each product component required to assemble the product has been properly identified, functions according to its description, and that the product–component interfaces comply with the interface descriptions." The entire practice gives a little more information as to what is expected than the practice label gives to the reader.

This process area is the favorite of one of the authors of this book. Why? Because this is where the product comes together and you get to see the results of your work. It is also where you deliver the product, and that means you get paid.

This process area expects the project to demonstrate each step to the user. This activity should probably be done by demonstrating one or a few modules at a time, rather than the entire system. If a phased approach for development has been used, then this process area would expect to build a little, test a little, demonstrate a little, and deliver a little, module by module. Integration testing (as defined by and used by software engineers) is *almost*, but not quite, discussed here. This process area talks about testing integrated modules as an example, but it seems to mean tangible products that are being tested, not just software modules. This process area also overlaps with the Verification and Validation process areas, which may occur in parallel.

This process area is not release management. Releasing products is covered somewhat in Configuration Management, Supplier Agreement Management, and Technical Solution.

Product Integration includes determining how to assemble the product and what the sequence of assembly should be; creating an operational environment in which to satisfactorily deploy the product; documenting procedures and criteria for integrating the product; ensuring adequate integration of interfaces; and delivering the product.

Verification

The purpose of Verification is to ensure that selected work products meet their specified requirements. Verification ensures that the requirements have been met, while Validation assures that the product meets its intended use. Verification ensures that "you built it right" while Validation ensures that "you built the right thing." Specific Goals and Practices for this process area include:

- SG1: Prepare for verification
  - SP1.1: Select work products for verification
  - SP1.2: Establish the verification environment
  - SP1.3: Establish verification procedures and criteria
- SG2: Perform peer reviews
  - SP2.1: Prepare for peer reviews
  - SP2.2: Conduct peer reviews
  - SP2.3: Analyze peer review data
- SG3: Verify selected work products
  - SP3.1: Perform verification
  - SP3.2: Analyze verification results and identify corrective action

This process area is advertised as answering the question: "Did you build the product right?" The next PA (Validation) answers the question: "Did you build the right product?" So, Verification is: "Did you meet the requirements"?

Peer reviews are included in this part of the text.

Verification expects the usage of test setups and test simulators. Sometimes, the same test setups and simulators can be used for Validation as well — you just use them for different purposes, looking for different things. Acceptance testing is mentioned here. The overall term "Testing" is used in this process area but never truly spelled out. Some examples of testing types are given — path coverage, stress, test case reuse, etc. — but testing by software life-cycle phase, or unit-integration-system-acceptance-regression, is not covered.

Verification includes selecting which work products are to be verified; creating the environment necessary for verification of those products; documenting procedures and criteria for verification, and then following those procedures; conducting peer reviews; and verifying the product and taking any corrective actions needed.

Validation

The purpose of Validation is to demonstrate that a product or product component fulfills its intended use when placed in its intended environment. Specific Goals and Practices for this process area include:

- ■ SG1: Prepare for validation
  - – SP1.1: Select products for validation
  - – SP1.2: Establish the validation environment
  - – SP1.3: Establish validation procedures and criteria
- ■ SG2: Validate product or product components
  - – SP2.1: Perform validation
  - – SP2.2: Analyze validation results

Validation includes the same strategies as for Verification above, except this time we create what is necessary to *validate* the product, not verify that the requirements were satisfied. Validation involves creating an environment as close as possible to the environment in which the product will be used, in order to perform final testing of the product. However, this is not always a logical, practical thing to do. An example follows. When one of the authors of this book was working as a subcontractor on a defense contract, we were required, as part of the contract, to build the product and test the product in the same environment as it would be used. Well, the system under development was only going to be used by six people at any given time, although it could be used by up to 200 simultaneous users during peak loads. So, the powers-that-be overseeing the contract decided that, if only six people were going to use the system at any given time, then only six personal computers (PCs) would be necessary. The project managers had determined that to meet the time constraints for the project (a large, database-driven claims processing system), 15 programmers, three database administrators, five test personnel, and one database manager were needed. That adds up to needing at least 24 PCs. We were allowed six. The solution was to work shift-work and share the PCs. This contract was cancelled after three years and no usable code was produced.

Are we saying that it is a bad practice to create similar environments? No, not at all. It is very worthwhile to test products in their ultimate environment, and to design products for their ultimate use. We are in favor of this. Just remember that it can get expensive and complicated. Plan ahead and plan wisely.

Because this process area also requires simulators to be built, one might want to consider the unique training requirements necessary to build the intended-use environment.

Validation asks: "Are you building the right product?" It includes selecting products and approaches for validating products; generating the validation environment; documenting validation criteria and procedures; conducting the validation activities; and analyzing the results and any issues that arise from conducting the validation process.

Organizational Process Focus

The purpose of Organizational Process Focus (OPF) is to plan and implement organizational process improvement based on a thorough understanding of the current strengths and weaknesses of the organization's process and process assets. Specific Goals and Practices for this process area include:

- ■ SG1: Determine process improvement opportunities
    - – SP1.1: Establish organizational process needs
    - – SP1.2: Appraise the organization's processes
    - – SP1.3: Identify the organization's process improvements
- ■ SG2: Plan and implement process improvement activities
    - – SP2.1: Establish process action plans
    - – SP2.2: Implement process action plans
    - – SP2.3: Deploy organizational process assets
    - – SP2.4: Incorporate process-related experiences into the organization's process assets

Piloting processes is mentioned here, and process improvement proposals are mentioned here as subpractices. OPF introduces who should be doing process improvement and what process improvement is. The Engineering Process Group (EPG) is mentioned here — one of the few groups still retained in the model. The EPG is the group responsible for planning process improvement and implementing the plans. They may or may not be involved in any initial assessments comparing their organization to what is included in the CMMI. The process area essentially describes how to initiate, diagnose, evaluate, act, and learn from process improvement in an organization. Those of you familiar with the IDEAL^{SM} model will recognize the use of this model for the layout of the process area.

One recommendation we have in this area concerns the formation of the EPG. Some organizations have decided to form a separate EPG for each discipline — that is, one EPG for systems engineering, one for software engineering, one for IPPD, and one for supplier sourcing. Those organizations have quickly found that this separation of duties based on job discipline defeats the purpose of the EPG. The purpose of the EPG is to define an integrated process for process improvement, and to implement this process seamlessly throughout the entire organization. By forming separate groups, feedback and communication are not really there. We recommend that you form one EPG that has representatives from the various areas and disciplines. How big should it be? We have found that the optimum number of full-time, fully engaged people on this type of team should be about ten. Any more and decision making becomes too lengthy and obfuscated. Too few and there are not enough people to do the work.

Yes, you can have levels of EPGs, just like there could be levels of SEPGs when using the Software CMM. Just do not get too hierarchical or too bureaucratic. This group must do real work in the process improvement area.

For more information, see Chapter 13 concerning Roles and Responsibilities.

Organizational Process Focus includes establishing a fundamental understanding of what process is and why it is important to an organization; assessing current processes in the organization and identifying areas in need of improvement; creating and following action plans for improvement; determining how to institute process improvement in the organization and what plans and documentation will be needed; and reviewing the process improvement effort itself and instituting improvements in this area.

Organizational Process Definition

The purpose of Organizational Process Definition is to establish and maintain a usable set of organizational process assets. Specific Goals and Practices for this process area include:

- SG1: Establish organizational process assets
  - SP1.1: Establish standard processes
  - SP1.2: Establish life-cycle model descriptions
  - SP1.3: Establish tailoring criteria and guidelines
  - SP1.4: Establish the organization's measurement repository
  - SP1.5: Establish the organization's process asset library

The process area is Organizational Process Definition because this is where you define and document your organizational processes. No big surprises there. The process asset library is commonly referred to as the PAL.

The measurement repository discussed here is different from what is mentioned in Measurement and Analysis at Level 2. The measurement repository at Level 2 is primarily concerned with project-level data stored in project-level repositories. At Level 3, the information from the projects is now collected and stored at an organizational level, and combined and integrated into organizational metrics that are meaningful to the organization as a whole. For example, at Level 2, the repository may contain when the Requirements phase began, and when it ended; when the Design phase began and when it ended; when Construction began and when it ended; when Testing began and when it ended; and when Implementation began. The repository may also contain defects found in testing. Each project has a repository, and each project collects these data to run their own projects. At Level 3, these metrics are bubbled up from the projects, and studied cumulatively to try to predict trends across the projects. For example, if one project was late getting out of the Testing phase because many errors were found, did that project skimp on the Requirements phase? Is there a correlation? If all of the project data are studied from all of the projects, and all of the projects except one had the same problem, what is it about that one project that made it different? Was it better? Can we devise a "standard" length of time to be set for the requirements phase to improve functioning downstream (like in the Test phase)?

Once an organizational-level repository has been built (based on historical, project-level data from the past) any project-level repository can also use the organizational-level repository as its foundation for building or updating its own (project) repository. This gives the project manager an idea of how to plan his project, where the bottlenecks commonly occur (or occurred in the past), and how long to schedule activities.

Tailoring is also discussed here. The organization must document its criteria for when tailoring of the organization's processes can be done by a project, and what those tailoring guidelines and rules are. However, if you find that you are often tailoring the organization's set of standard processes (OSSP), can you really state that you have a *standard* organizational process? I do not think so. It does not sound very *standard* to me.

Organizational Process Definition includes generating the OSSP; describing various life cycles approved for use; documenting tailoring criteria and guidelines; and creating and maintaining the measurement repository and PAL.

Organizational Training

The purpose of Organizational Training is to develop the skills and knowledge of people so they can perform their roles effectively and efficiently. Specific Goals and Practices for this process area include:

- ■ SG1: Establish an organizational training capability
  - – SP1.1: Establish the strategic training needs
  - – SP1.2: Determine which training needs are the responsibility of the organization
  - – SP1.3: Establish an organizational training tactical plan
  - – SP1.4: Establish training capability
- ■ SG2: Provide necessary training
  - – SP2.1: Deliver training
  - – SP2.2: Establish training records
  - – SP2.3: Assess training effectiveness

This process area expects a Strategic Training Plan coming from the OSSP, as well as business plans, process improvement plans, defined skillsets of existing groups, missing skillsets of existing groups, skillsets needed for any nonexistent groups necessary to be formed, mission statements, and vision statements. And all of these things tied into training plans. That is a lot of documentation that many smaller organizations do not have and do not need. Small organizations tend to operate at the tactical planning level and not at the strategic level. This process area expects a Strategic Plan that leads to a Tactical Plan.

Organizational-level training plans bubble up from project-level training plans and needs. Organizations also need to evaluate the effectiveness of the training received. That does not necessarily mean that the class fills out an evaluation after the class has been given. It means that the organization must track the value of the training received. Is what you learned what you needed to learn to do the job?

This process area is not about knowledge management. While you may define core competencies and certifications necessary, the concepts are not that similar. For a clearer discussion of knowledge management, review the People CMM, which gives much more guidance.

Organizational Training includes determining the strategic training needs of the organization and how to achieve them; procuring or delivering the training; and tracking its effectiveness.

Integrated Project Management

The purpose of Integrated Project Management (IPM) is to establish and manage the project, and the involvement of the relevant stakeholders, according to an integrated and defined process that is tailored from the organizational set of standard processes. For Integrated Process and Process Development (IPPD), it also covers the establishment of a shared vision for the project and a team structure for integrated teams that will carry out the objectives of the project. Specific Goals and Practices for this process area include:

- SG1: Use the project's defined process
  - SP1.1: Establish the project's defined process
  - SP1.2: Use organizational process assets for planning project activities
  - SP1.3: Integrate plans
  - SP1.4: Manage the project using the integrated plans
  - SP1.5: Contribute to the process assets
- SG2: Coordinate and collaborate with relevant stakeholders
  - SP2.1: Manage stakeholder involvement
  - SP2.2: Manage dependencies
  - SP2.3: Resolve coordination issues
- SG3: Use the project's shared vision (Goal and practices associated with IPPD):
  - SP3.1: Define the project's shared vision context
  - SP3.2: Establish the project's shared vision
- SG4: Organize integrated teams (Goal and practices associated with IPPD):
  - SP4.1: Determine integrated team structure for the project
  - SP4.2: Develop a preliminary distribution of requirements to integrated teams
  - SP4.3: Establish integrated teams

There are two versions of this process area: Integrated Project Management and Integrated Project Management for IPPD. To include the second version, the model adds two more specific goals — that is, SG3 and 4 — with their associated specific practices.

The policies written for this process area should include when and when not to include IPPD activities.

This PA is supposed to be the evolution of Project Planning, and Project Monitoring and Control from Level 2, plus more sophistication for Level 3. That means that this PA involves more rigorous techniques for planning and monitoring projects within the organization. In this PA, each project reviews and tailors the OSSP to fit a project's specific needs. The result is called the project's defined process, and yes, it must be documented. This process is then used to help build the project plan.

The difference between the standard processes, tailoring guidelines, and procedures mentioned in Organizational Process Definition (OPD) and here in Integrated Project Management (IPM), is that the documentation is created and stored in OPD and *used* in IPM on the projects.

The difference between management at Levels 2 and 3 is that Level 3 uses a set of organizational plans, processes, and assets (templates, checklists) based on best practices and lessons learned. The measurement repository is used for generating achievable estimates based on past performance. The repository of project and organizational information discussed in this PA becomes the basis of the performance baselines at Level 4.

Risk is not really discussed much here, at least not as much as in the CMM for Software. Risk thresholds are not discussed in depth, only as an example in SP1.4 subpractice 2.

SG1: Use the project's defined process makes this process a required element. Previous definitions of process in the CMMI were simply informative, or expected as part of the OSSP.

IPPD focuses on establishing and using a shared vision of what the project is to accomplish by way of using the IPPD team structure (Integrated Product Teams — IPTs). SP3.1: define project's shared vision when expanded to its full practice reads: "Identify expectations, constraints, interfaces, and operational conditions applicable to the project's shared vision." If your organization is using IPTs, then please review Organizational Environment for Integration and Integrated Teaming.

Integrated Project Management includes defining a process or processes at the project level, when necessary to tailor from the organizational process(es); using the processes and documentation developed from the organization; integrating all plans (including plans for each process area as well as project management plans) with the project's defined process; managing the project according to the plan; incorporating measurements, documentation, and improvements into the project or organizational-level repositories and processes; ensuring stakeholder involvement; tracking critical dependencies; and resolving issues. For Integrated Project Management for IPPD, also include defining a shared vision of the project among all involved parties; determining the structure of the integrated team; establishing the team; and ensuring that team members have all relevant documentation and information needed to guide them in understanding the project and developing the product.

Risk Management

The purpose of Risk Management is to identify potential problems before they occur, so that risk-handling activities may be planned and invoked as needed across the life of the product or project to mitigate adverse impacts on achieving objectives. Specific Goals and Practices for this process area include:

- SG1: Prepare for risk management
  - SP1.1: Determine risk sources and categories
  - SP1.2: Define risk parameters
  - SP1.3: Establish a risk management strategy
- SG2: Identify and analyze risks
  - SP2.1: Identify risks
  - SP2.2: Evaluate, categorize, and prioritize risks
- SG3: Mitigate risks
  - SP3.1: Develop risk mitigation plans
  - SP3.2: Implement risk mitigation plans

Some sort of risk identification and control is touched upon in almost all of the process areas. In Project Planning and Project Monitoring and Control, risks are identified and strategies for handling the risks are introduced. Evaluating project risks and the impacts of probable risks are addressed. The Risk Management process area is much more proactive, involving identification of risk parameters, formal strategies for handling risks, preparing risk mitigation plans, and structured risk assessments. The Technical Solution process area discussed risk in terms of risks involved in selecting alternative solutions, and reducing risks in "make-buy-reuse" decisions. The Decision Analysis and Resolution process area discusses evaluation processes used to reduce risks made in making decisions and analyzing alternatives. Although preparing for risks can be considered an organizational-level task, mitigating risks is usually the responsibility of the project.

Periodic and event-driven reviews should occur on the project to summarize the most critical risks that might occur. Make sure you review risks during periodic reviews. Why? Because discussing risks only during an "event" (usually a bad thing — like the risk has already happened and now what do we do about it?) only gives exposure to your project when problems are about to occur. In addition, risk probability changes over time and over the course of the project. The risk culture of senior management in a Level 1 organization is simply, "Don't tell me — I don't want to know. Only tell me that things are fine." The risk culture in a Level 3 and above organization is more proactive. They want to hear what might happen and what to do about it.

Disaster recovery may be included as part of an organization's risk management culture but it is not included here. A risk repository can be built at the organization level that contains the risks that were most frequently realized on projects, and their solutions. This repository can help project managers avoid these known risks on their projects.

Risk Management includes identifying and categorizing risks; generating a risk management strategy; analyzing risks; documenting risk mitigation plans; mitigating risks; and monitoring the risk effort.

Integrated Teaming

The purpose of Integrated Teaming is to form and sustain an integrated team for the development of work products. Specific Goals and Practices for this process area:

- ■ SG1: Establish team composition
  - – SP1.1: Identify team tasks
  - – SP1.2: Identify needed knowledge and skills
  - – SP1.3: Assign appropriate team members
- ■ SG2: Govern team operation
  - – SP2.1: Establish a shared vision
  - – SP2.2: Establish a team charter
  - – SP2.3: Define roles and responsibilities
  - – SP2.4: Establish operating procedures
  - – SP2.5: Collaborate among interfacing teams

This process area coordinates the activities of the power brokers in the organization. The teams formed should have complementary skills and expertise to advance timely collaboration to produce the product. Relevant stakeholders should be part of the team, and communication channels should be built to communicate what is happening on the team to individuals not part of that team. It does no good to come up with a shared vision if that vision contradicts what other members of the project have devised who were not allowed to participate on the team.

This team is actually a specialized team (or teams) within the project itself. Team tasks are generated based on project objectives. Members should be selected based on their skills, expertise, and needs of the project. You may also need to train members to fill in the gaps of who is available versus who has the skills. Teamwork training is also a plus, as well as specific training or orientation as to how this team will function, and how it will function with other teams. It is not unusual to include customers and the marketing department on these teams. Be prepared to train and mentor, as people have different backgrounds, different skills, different perspectives, different cultures, and different roles in the organization, and bring them to the team. Establishing the shared vision is therefore critical and will require lots of work. It is not a trivial exercise. We suggest that when it comes to rewards, that the *team* be rewarded — not the *individual* — but you must ensure that everyone on the team actively adds value.

Each team should write a vision statement, plan, charter, and procedures. These documents should be written by the team as a whole, and not by selected members who just mandate usage because they had to write this documentation.

While this process area is top-heavy and formally structured, the basic concepts of this process area can be used and tailored to fit your organization's culture.

Integrated Teaming includes defining team tasks; identifying any knowledge or skill gaps among the teams and team members, and rectifying them; ensuring appropriate personnel are assigned to the correct team; establishing a shared vision of the product and of team objectives; defining team roles and responsibilities; documenting a team charter; and determining strategies for interfacing among teams.

Integrated Supplier Management

The purpose of Integrated Supplier Management (ISM) is to proactively identify sources of products that may be used to satisfy the project's requirements and to manage selected suppliers while maintaining a cooperative project-supplier relationship. Specific Goals and Practices for this process area include:

- ■ SG1: Analyze and select sources of products
  - – SP1.1: Analyze potential sources of products
  - – SP1.2: Evaluate and determine sources of products
- ■ SG2: Coordinate work with suppliers
  - – SP2.1: Monitor selected supplier processes
  - – SP2.2: Evaluate selected supplier work products
  - – SP2.3: Revise the supplier agreement or relationship

This process area is the evolution of Supplier Agreement Management from Level 2. Integrated Supplier Management (ISM) takes a much more proactive view when identifying sources and evaluating them formally. This process area feeds into Decision Analysis and Resolution. ISM looks for a more cooperative agreement with suppliers, a more defined and formalized process, and active participation in improving the relationship between suppliers and customers.

Integrated Supplier Management includes identifying potential sources and suppliers; evaluating these sources; selecting a product source or sources; monitoring the processes and outcomes provided by the source; and revising the supplier agreement as necessary.

Decision Analysis and Resolution

The purpose of Decision Analysis and Resolution (DAR) is to analyze possible decisions using a formal evaluation process that evaluates identified alternatives against established criteria. Specific Goals and Practices for this process area include:

- SG1: Evaluate alternatives
  - SP1.1: Establish guidelines for decision analysis
  - SP1.2: Establish evaluation criteria
  - SP1.3: Identify alternative solutions
  - SP1.4: Select evaluation methods
  - SP1.5: Evaluate alternatives
  - SP1.6: Select solutions

Some organizations, in response to this process area, have stated that they do not need a formal mechanism to make decisions, nor do they need formal guidelines for choosing alternatives. Appraisal teams must ensure that these mechanisms are *used,* which can also prove difficult. This area could prove useful in the vendor selection process. The choice of which alternative, platform, architecture, language, and new technology overlaps somewhat with Technical Solution. The type of testing mentioned here concerns testing the possible solution approaches.

Why is this process area needed? The rationale is to provide managers and analysts with a mechanism to make decisions. This mechanism requires a formal approach to determine which issues need the formal approach of DAR, as well as what that mechanism should be. However, if you are having trouble making a decision, it seems this process area simply gives you more things to consider when making a decision, which increases the difficulty of making that decision, so that no decision ends up being made or the decision may be delayed. It is like saying that "You need to make a decision about which decision to make. Now, decide how to make the decision for the decision, and then make the decision." Well, if you could make a decision in the first place, do you not think you would have? And does this area really help you do that? We think not. Another way to look at this process area is as follows. You ask your boss for a new server. If he agrees, he just says, "Yes — go get one." If not, he makes you follow the guidelines in this process area, hoping you will just give up and go away. However, large organizations tasked with initiating complicated systems may find this PA helpful.

Decision Analysis and Resolution includes determining which decisions will be part of a formal decision-making evaluation process; creating evaluation criteria; determining the types of evaluation methods to use; and determining alternative solutions.

Organizational Environment for Integration

The purpose of Organizational Environment for Integration is to provide an Integrated Product and Process Development (IPPD) infrastructure and manage people for integration. Specific Goals and Practices for this process area include:

- ■ SG1: Provide IPPD infrastructure
  - – SP1.1: Establish the organization's shared vision
  - – SP1.2: Establish an integrated work environment
  - – SP1.3: Identify IPPD-unique skill requirements
- ■ SG2: Manage people for integration
  - – SP2.1: Establish leadership mechanisms
  - – SP2.2: Establish incentives for integration
  - – SP2.3: Establish mechanisms to balance team and home organization responsibilities

This process area is where the infrastructure for the team is built. It supports integrated, collaborative behaviors. Shared vision is critical to success. The team must define this vision, and get commitment and buy-in before proceeding. This approach is difficult for low-maturity organizations, especially where individuals are rewarded for their individual — not team — efforts. The major points of this process area are:

- ■ Communication
- ■ Reward structure
- ■ Physical location of the team
- ■ Appropriate facilities

Team building classes are promoted here. Decision-making responsibilities are defined and distributed between the team and senior management. Project responsibilities ("real work") versus process improvement responsibilities and other work must be defined and balanced. It helps if your organization has developed an organization-level plan that each team can use as a guideline when developing their own team plans, and tailor as necessary.

Organizational Environment for Integration includes defining, once again, a shared vision; empowering personnel; identifying unique skills and needs related to IPPD; creating leadership mechanisms and reward structures promoting effective integration of teams; and documenting guidelines to balance work and home activities.

Summary

Maturity Level 3 takes the best practices and lessons learned from Maturity Level 2 and integrates them at the organizational level. Level 3 requires more sophistication than Level 2. This sophistication is not achieved overnight; it is the result of maturing in your understanding of what the organization does, what it should do, what it can become capable of doing, and why it should do these things. Integrated Project Management can be considered the evolution of Project Planning and Project Monitoring and Control from Level 2. Risk Management can be considered the evolution of risk considerations in Project Planning and Project Monitoring and Control from Level 2 to Level 3. Integrated Supplier Management can be considered the evolution of Supplier Agreement Management from Level 2.

Level 3 has 14 PAs — twice as many as at Level 2. That is way too many areas to implement in one level.

Level 3 is divided into four basic process categories:

- *Engineering PAs:* Requirements Development, Technical Solution, Product Integration, Verification, and Validation
- *Process Management PAs:* Organization Process Focus, Organization Process Definition, and Organizational Training
- *Project Management PAs:* Integrated Project Management, Risk Management, Integrated Teaming, and Integrated Supplier Management
- *Support PAs:* Decision Analysis and Resolution, and Organizational Environment for Integration

Redundancies? Of course. Two that come to mind are Generic Practice 3.1: Establish a Defined Process, which overlaps with Organizational Process Definition; and Generic Practice 3.2: Collect Improvement Information, which overlaps with Organizational Process Focus.

One important concept must be discussed. The overview of Maturity Level 3 in the staged representation of the CMMI states that "Another critical distinction is that at Maturity Level 3, processes are typically described in more detail and more rigorously than at Maturity Level 2." We feel this sentence can lead to great misunderstandings and ultimate failure of your process improvement effort if interpreted incorrectly. Processes should always be defined at the level of detail necessary to be followed consistently. Procedures written can document how to perform the processes in more detail. However, some organizations have decided, based on this sentence in the CMMI, that processes do not have to be written until Level 3. That is not correct! We believe that what the authors of the CMMI are trying to say is that it is just natural that, as your organization matures and you become more adept at writing, you will get better at writing better process documentation. The Generic Practices support the view that processes are required at Level 2. Generic Practice 2.2: Plan the Process specifically states that "establishing a plan includes documenting the plan and providing a process description…. The plan for performing the process typically includes the following…. Process Description…." Generic Practice 2.3: Provide Resources describes ensuring that the resources necessary to perform the *process* as described by the plan are available. The remaining generic practices at Level 2 also support performing the process. To perform the process, it must have been written. Generic Practice 3.1: Establish a Defined Process (a Level 3 Generic Practice) relates to tailoring a project-specific process from an organizational-level standard process, not that Level 3 is where process documentation is written.

Chapter 7

Understanding Maturity Level 4: Quantitatively Managed

This chapter is designed to help the reader understand the basic tenets of Maturity Level 4 in the staged representation of the CMMI®. However, because this chapter consists of summaries of the process areas, anyone wishing to get a better idea of the model, no matter which representation is to be used, can benefit from this chapter. Once again, we are not attempting to teach the CMMI; we simply offer a condensed version of the various areas and key points to consider.

Moving from Level 3 to Level 4

Maturity Level 4 is all about numbers. The projects are managed "by the numbers." Organizational decisions are made "by the numbers." Processes, services, and product quality are all measured "by the numbers." At Level 4, the organization has achieved all of the goals of Levels 2 and 3. Processes, while *qualitatively* stable and predictable at Level 3, can be proved to be *quantitatively* stable and predictable at Level 4. The major difference between Level 4 and the next level (Level 5) is that Level 4 analyzes the data collected, determines *special* causes of variation from the norm, and supports quantitative management and control. You do this to make your processes predictable. Level 5 addresses *common* causes of variation. So, for Level 4, an organization needs data that are stable and consistent. The major preoccupation of assessors when reviewing Level 4 is: "Did this organization mix apples and oranges? Are the data really accurate? Did this organization collect the right data and did they collect the data right?" To get "good" data, an organization usually has to collect data for several years, or at least through several projects and several life cycles of the projects. And when you first begin collecting data, they will not be consistent data.

Measurement data are collected beginning with Level 2 in the staged representation and, in most organizations, actually begin being collected at Level 1. The problem is that the data are not clean and consistent because the processes used on the projects (where the data are collected and used) are not yet stable and consistent. Data in and of itself are not magical: they simply reflect what is going on in the projects. The point is that an organization cannot go to Level 4 overnight, and the focus is on the data.

What problems do we see in organizations when they decide to move from Level 3 to 4? At Level 3, measures are collected and preliminary thresholds are established, usually relating to size and effort. If the thresholds are exceeded, some sort of corrective action is undertaken. At Level 4, the control limits are based on years of historical data and trend analyses done on those data. More data are collected, and therefore more limits are established, monitored, and refined as necessary. At Level 3, the data may be somewhat inconsistent and "dirty." Although in a perfect world we would like to see "clean" data at Level 3, the focus in Level 3 is on organizational process, not necessarily on stabilized, normalized, statistically accurate data — which is exactly what Level 4 expects. One problem that we see in some organizations that have barely met the criteria for Level 3 are that the processes are not always followed consistently across the organization. Now, one author of this book has stated that, in that case, this organization is *not* Level 3 and should never have been awarded Level 3. The other author of this book, after many arguments and nights spent sleeping on the couch which he definitely deserved for having such a stupid opinion, finally agreed — with the following caveat: it all depends on what the organization does to enforce consistency, how important the consistency issue is to the appraisal team, what type of assessment is done to award the level, and who is on the team. So those of you new to process improvement, expecting black-and-white answers and no "wiggle room" in interpreting, implementing, and assessing this effort, are in for a letdown. Review Appendix B, entitled "Myths and Legends of the CMMI" and Chapter 11, entitled "Appraisals Using the CMMI," for more information.

At Level 3, we have also seen that tailoring the organizational process can get out of hand. That is, there is so much tailoring of the process that it cannot be judged to be a "standard" process. In addition, the measurement culture at Level 3 is not often well understood. People may not really understand why they are collecting the metrics they collect — only that they are "required" by the model, and so that is why they are collected. The metrics cannot be studied for consistency and clarity, or may not be closely analyzed to determine *why* the numbers are inconsistent, and whether that represents a potential problem or not. Because the numbers can be "wild," management decisions made using the numbers can be pretty much off-base. And with inconsistent data, you really cannot compare the performance of several projects against each other to truly analyze trends.

At Level 4, managers and analysts must use the data, and apply statistical and quantitative techniques to help monitor activities, identify potential problems, and note areas that need attention. The instructions for the CMM for Software at Level 4 basically said to keep it simple. The measurements here in the CMMI, and suggested techniques, are very sophisticated and are more difficult to implement.

Level 4 is about making processes stable and predictable. Level 5 is about making improvements to stable processes so as to improve the functioning of the organization.

Why do all this measurement stuff? Because it supports a proactive approach toward managing projects.

There are two process areas for Level 4:

1. Organizational Process Performance
2. Quantitative Project Management

Note that there are no additions to the list of generic goals at Level 4 from Level 3. What makes this Maturity Level different is the two process areas. The generic goals are listed below. We use the abbreviations GG for Generic Goal and GP for Generic Practice. The Common Features (Commitment to Perform — CO, Ability to Perform — AB, Directing Implementation — DI, and Verifying Implementation — VE) are also abbreviated.

- ■ GG3: Institutionalize a defined process
    - GP2.1 (CO1): Establish an organizational policy
    - GP3.1 (AB1): Establish a defined process
    - GP2.2 (AB2): Plan the process
    - GP2.3 (AB3): Provide resources

- GP2.4 (AB4): Assign responsibility
- GP2.5 (AB5): Train people
- GP2.6 (DI1): Manage configurations
- GP2.7 (DI2): Identify and involve relevant stakeholders
- GP2.8 (DI3): Monitor and control the process
- GP3.2 (DI4): Collect improvement information
- GP2.9 (VE1): Objectively evaluate adherence
- GP2.10 (VE2): Review status with higher-level management

To satisfy the goals for Level 4, the goals for Levels 2 and 3 must be satisfied as well. This mandate holds true for both the specific goals and the generic goals listed above.

The following pages discuss each process area for Level 4. We use the abbreviations SG for Specific Goal and SP for the corresponding Specific Practices.

The Process Areas for Maturity Level 4: Quantitatively Managed

Organizational Process Performance

The purpose of Organizational Process Performance is to establish and maintain a quantitative understanding of the performance of the organization's set of standard processes in support of quality and process-performance objectives, and to provide the process performance data, baselines, and models to quantitatively manage the organization's projects. Specific Goals and Practices for this process area include:

■ SG1: Establish performance baselines and models
- SP1.1: Select processes
- SP1.2: Establish process performance measures
- SP1.3: Establish quality and process performance objectives
- SP1.4: Establish process performance baselines
- SP1.5: Establish process performance models

This process area includes measurements for both process and product. It combines these measures to determine both the quality of the process and the product in quantitative terms.

Process performance baselines and process performance models are now included in goals for this process area, and not just as suggested best practices. A *process performance baseline* (PPB) documents the historical results achieved by following a process. A PPB is used as a benchmark for comparing actual process performance against expected process performance. A *process performance model* (PPM) describes the relationships among attributes (e.g., defects) of a process and its work products. A PPM is used to estimate or predict a critical value that cannot be measured until later in the project's life — for example, predicting the number of delivered defects throughout the life cycle. More information on PPBs and PPMs can be found in Chapter 19, A High Maturity Perspective.

Remember: do not wait until Level 4 to focus on measurements and to start collecting measures: that is way too late. The Measurement and Analysis process area resides at Level 2; so if you are attempting to achieve a Level 2 Maturity Level rating, this is probably not a process area to tailor out. And if you are using the continuous representation, which supposedly allows you to select which process areas to use, Measurement and Analysis should also be selected.

At Level 2, measures are collected, stored in a database per project, bubble up to an organizational database in Level 3, are reviewed for consistency and accuracy at Level 3, and then, at Level 4, have statistically based controls applied to them. What to put under statistical control depends on where the problems are in your organization, and which processes and measures will add value to your management techniques. This statement implies that not all processes must be put under statistical control. However, we do suggest that, for Level 4 and for this process area in particular, the organization's set of standard processes (OSSPs) must be understood from a statistical point of view.

The most common measurements we see in use for this process area are size, effort, cost, schedule, and product defect density. The measurements for these data points are usually displayed in ranges, and not by absolute points. Subsets of measures can be generated to be applied based on domains, new development versus maintenance, and type of customer.

Performance-related measurements can include schedule variance (lateness), effort variance, and unplanned tasks. Quality-related measurements can include rework and defects. These defects can be collected during all life-cycle phases, including requirements inspections, design inspections, code inspections, unit testing, integration testing, and system testing. Process-related measures that we commonly see can be found by reviewing Productivity at the different phases of life cycles. For example, in Testing, how many hours were spent deriving test cases versus how many tests were actually completed?

To be even more confusing, this process area refers to *process* performance as including both *process* measures and *product* measures. Then later, it refers to "*quality* and *process*-performance objectives" to emphasize the importance of *product* quality. The confusion comes in because product measures are primarily used in organizations to demonstrate quality. This process area refers to process measures as including effort, cycle time, and defect removal effectiveness. Product measures include reliability and defect density. However, the same source data (e.g., defects) can be used for both product and process measures. A process measure would be defect removal effectiveness — the percentage of existing defects removed by a process, such as the inspection process or the testing process. A product measure would be defect density — the number of defects per unit or product size, such as number of defects per thousand lines of code — that reflects the quality of the product. Basically, it might help to translate in this process area that Quality measure = Product measure.

Training is critical in this process area, in both modeling techniques and in quantitative methods.

There are no new generic goals for Levels 4 and 5 in the staged representation because the process areas include the basic tenets. The continuous representation *does* have generic goals because the continuous representation allows the selection of various process areas. So, you may decide not to select the process areas in Maturity Level 4. If you do that, then the generic goals of the continuous representation have been added to ensure that the basic concepts of statistical control and application will be met.

This process area covers both project-level and organization-level activities. Selecting processes to measure and selecting appropriate measures themselves can be iterative to meet changing business needs. Establishing quality and process objectives can be iterative as well, based on fixing special causes of variation.

An example of the importance of not mixing "apples and oranges" in this process area follows. Suppose you are collecting peer review data. You collect defect data resulting from peer reviews. You may collect the number of defects found and the type of defect (code, requirement, design, etc.). Be sure to analyze that data appropriately. For example, if one review of code produces 17 defects, that may not sound like much, while another review of another program results in 25 defects, which is obviously more than from the first product reviewed. However, by reviewing the number of lines of code for each product, you discover that the first review resulting in 17 defects occurred in a program with only 11 lines of code, while the second review that resulted in 25 defects was conducted on a program of 1500 lines of code. The 17 defects were so severe that the program needed a total re-write, while the 25 defects were mostly cosmetic, with only one or two potential problem areas. So, you must study the data produced in terms of the number of defects, type, severity, number of pages or lines of code reviewed, complexity, domain, and type of technology used.

Measures can usually be traced back to life-cycle activities and products. For example, the percent of changes to the Requirements Document, while reviewing the product itself, can demonstrate problems with the process used for collecting requirements and physically writing the document. These numbers can then be used to include more rigorous training in this area of weakness. You might also consider reviewing the number of defects out of the Requirements phase versus the number of defects out of the Test phase. One study has determined that 85 percent of defects found in the Test phase were introduced in the Requirements phase.

We admit that measurement programs can become onerous. The CMMI response to this criticism is that measurements should be tied to the business objectives of the organization. So, if you are highly driven by time-to-market, you would focus on product defects and the scheduling effort. Decisions to release the product with an "appropriate" limit of defects would be made by senior management in order to make the schedule date. That "appropriate" part should be determined based on historical data (and analysis of that data and your measurement repository) for the *number* of defects that can be released into the marketplace, and the *types* of defects that can be released into the marketplace and still satisfy the customer and make the product work.

Organizational Process Performance includes deciding which processes to include as part of statistical performance analyses; defining metrics to use as part of the process performance analyses; defining quantitative objectives for quality and process performance (quality and process "by the numbers"); and generating process performance baselines and models.

Quantitative Project Management

The purpose of Quantitative Project Management is to quantitatively manage the project's defined process to achieve the project's established quality and process performance objectives. Specific Goals and Practices for this process area include:

- SG1: Quantitatively manage the project
  - SP1.1: Establish the project's objectives
  - SP1.2: Compose the defined process
  - SP1.3: Select the subprocesses that will be statistically managed
  - SP1.4: Manage project performance
- SG2: Statistically manage subprocess performance
  - SP2.1: Select measures and analytic techniques
  - SP2.2: Apply statistical methods to understand variation
  - SP2.3: Monitor performance of the selected subprocesses
  - SP2.4: Record statistical management data

In this process area, usage of the organizational-level measurement repository is refined. This process area describes what projects need to do to manage quantitatively. Generally speaking, we have seen that the distribution of labor is that experienced managers and measurement personnel identify measures, senior-level project personnel collect the measures, and projects use the measures. Training for each role needs to be addressed.

Project managers should do, at least, a weekly review of the project measures and how they are being used. This information is usually communicated to senior management. A measurement group is usually needed to support measurement activities. Collection of data is easier if automated tools are used. Manual collection of data can be burdensome and can lead to abandonment of this effort. Automated tools are very helpful, but remember — do not go out and buy a tool willy-nilly. Most tools cannot support the very project-specific and organizationally specific measures that need to be taken. And remember the Level 3 process area, Requirements Development? Well, before you buy a tool, you are supposed to define the requirements of that tool — not buy a tool and then define the requirements that it happens to meet. We have found that the best tools for collecting and storing metrics have been developed by the organization itself. So, you have programmers — use them. Get them to develop a tool or tools. This approach also gets buy-in from them for some of the process improvement activities. What is the best tool? Your brain. God gave you a brain — now use it. Remember: not only do you need to *collect* the data, but you also need to *analyze* them. Your brain will certainly come in handy for that part.

There can be several organizational measurement repositories, or layers within one overall repository, so as to not mix data that may lead to misleading numbers and bad decisions. Repositories require years of historical data using the same, normalized data, and reviews and analyses of these data. Training and practice in this effort need to occur. Running projects quantitatively is not an overnight transition.

A bad example of collecting data and using them follows. Most organizations simply ask, "How many years must we collect data to prove that we have met the criteria for historically accurate data?" Wrong question. One organization collected data for 15 years about its projects. The data collected for 14 years were simply when the project started and when it ended. Each project took about seven years to complete. We find it difficult to imagine any real value that was added to these projects by simply collecting start and end dates. The 15th year of data collection included the start of each phase of software development, and the end — Requirements start and end, Designs start and end, Codes start and end, Tests start and end, and Installations start and end. While we can find much more value in these types of data and their collection, we believe that having only one year of that data was not enough, especially since each project ran almost seven years, and most of the projects were only in the Requirements phase. So, comparisons for bottlenecks and other trends were almost impossible, and would be inaccurate. However, the organization tried to advise us that these data met the criteria for stable, consistent data because they had data from as far back as 15 years. Sorry — no cigar. By the way, this example occurred during an external evaluation of an organization seeking a Maturity Level 4 rating.

Quantitative Project Management includes quantitatively defining project objectives; using stable and consistent historical data to construct the project's defined process; selecting subprocesses of the project's defined process that will be statistically managed; monitoring the project against the quantitative measures and objectives; using analytical techniques to derive and understand variation; and monitoring performance and recording measurement data in the organization's measurement repository.

Summary

The previous version of the CMM for Software said of Level 4 — Keep It Simple. Organizations involved in piloting CMMI have admitted that the bar has been raised significantly. Do we believe that measurement is necessary? Absolutely! However, Level 4 is where senior management commitment and participation really come to the forefront. Business decisions are supposed to be made based on the numbers. Have you ever sat in any senior- or executive-level meetings? You are lucky if you get ten minutes with these people. And they are not overly fond of viewing slide after slide of esoteric charts and graphs. They want to know the bottom line — that is, are we making money? And the one chart that they all love, which is not particularly popular in the world of statistics, is the pie chart.

Our recommendation is still to start simple. If you can then refine your approaches and include more complicated approaches as needed, then fine — go for it. But most small organizations will find Maturity Level 4 very difficult to implement as written, based on the number of people needed to make this run smoothly, and based on the type of expertise needed. And Maturity Level 4 may not prove all that beneficial (using cost-benefit analyses) to these organizations anyway.

Chapter 8

Understanding Maturity Level 5: Optimizing

This chapter is designed to help the reader understand the basic tenets of Maturity Level 5 in the staged representation of the CMMI®. However, because this chapter consists of summaries of the process areas, anyone wishing to get a better idea of the model, no matter which representation is to be used, can benefit from this chapter. Once again, we are not attempting to teach the CMMI; we simply offer a condensed version of the various areas and key points to consider.

Moving from Level 4 to Level 5

At Maturity Level 5, an organization has achieved all of the goals of Levels 2, 3, and 4. Level 5 concentrates on improving the overall quality of the organization's processes by identifying common causes of variation (as opposed to special causes of variation at Level 4), determining root causes of the conditions identified, piloting process improvements, and incorporating the improvements and corrective actions into the organization's set of standard processes or, as appropriate, just the project's defined process. While innovative, radical approaches to introduce change into an organization are often undertaken, most organizations have found that an incremental approach works better, and has longer-lasting results.

There are two process areas for Level 5:

1. Organizational Innovation and Deployment
2. Causal Analysis and Resolution

Note that there are no additions to the list of generic goals at Level 5 from Level 3. What makes this Maturity Level different is the two process areas. The generic goals are listed below. We use the abbreviations GG for Generic Goal and GP for Generic Practice. The Common Features (Commitment to Perform — CO, Ability to Perform — AB, Directing Implementation — DI, and Verifying Implementation — VE) are also abbreviated.

- GG3: Institutionalize a defined process
  - GP2.1 (CO1): Establish an organizational policy
  - GP3.1 (AB1): Establish a Defined Process
  - GP2.2 (AB2): Plan the process
  - GP2.3 (AB3): Provide resources
  - GP2.4 (AB4): Assign responsibility
  - GP2.5 (AB5): Train people
  - GP2.6 (DI1): Manage configurations
  - GP2.7 (DI2): Identify and involve relevant stakeholders
  - GP2.8 (DI3): Monitor and control the process
  - GP3.2 (DI4): Collect improvement information
  - GP2.9 (VE1): Objectively evaluate adherence
  - GP2.10 (VE2): Review status with higher-level management

To satisfy the goals for Level 5, the goals for Levels 2, 3, and 4 must be satisfied as well. This rule holds true for both the specific goals and the generic goals listed above.

The following pages discuss each process area for Maturity Level 5. We use the abbreviations SG for Specific Goal and SP for the corresponding Specific Practices.

The Process Areas for Maturity Level 5: Optimizing

Organizational Innovation and Deployment

The purpose of Organizational Innovation and Deployment (OID) is to select and deploy incremental and innovative improvements that measurably improve the organization's processes and technologies. The improvements support the organization's quality and process performance objectives as derived from the organization's business objectives. Specific Goals and Practices for this process area include:

- ■ SG1: Select improvements
    - − SP1.1: Collect and analyze improvement proposals
    - − SP1.2: Identify and analyze innovations
    - − SP1.3: Pilot improvements
    - − SP1.4: Select improvements for deployment
- ■ SG2: Deploy improvements
    - − SP2.1: Plan the deployment
    - − SP2.2: Manage the deployment
    - − SP2.3: Measure improvement effects

Process improvement proposals to improve the process of process improvement are included in this process area. Technology improvement proposals are also included. If readers review the Organizational Process Focus process area, they find that process improvement proposals are used there as well. What is the difference? In this PA, the proposals are subjected to quantitative analysis of proposed improvements. Metrics residing in the historical database, as well as defects and where they were introduced, are reviewed as well, in order to determine where, when, and how to make improvements. Costs and benefits of the proposed versus actual improvements are also studied.

Some people have interpreted this process area as including both process and product improvements. This opens up a can of worms for assessment teams. What was expected in the CMM for Software was process improvements *and* improvements in technology to support the processes. Technologies, such as a new requirements traceability tool or a new unit test tool, were included. Technologies that were to be part of a product, such as a new database management system or a new algorithm, were not included. With CMMI, these concepts become an even bigger issue. The systems that we may be building can include a lot of technologies. The question then becomes: how far should an assessment team go? Is the organization expected to have a defined process to select technologies? When selecting the type of phones for staff members, is that covered by OID? When selecting which type of interface to put on the new phone system, is that covered by OID? Or is that covered in Technical Solution at Level 3?

The steps in this process are as follows:

1. Submitting improvement proposals
2. Reviewing and analyzing the proposals (including a cost-benefit review)

3. Piloting the proposed improvement
4. Measuring the improvement to see whether it has been effective in the pilot
5. Planning the deployment of the improvement
6. Deploying the improvement
7. Measuring the effectiveness of the improvement across the organization or project

For example, a Level 1 organization will simply mandate that a certain change control tool is now to be used. There is no piloting of the tool, no requirements study to see which tools out there fit the organization, and no training is given. This introduction of the new tool causes chaos. A Level 5 organization will follow the steps above, and should the pilot prove effective, will probably deploy the tool one or a few projects at a time (not en masse) into the entire organization. A "go/no-go" decision will be made at each step.

Do not wait until Level 5 to introduce these concepts into your organization. The difference in introducing this approach at Level 1 or 2, versus Level 5, is that at Level 5 you absolutely know your organization's processes and you can be more proactive about predicting the level of uncertainty that the tool (in the example used) will create. You can plan its introduction better, and pinpoint areas that will need more attention — such as training and, perhaps, contracts.

Organizational Innovation and Deployment involves coordinating process improvement proposals submitted from the staff at various levels (improvement proposals may be related to innovative technology improvements); piloting selected improvements; planning and implementing the deployment of improvements throughout the organization; and measuring the effects of the improvements implemented.

Causal Analysis and Resolution

The purpose of Causal Analysis and Resolution is to identify causes of defects and other problems, and take action to prevent them from occurring in the future. Specific Goals and Practices for this Process Area include:

- SG1: Determine causes of defects
  - SP1.1: Select defect data for analysis
  - SP1.2: Analyze causes
- SG2: Address causes of defects
  - SP2.1: Implement the action proposals
  - SP2.2: Evaluate the effect of changes
  - SP2.3: Record data

Proposals and plans to improve defects in the processes used to produce products are included here. Defect Prevention in the previous CMM for Software included integrating project work with kickoff meetings. This activity is no longer included here. We recommend this activity be performed as a best practice, as found in other organizations.

This process area looks at defects and determines their root cause. The most simple definition of a root cause is simply the one, most basic reason why the defect occurred (or the source of the defect); and if that cause is removed, the defect vanishes. This process area identifies the root cause(s) and addresses the cause using a structured approach. The steps in this approach are:

1. Look at the defects and problems in the organization
2. Select data to analyze
3. Analyze causes
4. Prepare proposals to address the problems
5. Implement the proposals
6. Evaluate the effects of the changes

You should already be analyzing defects and problems during Project Planning and Project Monitoring and Control at Level 2. Training to perform the more sophisticated studies required for Level 5 should be considered.

We recommend that users of the CMMI for process improvement also review the CMM for Software for more advice or suggestions on other activities, and including them to satisfactorily complete this process area. Kickoffs, sharing among projects, roles in the organization, rolling up project data/causes/problems into organizational-level data, and integrating changes into the processes are described somewhat in the previous model, and may benefit the reader in understanding this process area.

Causal Analysis and Resolution includes identifying defects and where in the process they were introduced; determining the causes of defects and their resolution; and defining methods and procedures to avoid introducing defects into the processes in the future.

Summary

The focus at Maturity Level 5 is on improving processes, but now the organization's set of standard processes (OSSPs) is the controlling document that provides the primary focus. Using the OSSP (which by now must surely reflect true organizational functioning), process improvement can be engineered into the organization in a much more reasonable and efficient manner.

Level 4 focuses on special causes of variation in the processes of the organization. Level 5 tries to find common causes, and fix them, that will result in overall improvements. Measurements are used to select improvements and reliably estimate the costs and benefits of attempting the improvements. Measurements are used to prove the actual costs and benefits of the improvements. These same measurements can be used to justify future improvement efforts.

There are two types of improvement strategies: innovative and incremental. Incremental builds on the foundation of earlier improvements. Innovative tends to introduce more radical and drastic methods of improvement. Both can work in an organization, depending on the culture of the organization and the strength of its leaders, both politically and charismatically. However, most organizations have reported that incremental approaches to process improvement tend to have more long-lasting effects and lead to easier institutionalization.

At Maturity Level 5, the focus is constantly on reviewing and improving the processes, but these improvements must be introduced in a disciplined manner in order to manage and maintain process stability.

Chapter 9

Alignment of Multiple Process Improvement Initiatives

It is not uncommon to find multiple process improvement initiatives within even a moderately sized organization. These separate initiatives are going to be using different methods, techniques, and models as a basis for their work. Using the CMMI® has the potential to bring together existing process improvement initiatives covering software engineering, systems engineering, and supplier sourcing activities within an organization.

Organizations that we work with have reported problems between groups because of the different maturity levels of their processes; different expectations from senior management; different levels of training; and a mismatch of policies, processes, and procedures. These problems are often more difficult to resolve because of the separate initiatives occurring at the same time within the organization.

This chapter covers some of the things to consider when combining or aligning multiple process improvement initiatives. The topics covered are process improvement team structure, integration of existing procedures, measurement program, and training program. Following the topics, example real-world scenarios are described.

Process Improvement Team Structure

We often find different groups working on process improvement activities in an organization. For example, an organization may have a Software Engineering Process Group (SEPG) for software processes, a Systems Engineering Process Initiative (SEPI) for systems engineering processes, and an Engineering Process Group (EPG) for processes covering other disciplines such as electrical, mechanical, safety, and reliability. In addition to these explicit process improvement groups, organizations may have other existing groups, such as Quality Improvement Councils, Business Re-engineering Teams, and Six Sigma programs.

Given this wide range of groups interested in process improvement, it is not surprising that organizations find that, regardless of their current approach, they will need to clarify the roles and responsibilities of each team, increase communication between these teams, and often simplify the effort by eliminating some teams.

To address the structure, you need to know what structure already exists. Exhibit 1 lists some questions to consider.

Once you collect this information about your teams, you should be in a position to restructure your teams for better alignment. Make sure whatever teams you keep have a charter, a plan (not just a schedule — see Chapters 12 and 15), a budget, a management or an executive sponsor, and a communication plan. The section entitled "Scenarios" discusses two scenarios related to team integration.

Integration of Existing Policies, Processes, and Procedures[1]

The separate process improvement initiatives in an organization are likely to have developed separate processes and procedures. Some organizations have written their policies, processes, and procedures to map directly to their process improvement model (e.g., CMM for Software, CMMI, SA-CMM), so one of the negative side effects of different process improvement models has been an incompatible set of policies, processes, and procedures. To resolve these problems, we offer the following questions and suggested approaches.

Questions you should ask regarding your process-related documentation include:

- Do your current policies cover your selected CMMI scope?
- Do you need more detailed procedures?
- Do you have overlap in your procedures?

- What procedures should be merged?
- What procedures should remain separate?

Here are some suggested approaches.

Collect and Review the Policies, Processes, and Procedures

The first thing you need to do is collect, in one place, all the documentation that makes up your policies, processes, and procedures and conduct a

---

Exhibit 1. Questions to Consider to Determine Current Structure

---

What teams do you currently have? Take an inventory of the teams. Some organizations are surprised to find that they have a significant number of teams involved with process improvement across the organization. You may need to survey a number of people to identify all the teams. If it is difficult to identify all the teams, you will want to improve the communication and visibility of your teams. Process improvement teams need to be visible — stealth process improvement rarely works.

How many teams are real? For a team to be real, it should have a plan, a charter, a budget, and active members (see Chapters 12 and 13 for more information). In addition, teams should have an executive sponsor, and the team should have produced something. Look at the processes, procedures, templates, training materials, etc., coming from each team.

What overlap exists between your teams? It is not unusual to find multiple teams with many of the same members. This may not be a bad thing when the teams have a clear charter and know their responsibilities. If you have an overlap of team members and an overlap of responsibilities, it usually means nothing is going to get done, or something will get done but twice in slightly different ways.

At what level do your teams communicate and how often? Even separate teams working in unique areas should be exchanging ideas and leveraging from each other. Ways to encourage communication include joint meetings on topics of mutual interest, peer reviews of team-developed work products across teams, and assigning a representative from a related team as a member of the team.

Do your teams have an unhealthy competition? Multiple teams within an organization have been known to spend an unbalanced amount of time protecting their spheres of influence, their budgets, and their unique processes. You need to be sensitive to this situation. If you are a member of one or more of these teams, you may need an impartial third party to look at and evaluate your work, and determine the value of what has been accomplished.

---

review. Hopefully it will be as easy as it sounds. Make sure you have a good working definition of policy, process, and procedure: if in doubt, refer to Chapter 14 for documentation guidelines (this was written by one of the most intelligent people I know). Not everything you find will be labeled correctly. For example, we have seen lots of documents with the title "Process for X" that are really policies stating that you are expected to do X. These documents may still be helpful. Also look at your training courses — sometimes a process or a procedure is only documented in a training course. (Note: We do not recommend only documenting processes and procedures in training courses; however, we recognize that it happens.) Identify the correct title, author, change authority, and sponsor of all documents. Create a document log with all the above information. Conduct a review and record your findings. Use the questions above and the rest of this section to give you ideas on what to look at.

Examine the Interfaces

Examine and consider the interfaces between procedures to ensure that artifacts produced in one process satisfy the requirements of the receiving process (e.g., Systems Requirements flowing into Software Requirements, Systems Requirements into Acquisition, and Software Requirements into Acquisition). Each of these processes represents a producer and a consumer part. The producer needs to provide part of what the consumer needs to do their job. What can be done to make your interfaces clearer and more productive? In one organization we worked with, the addition of a formal design review step between the Systems Requirements and Software Requirements improved not only the artifacts, but also the working relationship between the groups. It also resulted in savings of a staff year for a 15-person project.

Review the Roles

Review the roles people perform and the various disciplines within your organization. For example, configuration management and quality assurance often perform similar roles. These two disciplines (Quality Assurance and Configuration Management) exist at both the systems level and the software level, perform similar activities regardless of the discipline, and may or may not be performed by the same individuals. Can your procedures for these roles be improved by sharing ideas? For example, in most organizations we work with, the software quality group has much more experience in reviewing and auditing *processes* and the systems quality group has more experience in reviewing and auditing *products* — sharing best practices has proven useful.

Consider Life Cycles

Consider the life cycle of the disciplines and scope of the procedures. Systems procedures may cover total life-cycle "lust to dust" (i.e., conception through to disposal), yet software and acquisition-related procedures may only cover the requirements phase to the test phase. How do these different life cycles affect your procedure integration? One example: some organizations find that systems engineering has a better technique for understanding customer needs and expectations. This technique can be borrowed and reused in software-only systems.

Consider the Level of Detail

Consider the level of detail of the written procedures. Some disciplines may have written procedures to just "pass the test" and be at such a high level that they provide very little value. Some disciplines, such as purchasing, may have developed detailed procedures and supporting checklists that help provide a repeatable and improvable activity. Now may be the time to leverage more practical process architectures and procedural approaches from other disciplines.

Consider the Format

Consider the format of the documentation you have produced, that is, process-related internal documentation, and the documentation you turn over to your user. Again, now may be the time to implement consistent process architecture, formats, and styles.

Exhibit 2 contains an example of what you might find existing across an organization. This example is based on documentation we have reviewed from organizations in the past. The three rightmost columns indicate the disciplines of systems engineering, software engineering, and acquisition (or purchasing). Key characteristics for each discipline are identified in the policies, processes, and procedures in the left-hand columns.

Measurement Program

If the organization has not developed an integrated measurement program, it is likely that measures[2] and measurements will be unbalanced across multiple process improvement initiatives. Different improvement models place different levels of importance on measurements. To exploit some of the resulting differences, we offer the following questions and suggested approaches.

Exhibit 2. Example Characteristics of Policies, Processes, and Procedures by Discipline

	Systems Engineering	Software Engineering	Acquisition (or Purchasing)
Primary Standard	Systems Engineering Handbook: Focus on engineering practices Based on unique customer requirements and best practices from the organization	Organizational Standard Software Process: Focus on project management practices Based on best practices and Project Management Institute	Buyer Guidelines: Focus on open market acquisitions Based on government regulations, unique customer requirements, and corporate guidelines
Level of Tailoring	Very little tailoring allowed; requires contract change	Some tailoring done on most projects	Tailoring expressly forbidden
Process Architecture	Based on waterfall life-cycle phases plus unique phases for internal research and development	Based on CMM for Software Key Process Areas	Based on roles in acquisition process
Level of Detail	High-level process descriptions	Level of detail varies by process area: Detailed management processes High-level engineering processes	Very detailed guidelines with checklists
Review Approach	Formal reviews (with customer): systems requirements review, preliminary design review, critical design review	Internal peer reviews (some involve systems engineering and acquisition participants)	Process execution review by managers; technical details reviewed by engineering; all activities audited by customer
Configuration Control	Data management for all formal work products: plans, drawings, specifications, and prototypes	Configuration management procedures around change control boards and software library	Contracts library with limited access containing specifications, requests for proposals, proposal responses, contract and contract status, vendor performance and preferred vendor lists
Quality	Verification and validation by third party or with external witnesses	Both product and process review, emphasis on process assurance	All activities audited by customer or third-party representative

Questions you should ask regarding your measurement programs include the following.

What measures are being collected for each discipline?

Some measures can cover several disciplines, for example, effort measures and earned value. Other measures would be unique to a discipline, such as number of late deliveries from vendor X or lines of code per hour.

Are there measurement specifications defined for all measures?

A measurement specification should contain a definition of the measure, source of the data, collection mechanism, criteria for counting, unit(s) of measure, and expected range value. In addition, guidelines on interpreting the measurement information, including an analysis approach and criteria for decision making, should be documented. Why do we need all this stuff? Well, measures are like many things in life; "if it ain't written down, it ain't so." For example, when you ask someone, "How many requirements do you have in your system?", the only way to make sense of the answer, and for that matter the question, is to have a definition of what a requirement is.

What measures are being presented to management on a regular basis?

The approaches to presenting measurement to management vary widely across organizations. We have worked with groups that hold a formal monthly measurement review with senior management and we have worked with groups that simply provide measures in quarterly project status reports. The key to success with measures is to be provide accurate measurement data to management on a regular, periodic basis — during both good times and bad — showing both the good news and bad.

How mature are the measurement systems for each discipline?

Many of the organizations we work with began their measurement initiatives in the software area and did not place as much emphasis on other disciplines. Therefore, software measurement in these organizations is often more mature.[3] Measurement maturity shows up in several ways, such as how well measures are defined, how consistent measurements are taken and used, and how well the actual data collected reflects the processes being executed.

You will want to understand these issues and the success individual disciplines have had in your organization in order to share best practices across the organization. Some organizations have software data identifying critical components, attributes, and measures of the standard processes based on critical business issues. If that is the case, showing the value the organization has gotten from more mature software measures may be helpful in getting buy-in from the other parts of your organization that have not been as intensely involved in process improvement or are just starting their own process improvement initiative.

How are the measures collected within the disciplines?

Again, we often find wide variation in how measures are collected across the disciplines. For example, you might use a manual method for calculating and collecting critical performance factors for formal reviews, or you might have a fully automated, integrated development and time tracking environment that produces weekly and on-demand measurement charts. These charts may include effort, earned value, requirements changes, size (code and documents), number of reviews, number of defects, and productivity measures. As a rule, you should make collecting measures as painless as possible. Remember that "if it is too damn hard, people won't do it." Automate data collection as much as possible, but do not forget to verify, validate, and monitor collection to be sure you are getting the right stuff. A brain is required to analyze and comprehend information, and a brain is required to ensure that the data collected makes sense. An automated tool does not have a brain.

Following are some suggested approaches to get answers to the questions.

Collect and review the related documentation

The first thing you need to do is collect all the documentation related to measurement policies, processes, and procedures. Some of this may be embedded in documentation for project planning and tracking or other process areas. Some disciplines will have developed measurement handbooks containing measurement specifications. Collect whatever you can find.

Collect examples of measures presented to management

Collect copies of status reports and briefings prepared for and presented to management. These include status from projects, major programs, functional areas, and the entire organization or division. Identify which measures are being reported and how often.

Identify all the groups (or individuals) with measurement responsibility

You need to know which groups and individuals are actually doing jobs related to measurement. You may find groups within individual disciplines, for example, a Process Action Team for Measurement chartered by the SEPG. You may find groups or individuals responsible for collecting and maintaining time-reporting data. You may find groups or individuals responsible for maintaining data used in bid and proposal activities. Go through the questions in Exhibit 1 and answer them for the groups and individuals with measurement responsibility.

Identify how the measures are being collected

You may find this information in a measurement specification. You may find this as part of the status report. You may have to interview the individuals responsible for the measures to see how they really do it. It is not unusual to find people "guesstimating" — guessing at a number and calling it an estimate, or worse, presenting it as actual data. (*Note:* We do not encourage this behavior; however, we recognize its existence.) You need to be somewhat understanding and flexible during this data collection phase. In some cases we have had to get senior management to declare an amnesty for all past behavior.

Create a measurement log

Create a measurement log summarizing the information identified above. At a minimum, this log should contain the measure, how it is documented, group or individual responsible for collecting it, tool or method used to collect it, and how often, to whom, and how it is reported.

Our experience is that if you go through all the steps above, you document your results, and review your findings with management, you will be able to identify the business case for merging your measurement programs, collection systems, and measurement databases. The primary business reasons that we have found for integrating measurement programs are removing duplication of effort, leveraging best practices, and establishing consistency.

Training Programs

Training programs need to include defining required training, planning the training, and executing the training plans. Different improvement models have placed different levels of importance on training. Some disciplines will have separate training programs, with some of them being more formal than others. With multiple training programs, it is not unusual to have several related courses. To exploit some of the resulting differences, we offer the following questions and suggested approaches.

Questions you should ask regarding your training programs include:

- Does your current training cover your selected CMMI scope?
- Do you need more detailed training in some disciplines?
- Do you have overlap in your training?
- What training should be merged?
- What training should remain separate?

Here are some suggested approaches to get to the answers.

Identify which training programs are in scope

You need to know what training programs exist within the CMMI scope that you have selected. These training programs may exist at the enterprise level, the organizational level, and within the disciplines (systems, software, and purchasing). For example, the enterprises through corporate human resources may train individuals in project management as they take their first management assignments; the organization may have orientation and training covering the specific domain of their major customers; and purchasing may have training in contract law and negotiations.

Identify all sources of training

Understanding the sources of the training courses helps ensure that you do not leave anything out. The sources of training are likely to include in-house training conducted within specific disciplines, enterprise- or organizational-level training (often within human resources), and training provided by specialist consultants (i.e., if you have been using a process improvement consultant, they are likely to be doing your model training).

Identify and collect all training plans and schedule

Some training plans will be easy to identify, as they will have the title Training Plan. Some training plans will only have a schedule. A schedule is not enough. Any training program should be managed as a project with a plan identifying what training is required, who needs the training, what resources (budget, participant hours, facilities, etc.) are required to perform the training, how training will be provided, and a schedule.

Identify all training courses

Create a course log summarizing the information identified above. You may need to survey the groups you have identified. At a minimum, this log should contain:

- Course description and syllabus
- What form it is in (video, PowerPoint slides, or interactive computer training module)
- Group or individual responsible for course content
- Group or individual responsible for course materials
- Method used to deliver the training
- How often it is taught, to whom, and how it is recorded
- How the course is evaluated

Our experience shows that if you go through all the steps above, and you document your results and review your findings, you will be able to identify two major opportunities for alignment:

1. *Merging training programs.* For example, you might merge a systems engineering training program and a software engineering training program for the same reason you merge process improvement groups to eliminate overlap, simplify the efforts, increase communication, and focus your resources
2. *Merging courses with similar content, roles, and level of detail.* For example, you might merge data management and configuration management courses to eliminate redundancy, improve consistency, and increase knowledge across two similar groups. Caution: some courses, for example a QA orientation and a QA techniques course, are similar but with a different level of detail for different audiences. Those would not be merged.

The other outcome of this effort is identifying courses that need to be developed to address the expanded scope of the CMMI. For example, if you have a software project manager course but do not have a systems or purchasing project manager course, you will either want to expand the scope of the software course or create new courses for systems and purchasing.

Scenarios

Here are two scenarios to consider. Our lawyers tell us that we have to include the following statement: This is a work of the imagination depicting organizations and events that have not happened. Any resemblance to actual companies or persons, living or dead, is purely coincidental.

Scenario One: Merged Teams

Background

Roadrunner Software Enterprises is a development organization with products that contain both custom hardware and software. They produce mainly embedded software for their primary products and some automatic test equipment software to test the final product. They do a lot of what they consider to be systems engineering, including the analysis of customer requirements, total systems design, and verification/validation activities throughout the development and installation life cycle. They have a large purchasing group that covers everything from buying paper clips to buying aircrafts to use as test platforms.

Existing teams

They have been doing process improvement with the software CMM for over 10 years, and they have a classic Software Engineering Process Group (SEPG) sponsored by the Director of Embedded Software. They have an ISO program in place for the hardware manufacturing activities that is part of their standard quality process that has been going on for five years managed by the Vice President of Quality. They began a systems engineering process improvement activity two years ago using the Systems Engineering Capability Model (EIA/IS 731), and they have an Engineering Process Improvement Group (EPIG) that is sponsored by the Director of Engineering. The Chairman of the EPIG is a member of the SEPG and the Chairman of the SEPG is a member of the EPIG. Training comes from two sources — a Software Training Group and an organizational-level training function within the Human Resource Department.

Approach

They have defined their organizational scope for the CMMI initiative to include all of engineering (systems, software, mechanical, electrical, and avionics), training department, quality assurance, and purchasing. As part of the new initiative, they have merged the SEPG and EPIG into a new group called the Engineering Process Group (EPG) and expanded their charter to cover all of engineering and purchasing plus related quality assurance functions. They have assigned sponsorship of the EPG to the newly identified Vice President of Technology. They have renamed the Software Training Group to the Engineering Training Group (ETG) and given them responsibility for training unique to engineering and purchasing. They decided to leave the ISO program as is but have assigned the senior in-house ISO auditor as a full-time member of the EPG.

Rationale

The rationale for the merged team approach is that:

- They found that they had many of the same members and stakeholders in the SEPG and EPIG.
- They have very similar processes and procedures for systems and software in requirements, design, integration, verification, and validation with some understandable differences in specialty engineering.
- The newly assigned VP of Technology sees this merged EPG and ETG as a way to improve communications between systems, software, and purchasing, and is looking for a way to reduce rework.

Scenario Two: Separate but Equal

Background

Wily Coyote Industries, a division of Kannotgetabrake, Inc., is an organization that produces major systems containing both custom hardware/software and significant amounts of purchased hardware/software. They produce a variety of custom software including embedded, information systems, and command/control applications. They do a lot of what they consider to be systems engineering, including the analysis of systems requirements, specification writing for components and subsystems, verification and validation activities, and product integration. A group at corporate headquarters, over 900 miles away, performs most purchasing activities.

Existing Teams

They have been doing software engineering process improvement with the CMM for Software for six years and have recently been assessed at Level 4 against that model. They have a classic SEPG sponsored by the Director of Engineering. The SEPG is responsible for all software processes, procedures, and training. They started a systems engineering process improvement initiative four years ago and formed a Process Improvement

Group (PIG) sponsored by the Senior Engineering Scientist. The PIG is responsible for systems process and procedures. The corporate training department covers systems engineering training activities. There is very little formal interaction between the SEPG and the PIG, but a lot of competition. Each group has its own logo, t-shirts, and coffee cups.

Approach

They have defined their organizational scope for the CMMI initiative to include systems engineering and software engineering. They have left the SEPG and PIG separate but have assigned a member of the SEPG to attend all PIG meetings and a member of PIG to attend all SEPG meetings. They have moved the responsibility for software training to the Corporate Training Department and have transferred the old software training group to corporate.

Rationale

The rationale for the separate teams is that:

- The SEPG is planning a Level 5 assessment against the CMM for Software next year and sees this as priority over the CMMI initiative.
- The competition between the groups was determined to be healthy by executive management.
- The processes and procedures for software are quite varied, with very different approaches in each domain (embedded, information systems, and command/control applications).
- The processes and procedures for systems engineering are very formal and unique to the major client.
- The move toward a total corporate training approach supports a corporate goal of leveraging training across divisions.

Summary

This chapter covers some of the things to consider when combining or aligning multiple process improvement initiatives. Considerations include process improvement team structure, integration of existing procedures, measurement programs, and training programs. Different improvement models have placed different levels of importance on some of these areas. This has naturally resulted in different levels of implementation across the disciplines.

None of the ideas presented in this chapter are difficult to understand. Mainly, they concern understanding the policies, processes, procedures, plans, courses, and people you currently have in place, understanding how they fit together within the expanded scope of the CMMI, and the vision the organization has created for its process improvement journey.

While we have presented these concepts in a simple, straightforward fashion, this effort actually will take many hours of hard work. Do not underestimate the level of effort required to successfully accomplish these tasks.

Notes

1. Chapter 16 is our "meat and potatoes" chapter on policies, processes, and procedures that will give you more details on some of these concepts, along with Chapter 14 that discusses documentation guidelines.
2. Measures in this section refer to both base and derived measures. Base measures are simple values of some attribute, for example, the size of a document in pages or effort to produce a document in hours. Derived measures are defined to be a function of two or more base measures, for example, productivity in hours per page to produce a document.
3. We really do mean many, but not all. We have had the opportunity to work with both systems and acquisition program that exhibit high measure maturity but these are the exceptional cases; and while it may be politically incorrect to talk about software success and systems and acquisition, we think it is important to share our experiences.

Chapter 10

Is the CMMI® Right for Small Organizations?

This chapter presents two viewpoints concerning implementing the CMMI® within a small organization. A small organization is defined as an organization with 20 or fewer technical personnel developing systems. In a small organization, it is not uncommon for a project to consist of three people. One individual may serve as the project manager, developer, and tester; another individual may serve as a coder, tester, and database administrator; and the third individual may serve as a part-time quality assurance representative. The project may only last from three to six weeks.

A point-counterpoint approach is presented to discuss the pros and cons associated with various issues and their operational impacts. The reader should be somewhat familiar with both the CMMI effort and the previous models developed by the Software Engineering Institute (SEI).

The authors of this book do not make any claims as to these arguments. We believe the readers should be able to make up their own minds.

Definitions

Before continuing, let us discuss some basic terms to avoid any confusion later.

Systems Engineering

There seems to be no real agreement as to what systems engineering really is. The Systems Engineering Capability Maturity Model, version 1.1, states that "Systems Engineering is the selective application of scientific and engineering efforts to:

- Transform operational need into descriptions of the system configuration which best satisfies operational need according to measures of effectiveness
- Integrate related technical parameters and ensure compatibility of all physical, functional, and technical program interfaces in a manner that optimizes total system definition and design
- Integrate efforts of all engineering disciplines and specialties into the total engineering effort."

The definition of Systems Engineering from the draft version 0.5 of the Systems Engineering Capability Model EIA 731–1 states that "Systems Engineering is an inter-disciplinary approach and means to enable the realization of successful systems."

The CMMI v1.1 defines Systems Engineering as:

> The *interdisciplinary approach* governing the *total technical* and *managerial effort* required to *transform* a set of customer needs, expectations, and constraints *into a product solution,* and support that solution, throughout the product's life. This includes the *definition of technical performance measures,* the *integration of engineering specialties* towards the establishment of a product architecture, and the *definition of supporting life-cycle processes* that balance cost, performance, and scheduled objectives.

What do these definitions mean as they relate to CMMI? Basically, Systems Engineering covers the development of total systems, which *may* or *may not include* software. Systems Engineering integrates all parts, areas, personnel, and characteristics of a project that are necessary to produce a completed system for delivery to the customer. Projects may begin with feasibility, cost-benefit, and concept of operations analyses to justify any subsequent software or non-software activities.

Software Engineering

This covers the development of software-focused systems. Projects begin once a software project manager is assigned and funding has been received. Software Engineering may be a subset of Systems Engineering — or it may stand alone as its own area of focus. It is possible to have some systems that are entirely made up of software-only tasks.

Integrated Product and Process Development

This covers the usage of large product development teams, with each team member focusing on specific areas of expertise. Each team's results are then integrated into one product.

Acquisition

This covers the identification of a need, selection of vendors, and monitoring their ability to produce the system according to contract constraints.

The Staged Model Representation

This is the architecture in use by the Software CMM. This structure focuses an organization's improvement activities on undertaking the practices depicted in each process area (PA) within each level. For example, an organization would choose to attain Level 2 (by satisfying the goals for each process area in Level 2) before trying to undertake Process Areas in levels 3, 4, or 5. Each level provides the foundation for further improvements. This representation begins with basic management practices, and continues with increasingly sophisticated focus areas that belong within a specific level. Practices reside within Process Areas within levels. There are five maturity levels, each serving as process boundaries.

Staged models provide guidance to organizations on the order of improvement activities they should undertake, based on (Key) Process Areas at each stage/maturity level. Performing practices in the appropriate process area at a given level will help stabilize projects, thus allowing the execution of further improvement activities. Incremental improvement is supported in each maturity level/stage because that stage contains a collection of process areas on which to focus current activities.[1]

The Continuous Model Representation

This is the architecture in use by the systems engineering models. This structure focuses process improvement on actions to be completed within process areas. Organizations are expected to select the process areas of interest to them. Processes may span different levels and are grouped by functional categories. More sophistication in implementing the practices for each process area is expected at the different levels. There are six capability levels, which group process areas into functional categories of increasing evolution.

Continuous models provide more flexibility in defining process improvement programs. They recognize that individual Process Areas are performed at distinct capability or maturity levels. Organizations need to perform an analysis of how the various process areas address the needs of the organization. This exercise also provides an opportunity to gain consensus on the sequence of improvement activities that are appropriate to the organization as a whole.[2]

Maturity Levels

These belong to the Staged Representation. These apply to an organization's *overall* process capability and organizational maturity. Each maturity level comprises a predefined set of process areas and generic goals. There are five maturity levels, numbered 1 through 5. These components suggest a recommended order for approaching process improvement in stages by grouping process areas into actionable groups.[3]

Capability Levels

These belong to the Continuous Representation. These apply to an organization's process improvement achievement for *each* process area. There are six capability levels, numbered 0 through 6. Capability levels focus on maturing an organization's ability to perform, control, and improve its performance in a process area.[4] These levels enable an organization to track, evaluate, and demonstrate an organization's progress as it improves its processes associated within a specific process area. A recommended order of process improvement is also suggested by these levels, due to the groupings of the process areas into functional categories.

SCAMPI

This stands for Standard CMMI Assessment Method for Process Improvement, an assessment technique that is similar to both the former CBA-IPI and Software Capability Evaluation methods. SCAMPI uses the CMMI as its reference model. (See Chapter 11 for more information.)

Small Organizations

This encompasses those organizations having 20 or fewer people, in total, supporting software or system development. Each member of a project may wear several hats (i.e., may perform several different roles) as part of normal daily tasks. Projects are short-lived, that is, between three and six weeks.

Point-Counterpoint

A point-counterpoint approach is presented to discuss the pros and cons associated with various issues and their operational impacts. The reader should be somewhat familiar with both the CMMI effort and the previous models developed by the Software Engineering Institute.

The authors of this book do not make any claims as to these arguments. We believe the readers should be able to make up their own minds.

Issue: No tailoring guidance is given for tailoring the CMMI for small organizations.

Point: The previous CMM was often criticized as having been written *by* large DoD organizations *for* large DoD organizations. Projects within the DoD realm generally consist of many people devoted full time to one project, or many people devoted full time to one of several sub-projects. These projects run for years, and cost millions of dollars. This type of thinking is completely opposite to that of small organizations. One example of problems that small organizations currently have with the CMM is the number of "groups" suggested by the CMM to achieve Level 3. The number of groups suggested is 13. Even if a group ranges from one person, part-time, to several people full-time, if your entire organization only consists of 20 people maximum, 13 groups become quite an expenditure of resources. The CMMI, relying heavily on practices maintained by large organizations, will be even more difficult to implement in smaller ones. CMMI has been slow to catch on in the commercial community. CMMI tends to attract DoD/aerospace organizations. The only tailoring guidelines given are called "Discipline Amplifications," which reside in the margins of most Process Areas and consist only of one or two sentences. These are often not clear or detailed enough to follow. The tailoring guidelines suggested in Chapter 6 are similar to those found in the original CMM for Software; that is, the more tailoring done, the less likely an organization is to improve. This warning seems to address only the negative aspects of tailoring "out" a practice or process area. It appears as if tailoring is actively discouraged. Also, software shops are not necessarily interested in systems engineering — it just may not apply to them. So how and when can this be tailored out?

Counterpoint: While it is true that more guidance is needed as to how to select those Process Areas and practices that are most relevant to a small organization, the CMMI still allows the organization to tailor its process improvement objectives to the organization's business goals. The point of the CMMI is to improve the processes of the organization, not to just worry about maintaining fidelity to the model for Maturity Level ratings.

Issue: CMMI is simply too big for small organizations to handle.

Point: The CMM was criticized for having too many Key Process Areas and too many Key Practices. Just doing a visual comparison of CMMI against the CMM, CMMI appears to be three times as big. Also, the CMM was criticized for not containing everything necessary to promote the development of effective, efficient systems. So, the CMMI has removed the term "key" from its Process Areas and Practices. It now seems as though the CMMI is trying to prescribe *everything* necessary to produce good systems. The CMM has over 300 Key Practices. Processes and supporting procedures needed to be written by the organization in order to describe how these practices were to be followed. This effort was seen by most organizations as a major part of the time it took for their software process improvement efforts. The CMMI contains more Practices, and most of these are not detailed enough to be understood in such a way as to promote consistent application across organizations. Writing procedures will be long and difficult. The time, resources, and costs associated with implementing the CMMI appear to have expanded exponentially, compared to the already major investment required by the CMM.

One response heard at an SEPG Conference was that an organization no longer had to write as many procedures. That response was based on the fact that the CMMI rarely uses the word "procedures," whereas the CMM did rely on that word. However, a close reading of the CMMI will reveal that most of what an organization used to call "procedures" is now included in the "plans" that are a major part of each Process Area. Without the detail included in documented procedures, it is very difficult to ensure that processes are being followed in a consistent manner across your organization. So, whether they are called "procedures" or "plans," an effective process improvement program still has plenty of documentation to prepare.

Counterpoint: The CMMI allows small organizations, as well as large ones, to realize the benefits of following a structured process. CMMI allows for tailoring of the process, and for aligning the process to the needs of the organization. However, this alignment requires more thought than was previously required with the CMM, as the CMM was directed specifically at software engineering. As stated previously, the SEI responded to the cries from the marketplace for more information regarding those areas where the CMM was lacking — specifically systems engineering. The organization can also choose how much of the model it wishes to follow. For example, if an organization is not interested in applying the Systems Engineering guidelines cited in the model, that organization may select the continuous representation of the model, or only the Software Engineering aspects.

Issue: Return on Investment (ROI) from CMMI has not been validated, especially as it relates to small organizations.

Point: The Return on Investment (ROI) quoted by proponents refers to the ROI gained from the CMM, not for the ROI from the CMMI. With some organizations reporting that it takes three to five years to realize its ROI from following the CMM, how long will it take an organization to realize its ROI from following the CMMI? Small organizations do not have the deep pockets and overhead of the larger organizations. Small organizations must worry about meeting payroll every two weeks. Expected ROI from using a model is often the argument used to justify the large expenditures necessary to institute and maintain a process improvement effort. Yet no real studies are available (at time of print) that can help a small organization calculate ROI from using this model.

Counterpoint: As for citing statistics for ROI from usage of the CMMI, it is still too early to have enough data points gathered to be statistically accurate. However, the SEI is conducting pilots and gathering this information. As both models are predicated on applying common sense to the practice of developing systems, one can extrapolate the benefits from one model to the next.

Issue: CMMI emphasizes Systems Engineering over Software Engineering.

Point: Historically, the biggest seller of all the models was the CMM for Software. For those customers who bought into and applied the CMM for Software, Systems Engineering may not be part of their work, and simply may not apply. The biggest growth sector in the marketplace right now for technical work is not large, bureaucratically structured organizations, but small, *software*-oriented shops. Why make taxpayers pay for a model that is not universally needed?

Counterpoint: Systems Engineering is necessary, no matter how large or small the organization. Very few organizations develop just software — there are always systems issues to be taken into consideration, platform and hardware requirements, as well as interfacing with other groups or individuals responsible for some part of the system being built. Good systems engineering practices flowing into and out of software engineering tasks can only improve the software engineering effort.

Issue: CMMI is too prescriptive for small organizations.

Point: The CMM was sold as being *what* to do, with the organization responsible for defining *how* to do the *whats*. The CMMI is structured so similarly to large, bureaucratically controlled efforts that there seems to be little room to maneuver. For example, published results of CMMI pilot assessments have reported that the assessors had difficulty not asking interviewees leading questions, because the model is basically black or white, yes or no, do you do this or not. As for examples in the Process Areas themselves, Risk Management seems to require a risk mitigation plan. Is this really necessary if you are a maintenance shop and your projects only last three weeks? Verification and Validation may be too rigorous for small teams. Can independent testing and configuration audits satisfy the tenets of these Process Areas instead?

Counterpoint: The CMMI is a balanced model, promoting not only Systems Engineering concepts, but also Software Engineering, IPPD, and Supplier Sourcing. The organization may choose which areas to focus on, as well as the degree of focus that fits their business objectives. The developers of the CMMI realized that small organizations, as well as those organizations not as mature as early adopters of the SEI process improvement approach, should not be penalized. Therefore, Level 2 in the Staged representation mostly mirrors the basic concepts expressed in the CMM itself at Level 2, that is, basic project management. Because going from Level 1 to Level 2 is generally the most difficult for most organizations, Level 2 remains basic. Small organizations may also choose to follow the Continuous representation, although these shops may need more time to implement the concepts and to understand the terminology (as most software shops used the Staged Model of the CMM for Software). With the Continuous representation, an organization may select which Process Areas best fit their needs and concentrate on those areas only. Organizations may also elect to focus on only one discipline. So, the CMMI is actually much more flexible than the original CMM.

Issue: Small organizations are run differently from large organizations and face different challenges.

Point: The *primary* business driver in small, high-tech companies is time-to-market. Decisions must be made quickly, and all relate to the bottom line. While CMMI promotes quality by elongating the process used to develop and deliver systems (because of preplanning and embedded checkpoint mechanisms), time-to-market does not seem to be considered. Ignoring time-to-market concerns is simply not practical in today's marketplace. Although the public decries poor-quality systems, it seems to prefer speed over functionality. And delivering products quickly is the life-blood of small organizations.

Counterpoint: This is the reason models such as the CMMI were written. What good does it do to deliver a system on time if it does not work? While small organizations may need to consider time-to-market questions, inevitably, if the organization cannot deliver good products, it will go out of business. The CMMI is written based on the best practices of highly mature organizations that have used the various models and methodologies, and have learned from them. The CMMI has leveraged this information, consolidated it, and presents it in a format that can be tailored to the needs of any organization. While several Process Areas within CMMI may prolong the development and delivery of systems, using the Process Areas of this model will result in better products delivered and better decision making by executives.

Issue: CMMI was written for already-mature organizations.

Point: Early, introductory material from the Staged Representation of an earlier version of the CMMI states that organizations currently rated at the higher maturity levels, or pursuing Malcolm Baldridge or ISO 9000 certification, should consider using the CMMI. These organizations are already working on, or have achieved, some notion of process improvement. But is it not true that most organizations are still functioning at the lower levels? Is this an elitist model?

Consider the following example. The Measurement and Analysis Process Area is now a stand-alone PA. Measurement and Analysis used to be a Common Feature in the previous CMM. As such, it served as an effective check-and-balance for the entire Key Process Area (KPA). If an organization had performed the activities preceding it, then that organization should have been able to measure those activities. Then, the measurements could be reported to Management and Software Quality Assurance (as discussed in the Verifying Implementation Key Practices). The effectiveness of the processes for a particular KPA, as well as any deficiencies, could then be determined by reviewing the metrics collected. In the CMMI, we now have Directing Implementation. This Common Feature has far fewer examples of practical metrics. While the Measurement and Analysis PA has useful information, much of this information seems to relate to higher maturity levels. If an organization is just beginning the road to process improvement, how much of this PA must be implemented? The reason this PA was pulled out of each Key Process Area and is now its own PA came as a result of input from higher-maturity organizations. They all stated that measurement is the key to successful improvement efforts. But is creating this as a stand-alone PA the answer? Hindsight is a wonderful thing. Most organizations at Levels 4 and 5 are large organizations with deep pockets. Do these organizations really believe that they can institute this PA in their organizations, as they were back when their organizations were not quite as sophisticated as they are today? Do they believe that small organizations can implement this PA as written? Comprehensive metrics programs for small organizations, while beneficial, are too difficult and expensive to implement at Level 2.

Counterpoint: Level 2 in the CMMI still remains somewhat comparable to what it was in the CMM for Software. This should allow organizations, no matter what their size, to readily achieve this level if they had already been assessed at Level 2 or above using the CMM. Measurement truly is the key to focused improvement. As stated, if you have done it, you should be able to measure it. *Using* the measurements is also key. It does no good to simply collect the numbers and report them — the numbers must be used. At the lower levels and in less-mature organizations, the metrics were not always used. Most organizations only began focusing on metrics when they were attempting to reach Level 4; and not all organizations continued in process improvement once they achieved Level 3. They dropped out before really turning their attention to measurement. By separating out this PA, emphasis is placed on collecting, analyzing, reporting, and using the measurements. Once again, an organization can tailor its process improvement efforts and the usage of this PA, as related to business goals.

Issue: The CMMI is too vaguely written to be used in assessments.

Point: Organizations attempting to use the model for an assessment report greatly extended timeframes. Interpretation appears to be based on personal experience, not on careful reading of the model. Most assessment teams have difficulty interpreting the model and state that the model is too vaguely written. Therefore, they *must* rely on their own personal experience. Because individuals have different experiences, this reliance does not promote consistent assessment results across organizations. While this consistency has always been a problem with CMM-based assessments and evaluations because of their dependence on the individuals who make up the appraisal teams, it is magnified with this model. Assessment teams could go to the CMM and read its practices and subpractices for guidance. Users of the CMMI report that this guidance cannot be found. Also, assessment teams have been directed to assess three projects from the Software area — and then three different projects from the Systems area. Where is the integration?

This is not just a problem for small organizations.

Counterpoint: These issues have been raised by early pilot assessments and have been addressed in the SCAMPI method. Early CMM-based assessments had significant interpretation issues, so this is nothing new.

Summary

Regardless of an organization's size, process improvement must use a structured approach to be successful. The CMMI includes more information and more areas that promote the development of high-quality systems. However, professional judgment in determining how to implement the model must be used.

It can also be said that the CMM is always right for an organization; the CMMI is always right for an organization; SCAMPI/SCE/CBA-IPI is always right for an organization. What is *not* right for an organization is basing contract awards or contract bid opportunities solely on assessment results.

Notes

1. Capability Maturity Model (CMM) for Software, version 1.1.
2. Capability Maturity Model — Integration (CMMI) for Systems Engineering (SE)/Software Engineering (SW)/Integrated Product and Process Development (IPPD), version 1.1.
3. Architectural and Functional Comparison of the CMMI Model Representation, Draft, Mike Konrad and Sandy Shrum, December 1999.
4. Expanding the Focus of Software Process Improvement to Include Systems Engineering, Kent Johnson and Joe Dindo, TeraQuest Metrics, Incorporated, Crosstalk, October 1998.

Chapter 11

Appraisals Using the CMMI®

This chapter discusses the Software Engineering Institute's (SEI's) defined approaches to CMMI®-based appraisals. Appraisals, assessments, and evaluations are by no means a new subject. There are a number of appraisal methods[1] that have been developed to measure and evaluate an organization against the family of Capability Maturity Models (CMMs) in addition to other models and standards. A community of assessors and evaluators has grown around these methods. The CMMI product suite introduces some new concepts, but mostly builds on the history of these previous methods and the best practices of the assessor and evaluator community.

The SEI has released two guiding documents for CMMI assessments:

1. Appraisal Requirements for CMMI (ARC): contains the requirements for three classes of appraisal methods Class A, Class B, and Class C. These requirements are the rules for defining each class of appraisal method.
2. Standard CMMI Appraisal Method for Process Improvement (SCAMPI) Method Description Document (MDD): currently the only approved Class A appraisal method.

This chapter is based on version 1.1 of both the ARC and the SCAMPI MDD that were released in December 2001.

We need to emphasize one point: SCAMPI is currently the only approved CMMI Class A Appraisal Method. That is, SCAMPI satisfies all the requirements of an ARC Class A Appraisal Method and has been approved by the SEI.[2] There are three classes of CMMI Appraisal Methods: Class A, Class B, and Class C. We emphasize this point because we have heard and seen numerous references to a SCAMPI Class B or SCAMPI Class C. These are incorrect usages. A Class B or Class C Appraisal Method would be something other than a "SCAMPI."

Definitions

The following definitions may be helpful when considering this subject.

- *Assessment:* An appraisal that an organization does to and for itself for the purpose of process improvement. (ARC v1.1)
- *(Process) appraisal:* An examination of one or more processes by a trained team of professionals using an appraisal reference model as the basis for determining, at a minimum, strengths and weaknesses. (ARC v1.1)
- *Evaluation:* An appraisal in which an external group comes into an organization and examines its processes as input to a decision regarding future business. (Note: This definition is somewhat misleading because evaluations can be either Acquisition/Supplier Selection or Process Monitoring. Process Monitoring includes incentive/award fee decisions or risk management planning.)
- *Organizational unit:* That part of the organization that is the subject of an appraisal (also known as the organizational scope of the appraisal). An organizational unit deploys one or more processes that have a coherent process context and operates within a coherent set of business objectives. An organizational unit is typically part of a larger organization, although in a small organization, the organizational unit may be the entire organization. (ARC v1.1)
- *(Appraisal) rating:* The value assigned by an appraisal team to (1) a CMMI goal or process area, (2) the capability level of a process area, or (3) the maturity level of an organizational unit. The rating is determined by enacting the defined rating process for the appraisal method being employed. (CMMI v1.1)

We offer some words of caution. Although the definition of an assessment says "to and for itself for the purpose of process improvement," we will see that SCAMPI can also be for purposes other than process improvement.

There is also no clear definition of what it means for "the organizational unit to be part of a larger organization" under the definition of an organizational unit. Some companies game the assessment by defining the organizational scope to be only a small number of well-managed projects for the assessment to fit their agenda for securing the level rating and "passing" the assessment. With all assessments, some planning must be done to align model scope and method details to the organization's business needs and objectives. However, it is up to the Lead Appraiser to keep the organization honest and to ensure that the organizational unit is clearly identified in the appraisal report.

As discussed in previous chapters, appraisals consider three categories of model components as defined in the CMMI:

1. *Required:* specific and generic goals only
2. *Expected:* specific and generic practices only
3. *Informative:* includes subpractices and typical work products

The appraisal team must find an indication that projects and organizational groups within the organization unit are satisfying the required specific and generic goals. Appraisal teams generally look at the practices associated with the goals to decide whether or not the goals have been met. This is done through examination of project and organizational practices to see that they are "compliant with" or support the specific and generic practices. All the practices are really expected. Because a lot of practices are written to cover all kinds of situations, the informative material provides clarification. The appraisal teams use subpractices and typical work products to clarify the meaning of the practices and goals.

SCAMPI Fundamentals

As identified above, SCAMPI is an acronym that stands for Standard CMMI Appraisal Method for Process Improvement. A SCAMPI assessment must be led by an SEI Authorized SCAMPI Lead Appraiser. SCAMPI is supported by the SCAMPI Product Suite, which includes the SCAMPI Method Description, maturity questionnaire, work aids, and templates. Currently, SCAMPI is the only method that can provide a rating, the only method recognized by the SEI, and the method of most interest to organizations.

SCAMPI is based on experience from previous methods, including:

■ CBA IPI: CMM-Based Appraisal for Internal Process Improvement
■ SCE: Software Capability Evaluation

- EIA/IS 732.2: the interim international standard entitled Systems Engineering Assessment Method
- SDCE: Software Development Capability Evaluation
- FAA Appraisal Method

Non-Process Improvement Appraisals

A stated goal of SCAMPI v1.1 was to support two non-process improvement uses often associated with Software Capability Evaluations:

1. Acquisition/supplier selection
2. Process monitoring (often contract monitoring)

Note: SCEs may be, and have also been, used for internal process improvement.

SCAMPI v1.1 does not make the use of only external team members a requirement for these non-process improvement types of evaluations. However, it would be reasonable to expect that this external-only requirement will continue to be imposed by both federal, individual corporate, and other acquisition policies to avoid conflicts of interest.

Appraisal Classes

As mentioned, there are three classes of CMMI Appraisal Methods. Each class is distinguished by the degree of rigor associated with the application of the method. Class A is the most rigorous. Class B is slightly less rigorous; and Class C is the least rigorous. Exhibit 1 gives some idea of the expected differences between the methods in each class. The paragraphs that follow describe some of the details.

Class A Appraisal Methods must satisfy all ARC requirements. A Class A Appraisal Method is the only method that can provide a rating. It requires three sources of data: instruments, interviews, and documents. An instrument is a survey or questionnaire provided to the organization, project, or individuals to complete prior to the on-site visit. It helps the organization define and document the scope of the appraisal, and gives the appraisal team members a "quick look" into the organization's structure and culture. An interview is a formal meeting between one or more members of the organization and the appraisal team or mini-team. During this interview, the interviewee represents the organization in some capacity, based on the role he performs. For example, the SCAMPI team may interview a project manager, a quality assurance representative, and the director of

Exhibit 1. Appraisal Class Characteristics

Characteristics	Class A	Class B	Class C
Amount of objective evidence gathered (relative)	High	Medium	Low
Rating generated	Yes	No	No
Resource needs (relative)	High	Medium	Low
Team size (relative)	Large	Medium	Small
Data sources (instruments, interviews, and documents)	Requires all three data sources	Requires only two data sources (one must be interviews)	Requires only one data source
Appraisal team leader requirement	Authorized Lead Appraiser	Authorized Lead Appraiser or person trained and experienced	Person trained and experienced

Source: Adapted from Appraisal Requirements for CMMI, Version 1.1, December 2001, Table 1: Characteristics of CMMI Appraisal Method Classes.

systems engineering. Many interviews are held with many members of the organizational unit. A document is just that — a written work product or artifact that is used as evidence that a process is being followed. It can be a plan, meeting minutes, or a process description. The document can be either hard-copy or electronic.

A Class A Appraisal Method can additionally be either EIA 15504 conformant or non-EIA 15504 conformant. EIA 15504 is an international standard covering software process assessments. When an EIA 15504 comformant appraisal method is desired, there are additional requirements introduced to document how well processes perform. These include process profiles and product quality characteristics. Process profiles summarize the performance of processes found in the reviewed projects. Quality characteristics summarize the quality of the products and services provided, (e.g., defect density, reliability). Measuring and reporting process performance and quality characteristics is a fundamentally different approach to appraisal from previous CMM-related approaches.

A Class B Appraisal Method has fewer requirements than a Class A method. Class B requires only two sources of data (interviews and either instruments or documents). Data sufficiency and the draft presentation are optional with Class B. Data sufficiency means that for all specific and generic practices reviewed, validated observations exist. These observations are adequate to understand the extent of implementation of the practice, are representative of the organizational unit, and are representative of the life-cycle phases in use within the organizational unit. Draft presentation of findings (strengths and weaknesses based on valid observations) is used to get feedback for the people interviewed by formally presenting the draft findings before finalizing the findings. Data sufficiency and draft presentation are optional in Class B in order to reduce the amount of time needed for the appraisal. The result of an appraisal without data sufficiency and a draft presentation is an appraisal done in a shorter amount of time and effort, but with possibly less confidence in the findings.

A Class C Appraisal Method has even fewer requirements than a Class B method. Class C requires only one source of data (interviews, instruments, or documents). Team consensus, observation validation, observation corroboration, data sufficiency, and draft presentation are optional. Team consensus refers to a technique of team decision making regarding observations and findings that result in decisions that all team members are willing to support. Making observation validation and observation corroboration optional means that the team does not need to agree that enough data has been gathered for an observation and that observations need not be consistent with other observations. The result of an appraisal without team consensus, observation validation, observation corroboration, data sufficiency, and draft presentations is an appraisal done in a shorter amount of time and effort, but again, with much less confidence in the findings.

As of February 2003, only one "officially recognized" method is defined for any of these classes, and that is the SCAMPI, which satisfies the ARC requirements for a Class A Appraisal Method. Class B and Class C methods are left as an exercise for the reader by the SEI — in other words, no approved methods currently exist. Many groups and organizations have created their own methods. A few words of caution: most groups and organizations have not really defined their methods in detail. They have just put the label of Class B and Class C on approaches that they previously employed to assess themselves and their clients.

Which Appraisal Method Class Should I Use?

Organizations involved in process improvement often use a range of methods to assess their improvement progress. Many organizations undergo process improvement using the CMMI in order to be rated at a particular level. Therefore, these organizations will need a Class A Appraisal Method at some time, and today that means a SCAMPI. The use of a Class B or Class C appraisal will depend largely on the organization's process improvement and appraisal strategy. Examples follow.

- *Strategy One*. A Class B appraisal is used to initiate an organizational-level process improvement program by identifying the majority of weaknesses against the CMMI. The process improvement plan is based on the identified weaknesses. Class C appraisals would then be performed periodically to measure progress against the process improvement plan and to determine readiness for a follow-on Class B or Class A appraisal.
- *Strategy Two*. Class C appraisals are used on subsets of the organization. These subsets are based on business areas or project size. The process improvement plan is based on the aggregation of the weaknesses found. Because the Class C appraisal is less detailed, the weaknesses are addressed across the organization, not just in the subset where found. A Class B appraisal would be performed after six months or a year of performing against the process improvement plan to determine readiness for a Class A appraisal.
- *Strategy Three*. A Class A appraisal is used to initiate an organizational-level process improvement program. The process improvement plan is based on the identified weaknesses. A Class B appraisal would be performed after six months or a year of performing against the process improvement plan to determine readiness for a second Class A appraisal for an official rating.

In most situations, Strategy Three would be recommended because:

- The most weaknesses are found in a Class A appraisal with the highest confidence level.
- More organizational learning occurs through the formal appraisal process.
- More organizational buy-in is possible, particularly for internal team members.

Using SCAMPIs in the Field

Pilots of SCAMPI v1.0 have indicated that the assessments took too much time. As a result, a performance goal of SCAMPI v1.1 was defined as follows. On-site activities should be completed within two weeks or 100 hours (excluding training and pre-onsite activities) for an assessment covering CMMI-Systems Engineering/Software Engineering version 1.1, through Maturity Level 3. Four projects would be reviewed that represent the organizational unit. Both the systems engineering and software engineering disciplines would be included.

"New" approaches taken to meet this goal included the development of the Practice Implementation Indicators (PIIs) that are collected prior to the on-site review in a PII Description (PIID). This approach is based on the best practice from many process improvement specialists, Lead Evaluators, and Lead Assessors of having the organization generate and maintain a compliance matrix showing how practices are performed in the organization. Exhibit 2 shows a sample PIID Element containing the three types of PII information collected: Direct Work Product, Indirect Work Product, and Affirmations. Direct Work Product and Indirect Work Product come from documents, and Affirmations come from interviews. This example contains information and appraisal team notes that have been collected for a Specific Practice of the Project Planning process area.

The initial PIIDs contain the direct and indirect work products that are prepared by the organization, and demonstrate how the practices of the CMMI are implemented in their organization via organizational documentation. In practice, often the PIID will contain the location of the work products, either hard-copy or electronic. Development of the PIIDs is nontrivial. This PIID development puts additional work on the organization to prepare for an appraisal.

The SCAMPI team is expected to conduct a Readiness Review of the PIIDs prior to the start of the on-site SCAMPI. The Lead Appraiser is responsible for giving the go-ahead at the Readiness Review to begin the on-site SCAMPI interviews. This go-ahead statement means that the SCAMPI team feels the organization is ready to have the SCAMPI team show up at the organization and begin the interview process. This step proved necessary because, in pilots, several false starts occurred, costing the organization and the SCAMPI teams time, money, and frustration.

SCAMPI v1.1 is designed to support a verification-based appraisal using the PIID to focus the team resources in areas needing further investigation. The SCAMPI team will need to verify the contents of the PIID. This is in contrast to an observation-based or discovery-based appraisal in which the team writes observations for all practices and discovers the existence of documentation through interviews and document reviews as part of the on-site review period.

The verification of the PIIDs may result in a more hostile environment being created between the organization and the SCAMPI team. The organization and the developers of the PIIDs are now stating that "X" on the PIID shows they are compliant. The SCAMPI team is now in the position of saying, "No you are not compliant because X does not match the intent of the CMMI practice."

SCAMPI also encourages mini-teams, a subset of the entire team, to interview independently. Mini-teams are given authority to reach consensus

Exhibit 2. Sample PIID Element for Project Planning Specific Practice 1.1-1

Practice ID		*PP SP 1.1-1:*	
		"Establish a top-level work breakdown structure (WBS) to estimate the scope of the project."	
PII Type	*Direct Work Product*	*Indirect Work Product*	*Affirmations*
Organizational Implementation Evidence	Top-level WBS, with revision history Task descriptions Work project descriptions	Minutes of meetings at which WBS was generated or used to develop project estimate Project estimates aligned with WBS elements	Developer 1 — "We used the WBS" Project Manager 2 — "I worked on the WBS Team"
Appraisal Team Notes	WBS found for all projects	Minutes found for two projects	

on practice implementation for each instance. The entire team remains responsible for consensus at the organizational unit level. This is a change over most previous methods that required the entire team to conduct interviews. Allowing mini-teams to interview independently may result in low-quality or inconsistent results during late-night rollups of findings. The mini-teams must be formed based on trust and experience working with the SCAMPI team members. It is not unusual for a mini-team to interview an individual, and come back and report to the rest of the SCAMPI team. The SCAMPI team may then respond by asking, "Well, did you then follow up with a question about x or y or z?" The mini-team might not have thought of those questions. The mini-team may also be allowed too much freedom. For example, the SCAMPI Lead Appraiser may allow the mini-team to interview one project manager, and another mini-team to interview another project manager, and another mini-team to interview yet another project manager. Each mini-team, if not immediately consolidating their results with the entire team, may find that the first project manager does something in agreement with a practice, the second one does not, and the third manager was not even asked a question relating to that practice. During the late-night, last-night on-site rollup of results to produce final findings, the team may be surprised to learn that is has inconsistent findings on a number of practices. So, while the concept of mini-teams sounds like it will promote time-savings by allowing more people to be interviewed in a shorter timeframe, the mini-teams must be managed closely by the Lead Appraiser — which puts yet another burden on the Lead Appraiser.

Some of the older assessment and evaluation methods had more specific guidance in some areas; for example, the number of focus projects and the assessment team size. This guidance is not as clear in the ARC and the SCAMPI. This leads the user of these new methods to make more decisions. And while one of the stated purposes of the ARC and the SCAMPI is to ensure more consistent results in assessments, this lack of guidance may, in fact, result in less consistent results.

Reusing Previous Assessment Results

Organizations often want to use previous assessment results when beginning a CMMI initiative. This has proven to be extremely difficult for many organizations, and in our experience has led to inappropriate actions. By previous assessments, we mean results from non-CMMI appraisals (CBA IPIs, SCEs, EIA 732, etc.). The reason for these problems in reuse include the following:

- Different levels of detail in assessment approach
- Some assessments did not consider institutionalization of practices
- Not all weaknesses were documented

Do not assume that because you did not have a weakness, that you have a strength. Often, only level-threatening weaknesses are documented. A threat to a level is only known after hours of consensus and team negotiations. Some assessment methods do not require these findings to be captured and documented. To use old results for any purpose, you need to understand the key differences between assessment methods and their results.

Most organizations using the CMMI will need a baseline SCAMPI assessment to obtain a consistent understanding across the expanded scope of the organization and of the model.

Frequently Asked Questions for Planning and Conducting a SCAMPI

The following questions are the most frequently asked questions that we have been asked to address. We have pulled them from lists of questions that prospective clients for SCAMPIs have sent us.

1. How will you determine the number of focus projects to include in an appraisal?

The primary criteria are that the focus projects are a representative sample of the organizational unit's overall behavior, provide at least two instances of the processes being investigated as sources of objective evidence, and provide representative coverage of the life cycles in use within the organization.

Our goal would be to keep the number of focus projects small (usually four). If the scope of your appraisal includes systems engineering and software engineering, or you have a large organization, it may be difficult to meet the stated criteria with four projects. Appraisals of very large organizations have required over 10 focus projects.

2. What is the minimum number of projects (we have three core businesses)?

We consider the minimum to be four projects; however as stated above, this may be difficult to accomplish. For example, if the three core business units use significantly different processes, methods, and tools to produce their products or provide their services, this could expand into a need for considering 12 projects.

3. Do you consider the organization as a separate project?

We do not understand exactly what this question means. As far as planning goes, we will need to interview organizational managers — middle managers responsible for technical development, process improvement, training, quality, and measurement.

4. Can projects that are partially through the product development life cycle be included in the appraisal? How many projects will have to provide full life-cycle coverage?

Yes, most projects should be ongoing and therefore are most likely partially through the product development cycle or some phase or iteration. There is no exact answer to this question — the selected projects need to provide representative coverage of the life cycles in use in the organization. That is, the sum of the selected projects' life cycles needs to cover the organization's life cycle.

5. How is model coverage determined?

If by "model coverage" you are referring to verifying and validating objective evidence, this is determined by reviewing documents and artifacts and affirmations for each practice.

If by "model coverage" you are referring to reference model scope, this is determined by the Lead Appraiser reviewing appraisal goals with the sponsor and ensuring the sponsor makes an informed choice.

6. Do you characterize implementation of model practice instantiation on the basis of specific and generic practices, or at the subpractice level?

Appraisals consider three categories of components as defined by the CMMI:

- *Required:* specific and generic goals only
- *Expected:* specific and generic practices only
- *Informative:* includes subpractices, discipline amplifications, generic practice elaborations, and typical work products

So, to be compliant with the model, we would characterize implementation based on specific and generic practices and use subpractices to guide interpretation of the practices.

7. Are typical work products, discipline amplifications, or generic practice elaborations listed in the model included in the instantiation decision?

Yes, as stated above, these are informative and would guide interpretation of the practices.

8. Can you conduct a two-week, eight-hour-a-day, on-site CMMI Target Profile 5 appraisal, covering systems engineering, software engineering, and supplier sourcing with six appraisal team members (including the lead appraiser)? Please be specific.

No, based on no additional knowledge of the organization and the time it takes to conduct a SCAMPI. Our estimate for a SCAMPI Class A Appraisal covering 24 process areas through Capability/Maturity Level 5 with six appraisal team members that have received Team Training to include Introduction to CMMI, SCAMPI Appraisal Team Member Training, and High Maturity Assessments is 13 days. In addition to the Lead Appraiser, we base our estimate on at least one additional external appraiser on the team. Even with 13 days, it is probable that some days may be longer than eight hours.

Only when we have worked with the organization and have a better understanding of the organization's processes, organizational structure, and qualifications of the appraisal team members would it be possible to decrease the proposed schedule.

9. How many participants do you plan to interview for an appraisal covering software engineering, systems engineering, and supplier sourcing? Please use a matrix to indicate, by function, the total number of staff involved, and estimate the total number of labor hours (e.g., project manager, middle manager, test, quantitative measurement specialists, etc.).

Because we have not performed detailed planning and do not have an understanding of your organization's processes, roles, and structure, this is very difficult to answer with any certainty. However, Exhibit 3 will give you an idea of what to expect.

Exhibit 3. What to Expect

Role	Estimated Number of Interviews	Hours per Interview	Number of Interviewees per Interview	Estimated Total Hours
Project managers	4	2	1	8
Measurement group (assumes separate organization and project groups)	2	1.5	4	12
Middle manager groups (assumes separate systems and software groups)	2	2	4	16
Training group	1	2	3	6
Requirements representatives	1	2	4	8
Development representatives	1	2	4	8
Test representatives	1	2	4	8
Integration representatives	1	2	4	8
Process improvement group (assumes separate leads and specialists)	2	2	4	16
Quality assurance group (assumes separate systems and software)	2	2	4	16
Supplier sourcing group	1	2	4	8
Tool group	1	2	3	6
Estimated total				120

10. How many follow-up interviews do you anticipate? Please estimate the level of effort (e.g., total number of labor hours).

Our goal is to have nearly no follow-up interviews. For planning purposes, you may want to consider allowing time for two one-hour follow-up interviews with four people each for a total of eight labor hours for the interviewees.

11. Do Lead Appraisers interpret the CMMI practices as required or expected? Please elaborate. Under what conditions is an "alternate practice" acceptable in satisfying the CMMI?

Specific and generic practices are expected model components. Expected components are practices an organization will typically implement when it is trying to satisfy a set of specific and generic goals. Ordinarily, an alternative practice has to contribute an equivalent effect toward satisfying the goal associated with the practice. In some cases, an alternative practice may not explicitly contribute an equivalent effect because a project's characteristics are different from the characteristics assumed in the model. An example of this might be where the project's customer performs requirements management. The alternative practice might be to review the customer's requirements management process and activities. The practices implemented by the project in this example might not contribute an equivalent effect toward the goals. The decision as to whether an alternative practice is acceptable is an appraisal team decision. The Lead Appraiser's role in that decision is to ensure the integrity of the SCAMPI process and help the team correctly interpret the model.

12. How do Lead Appraisers interpret "institutionalization" of a process area? Is it expected that all generic practices be performed? How is the generic goal judged in the absence of one of more generic practices? Is there any required time duration that a practice must be performed to consider it institutionalized?

Institutionalization in the CMMI is interpreted as satisfying the requirements of the Generic Goals (GG). For the staged representation, this means that GG 2: Institutionalize a Managed Process is satisfied for Level 2. In addition, GG 3: Institutionalize a Defined Process is satisfied for Level 3.

Yes, we expect generic practices to be performed. If one or more generic practices are not performed, the assessment team will determine the impact of the missing practice upon satisfying the required generic goal. Although each generic practice is expected to be performed, the implementation of the generic practices to individual process areas is often not distinguishable (one process area versus another), and they may appear to be absent for a process area or areas. This may be acceptable but the assessment team would have to understand and determine whether the implementation is reasonable.

While the SEI has not published specific guidelines for institutionalization, a number of appraisers consider a minimum of six months as a demonstration of basic institutionalization. Other appraisers expect to see that practices have been performed through several cycles. And other appraisers have considered the requirement to be a demonstration that the practices have been performed in the past and will continue after the appraisal. In addition, some Lead Appraisers consider how often a process can be performed. For example, on a 20-year-old legacy system, they would not consider it reasonable to expect that the initial customer requirements were captured using today's process; however, they would expect new requirement changes to use today's process. With no stated institutionalization requirement, a Lead Appraiser and Appraisal Team may consider any or all of the above guidelines.

13. How do Lead Appraisers interpret the need for documented procedures in the CMMI, now that the phase "...according to a documented procedure" is not used? Are documented procedures required, or can an acceptable alternative practice be to perform the practice without a documented procedure?

For any process area to satisfy Level 2 "GG 2: Institutionalize a Managed Process," a Lead Appraiser would expect that "GP 2.2: Establish and maintain the requirements and objectives, and plan for performing the process" is performed. Although documenting the process is only a subpractice of GP 2.2, it is quite implicit in the statement of GP 2.2 and hence is expected. The clearest way to meet the expectations of GP 2.2 is to have a documented process and plan covering the process area. An alternative practice of "just doing it" is generally not acceptable. The term "plan" in the CMMI has been expanded to include such documentation as processes and procedures.

Part of an acceptable process description is that it contains an appropriate level of detail. In some areas of the process, this means that a documented procedure is appropriate, but neither "expected" nor "required" in CMMI terminology. Note that there are only a very few mentions of "documented procedures" in the informative parts of the CMMI model. The test that the SCAMPI team will have to apply is not whether there is a documented procedure for "X," but whether the process, the plan, or supporting procedures are adequate in the area of "X." This is the same for both the project- and organization-level processes.

For any process area to satisfy "GG 3: Institutionalize a Defined Process," a Lead Appraiser would expect that "GP 3.1: Establish and maintain the description of a defined X process" is satisfied. The expectation is that a process from the organization's set of standard processes is tailored to address the needs of a specific instantiation. As defined in the Model Terminology section of the model, the phrase "Establish and Maintain" connotes a meaning beyond the component terms; it includes documentation as well as a usage component — that is, documented and used throughout the organization.

14. In which situations is the Supplier Agreement Management process area applicable/non-applicable? Please address Integrated Product/Process Teams ("badgeless" teams of multiple contractors), tool vendors, and hired labor ("bodyshop workers"). Please address customer-directed subcontractors.

The Supplier Agreement Management process area states that it is applicable to a "contract, a license, or a memorandum of agreement" for acquired products that are "delivered to the project from the supplier and becomes part of the products delivered to the customer." It applies primarily to both internal and external "arm's-length" relationships where the project manager is not directly involved in managing the activities of the supplier.

The Supplier Agreement Management process area does not apply to products that are not delivered to the project's customer, such as nondeliverable development tools. It does apply to commercial vendors if their product is included in the product delivered to the customer. It does not apply to hourly contract workers who are managed in the same way as any other member of the project team.

For all deliverable work not covered by the Supplier Agreement Management process area, the project management process areas (PP, PMC, ISM, RSKM, IPM, and QPM) and the IPPD process areas (if IPPD is implemented and that model is used) will apply.

15. What are the minimum contents of an organization's set of standard processes?

The OSSPs (Organization's Set of Standard Processes) must cover the processes for the engineering, project management, engineering support (e.g., QA and CM), and organizational activities (e.g., training and process group — limited to software if the assessment is limited that way). The OSSPs describe the fundamental process elements that will be part of the project's defined processes. It also describes the relationships (e.g., ordering and interfaces) between these process elements. Often, the OSSPs for the organizational processes are one and the same as the defined processes. The OPD process area provides specific information as to what might be in the process descriptions and how they might be defined (see Chapter 6). This information is reasonable for most organizations and would be considered by the SCAMPI team. However, there are no hard and fast rules as to the minimum content.

16. Some projects' defined software processes may pre-date the establishment of the organization's standard software process. Is a matrix showing the traceability sufficient?

It is expected that the majority of the organization's projects would be using the OSSP. However, an organization that is improving its OSSP is likely to have some number of long-term projects that pre-date the establishment of the current OSSP. For business reasons, these projects may not migrate to the new OSSP. All projects' defined processes should, however, be recognized as alternative processes by the organization. A Lead Appraiser would expect to see rationale for why projects were exempted from using the OSSP. A Lead Appraiser would expect to see an analysis of the existing process against the OSSP that may take the form of a traceability matrix. However, the existence of such a matrix would not in and of itself be sufficient to exclude a project from using the OSSPs. Furthermore, it should be recognized that a project's defined process that is not tailored from the OSSPs will have an impact on organizational learning and any efforts to establish performance baselines for the organization and for these projects. The organization would have to make appropriate accommodations for these shortfalls.

17. Some of our projects require special security clearances for access to any project documents. A subset of the internal assessment team members has these accesses. What is your approach for assessing such projects?

If the issue is limited to gaining access to the project documents, or if this also includes limiting the access during interviews, then we need to discuss this situation further. This represents a high risk that the team will not be able to achieve consensus on some process areas, that sufficient data collection may not be performed, and certain process areas would have to be "not rated." "Not rated" does not satisfy SCAMPI rating requirements and will result in the organization not receiving a level rating. What we have done in the past is make sure that all members of the team have the appropriate security clearances. Team members could also sign a nondisclosure agreement.

18. What metrics are required for each process area? Must separate time accounting be performed for every process area?

There is no simple list of required metrics for each process area (see Chapter 17). The requirement is for sufficient metrics to monitor and control the processes at Level 2, sufficient metrics to support the organization's needs at Level 3, and sufficient metrics to achieve reasonable predictability of the project's processes (relative to the critical business issues) at Level 4. Metrics should not be defined around CMMI process areas; they should be defined around the project's and organization's process and their need for metrics. Separate time accounting is not required for each CMMI process area. Hours to perform the individual processes is often not very useful; however, many organizations provide this metric because it is easy compared to collecting more interesting metrics. Some organizations at a lower maturity level also find this metric initially helpful in reviewing the time spent and dollars expended in doing process improvement work. It helps them build a preliminary case for return on investment (ROI).

19. How is the generic practice for collecting improvement information interpreted? What is the minimum information that must be collected?

This generic practice represents the "supplier" or input to several practices of the OPF and OPD process areas. There is no clear specification of the minimum information that must be collected. The types of information collected are defined in the model: the organization's common set of measures plus other measures, lessons learned, process improvement proposals, and process artifacts. For measures, the "minimum" is the organization's common set of measures applicable to the processes performed. The assessment team will have to judge whether what is collected, stored, and, more importantly, *used* is appropriate to the OSSPs, the projects, and the organizational and support groups. Too much can be as big a problem as too little.

Summary

Appraisals require planning. When planning an appraisal of your organization, determine the scope of the organizational unit, which disciplines to include, whether the appraisal team will consist of members internal or external to your organization, projects to be included, individuals to be interviewed, and the type or class of appraisal necessary. Remember that team training does not include CMMI training, and both CMMI and team training must be completed prior to the on-site visit. Plan enough time into your schedule for completing all of the necessary documentation required before the team appears on-site.

Notes

1. Not all these methods are called appraisals. Some are called assessments and some are called evaluations. We use the term "appraisal" in an attempt to be consistent with the CMMI product suite. Appendix A provides a comparison of CBA-IPIs to SCEs to SCAMPI.
2. We know of at least one organization that is working to get its incremental assessment method approved as a Class A method.

Chapter 12

Establishing Your Process Improvement Organization

Whether you are using the CMM® for Software, the CMMI®, ISO, or any other process-focused guidelines, this chapter is for you. This chapter presents the four basic phases of process improvement:

1. *Set Up:* establishing a process improvement group and organizational infrastructure. This includes baselining your processes, initial planning, and securing funding and commitment throughout the organization.
2. *Design:* writing policies and procedures, and identifying and writing standards and processes.
3. *Pilot:* training participants and trying out the procedures in a few areas. The procedures are then updated, as necessary, based on the results of the pilots.
4. *Implement:* following the procedures on all projects and measuring their effectiveness.

Set Up

Set Up, or initiation, involves selling the concept of process improvement to the organization, planning the effort, securing funds and staff, and structuring the effort. Most organizations become aware of process improvement through conferences, books, articles in industry magazines, or, most prominently, when achieving maturity levels becomes the basis for contract award. An individual is usually chosen as the "champion," who literally promotes the process improvement effort throughout the organization. This promotion may entail doing research on Return on Investment (ROI), budget allocations within the organization, and cost-benefit analyses. For those of you tasked with this responsibility, the SEI (Software Engineering Institute) provides information on its Web site, www.sei.cmu.edu. While the information on this Web site changes from time to time, you can find data under "Community Profiles" and under the Publications directory.

After the executives have been satisfied that process improvement should be attempted, initiate an Engineering Process Group (EPG). The EPG's role is to establish and prioritize process improvement actions, produce plans to accomplish the actions, and commit resources to execute the plans. The EPG also either writes the processes or assigns personnel to write the processes, and then reviews and updates them. More about roles and responsibilities in Chapter 13.

Planning is critical, and during Set Up, planning is the primary activity. While the plans for each organization differ, there are certain plans that seem to be commonly used among different organizations. They are:

- *Process Improvement (PI) Plan:* high-level strategic plans that document the organization's vision of process improvement and success factors, and justify the initial budget for this effort
- *Implementation/Operations Plan:* tactical-level plans that discuss the formation of specific groups and include deliverables and timetables
- *Action Plans:* very specific plans that address specific weaknesses and organizational problems discovered during an assessment or other organizational process baselining technique

Guidelines and templates for these plans are included in Chapter 15.

SCAMPI

Somewhere between the PI Plan and the Implementation/Operations Plan, an assessment is usually done. Before you can begin your process improvement effort, you really need to understand your organization. Most people would argue that they already know what is going on throughout their workplace. While that may be true for some people, we have found that people know their *own* jobs — they do not necessarily know *other people's* jobs and roles and duties; and they certainly do not know how everything done throughout their departments *fits* into the entire organization. Most senior managers (at the executive levels of an organization) also think they know what is really happening, but they do not. Just because a flurry of memos has been written mandating something to be done, does not mean that it is being done. (Our experience shows that things need to be communicated at least seven times and in three ways before people even hear the message.) It also does not mean that everyone is doing it the same way. The thing to remember about process improvement is that consistency is the key. While we do not expect people to mindlessly follow instructions like some sort of robots, we are looking for consistent application of policies, procedures, processes, plans, and standards. So, to truly understand what is going on at your place of business, we recommend that the first step in process improvement be to conduct some sort of organizational process assessment.

SCAMPI (Standard CMMI Assessment Method for Process Improvement) is the assessment method developed by the SEI. SCAMPI is an appraisal method for organizations that want to evaluate their own or another organization's processes using the CMMI as their reference model. SCAMPI consists of a structured set of team activities that includes conducting interviews, reviewing documents, receiving and giving presentations, and analyzing surveys and questionnaires. SCAMPI results are ratings and findings of strengths, weaknesses, and improvement activities using the CMMI. What are these results used for? To award contracts and to baseline processes for process improvement. Results are based on how the organization satisfies the goals for each process area. Several projects are investigated, including several process areas and several maturity levels (and possibly several capability levels). So, the steps in SCAMPI are basically:

1. Gather and review documentation.
2. Conduct interviews.
3. Discover and document strengths and weaknesses.
4. Present findings.

And the primary components of SCAMPI are:

- Planning and preparing for the assessment
- Collecting and consolidating data, both before and during the assessment
- Making judgments
- Determining ratings
- Reporting results

There are three classes of appraisals recognized by the SEI when using the CMMI: Classes A (SCAMPI), B, and C. Each class is distinguished by its degree of rigor. SCAMPI and appraisals are discussed in greater detail in Chapter 11. A comparison of other assessment methods can be found in Appendix A.

The Design Phase

The Design phase focuses on establishing the Process Action Teams (PATs) to build the organization's processes. The initial steps for this effort are:

1. Generate the PAT Charters.
2. Review, modify, and approve the charters.
3. Generate Action Plans.
4. Review, modify, and approve plans.
5. Assign work per the Action Plans.
6. Do the work according to the Action Plans (generate policies, procedures, standards).
7. Develop supporting metrics and measurement techniques.
8. Develop the required training materials.
9. Track status.
10. Review/recommend tools.
11. Facilitate, review, and monitor work.
12. Update Action Plans.
13. Attend meetings and support EPG.

We discuss creating the documentation listed above in Chapters 14 and 16.

The Pilot Phase

After the Design phase has completed, the processes developed by the PATs should be piloted across two or more projects. The Pilot phase consists of the following steps:

1. Select pilot projects.
2. Document success criteria and measurement techniques.
3. Orient and train pilot project members in CMMI concepts.
4. Orient and train pilot project members in the processes and procedures developed.
5. Perform the pilots.
6. Monitor the pilots.

7. Analyze results from the pilots.
8. Measure success.
9. Provide lessons learned.
10. Update procedures and re-pilot as needed.

As described below, the piloting effort consists of a structured approach to implementing a selected number of procedures in project(s) throughout the organization, and then evaluating the procedures throughout the project(s), as well as at the end of the pilot.

Select the Pilot Project(s)

The project or projects targeted for the pilots selected must be in the appropriate phase of the process, and must be in the appropriate phase of the life cycle. For example, you cannot adequately pilot your test procedures if none of the selected pilot projects have reached the test phase yet. To adequately test the procedures during the pilot process, the pilots have to be of sufficient duration and size, and have an appropriate number of staff members. The pilots also must last long enough to test all of the procedures piloted. For example, if the procedures being piloted were written for regular projects that were made up of 50 people, lasted ten months, and consisted of over a million lines of code, and involved systems engineering, software engineering, and software acquisition personnel, one would expect the pilot to take at least three months and involve members of those organizations mentioned. One would also expect the pilot projects to not be small, Web-based design projects, but match the type of projects for which the procedures were written. Typically, we request that the pilot project last between two and six months, and that at least five process improvement staff members be involved with the pilot on an ongoing basis.

Document the Success Criteria

To determine whether the pilots performed are going to be successful, the organization needs a clear-cut vision of what success really means. The following are some of the criteria that can be used to determine the success of a pilot project:

■ How long will the pilots last?
■ How many pilots will there be?
■ How will the use of the procedures be monitored?
■ How will needed changes to the procedures be identified and implemented?

Train Pilot Participants

Project staff from the pilots must be trained in the policies and procedures to be followed and the purpose of the intended pilot. Training does not consist of simply handing the pilot participants the written procedures and telling them to read them. The EPG may assist in the training. Process Action Team (PAT) members may also assist.

Monitor the Pilot Efforts

The EPG provides an ongoing program for monitoring and analyzing the pilot progress by monitoring and answering questions posed by the pilot project teams.

Refine Policies and Procedures Based on Pilot Results

The PATs must be prepared to make changes to the policies and procedures, both on an ongoing basis as the pilot progresses and afterwards as the pilot is evaluated.

After the Pilots

The pilot projects will last as long as there are process areas to be piloted, or significant changes to processes. The overall plan should be to use these initial pilot projects on as many process areas as possible. If the originally selected projects for piloting cannot be used again, then new pilot projects may need to be selected.

More information concerning checklists for the pilot effort can be found in the appendices.

The Implementation Phase

Once the EPG and senior management have decided that the pilots have been successfully completed, the Implementation phase begins. This phase focuses on implementing the new processes across the organization in a phased manner; that is, one or two projects at a time. Each project will be monitored to determine success, and procedures and plans will be modified to reflect the lessons learned from each project. For each project, a "go/no-go" decision will be made to determine whether the processes as written can be continued to be implemented across the organization. Any "no-gos" will result in review by senior management and the EPG, and will be considered for rewrites of the processes, retraining, or other remedial efforts.

The Implementation phase mirrors the Pilot phase, changing only in scope and duration. The Implementation phase consists of:

1. Selecting one or more actual projects
2. Documenting success criteria and measurement techniques
3. Orienting and training project members in CMMI concepts
4. Orienting and training members in procedures
5. Assisting in implementation as needed (by the EPG, PAT members, and the writers of the processes)
6. Monitoring and measuring success
7. Providing lessons learned
8. Updating procedures as needed
9. Implementing across more projects as needed
10. Signing off completion of the PATs

The EPG needs to determine whether the processes and procedures will be rolled out "en masse" or one project at a time. We do not recommend that all of the procedures for all of the PAs be rolled out for implementation on all of the projects at the same time.

Monitoring the Process Improvement Effort

The one area that makes upper management uncomfortable is the inability to see progress being made. To that end, we suggest the following measurements as a start to use as tracking mechanisms for PI efforts:

■ Actual size of deliverables (based on processes to be developed, as well as standards to be devised; all track directly to the requirements in the CMMI)
■ Actual effort (staff hours) expended for major activities
■ Start and end dates for major activities
■ Completion dates for identified milestones (Design-Pilot-Implementation for each PA)
■ Number and type of changes to the PI strategy

This is one of the ways that the process improvement effort can serve as a model for future projects. By tracking and communicating progress to upper management, the Process Improvement Program can lead through example. More tracking guidance is given in Chapter 15.

Different Approaches for Process Improvement

Now that we have presented the fundamentals of process improvement, let us compare two different approaches.

The Traditional Approach to PI

- Form the EPG (35 or more members).
- Define the "As-Is" process.
- Define the "To-Be" process.
- Gain consensus across the organization.
- Start up the PATs.
- Continue.

The benefits of this approach are that it promotes communication across large organizations, promotes organizational consensus, gives the players in the organization the "big picture," and can expand the focus on areas of improvement not called out specifically in the CMMI.

The disadvantages are that it takes a long time (up to a year or more to define the AS IS process, and then another six months to define the TO BE process). It is difficult to show progress to management (players leave before getting to the "real work," that is, the PATs), decision making with a large EPG is unwieldy and slow, funding runs out or the PI project is cancelled, and ideas do not always map to the CMMI.

An Alternate Approach

- Do an appraisal (SCAMPI).
- Set up the EPG (sometimes already done and the EPG participates in the SCAMPI).
- Proceed based on SCAMPI findings.
- Prioritize areas to concentrate on.
- Prioritize PATs.

The benefits of this approach are that it gets the organization involved quickly, gets the organization CMMI-aware quickly, can show progress to management more easily, proves to the organization that everyone does *not* do everything the same way, documents how things are currently done and ties it directly to CMMI practices, and sells the idea of appraisals to management.

The disadvantages are that this approach takes the organization longer to get the "big picture" (interdependencies of the CMMI and current organizational processes), and some people feel the program is pushed down on them with little input from the workforce.

Sample Process Improvement Program

Exhibit 1 shows a "typical" approach for process improvement.

Why should you begin with an appraisal? Most organizations just starting out on the path to process improvement already know that they are at Maturity Level 1 or Capability Level 0. Why do a SCAMPI? Because it is absolutely essential. You may not have to do a full SCAMPI, but at least do an appraisal against the CMMI practices. (The differences between SCAMPI and other CMMI appraisal methods are discussed in greater detail in Chapter 11.) This appraisal baselines processes and introduces the PI approach using the model. It helps the organization find, gather, and review existing documentation and standards, helps team members learn about their organization, helps the organization learn about the CMMI, and helps direct PI efforts based on SCAMPI results (and not someone's idea about what process improvement should be according to whim). This appraisal must be done by trained, certified individuals.

The other thing that the appraisal results will lead to is devising a schedule for improvement activities. Based on SCAMPI results and working with management, the EPG should devise the schedule, prioritize areas of weakness that need to be addressed and their sequence, and assign resources. Be prepared to change some of your approach as more knowledge of the organization becomes available, and as the organization learns the CMMI.

As for the schedule, management is going to be very interested in the schedule and resources. These days, they never give you enough time, resources, or staff. So, although you may be just casually reading this book, start lobbying management now! Make sure everyone involved — including management, the sponsor, the EPG, PATs, and organization members — have CMMI goals in their performance evaluations. Remember: if it is measured and reported to management, it will be done.

Summary

There are four phases of process improvement:

1. Set Up
2. Design
3. Pilot
4. Implement

Exhibit 1. ABC Corporation Process Improvement (PI) Program

Baseline current processes — SCAMPI.
Implement Virtual Organization for ABC Corporation PI Program.
Establish Process Action Teams (PATs).
Provide training for the Engineering Process Group (EPG) and PATs.
Conduct Process Area (PA) Workshops and develop Action Plans.
Implement and manage Action Plans.
Perform a mid-point mini-appraisal (e.g., using a Class C Appraisal Method).
Update plans.
Establish new baseline (conduct a SCAMPI) when mini-appraisal indicates
  readiness.
Update plans
Continue.

These four phases can be accomplished in as many ways as there are organizations. However, no matter which approach you take, or even which model you choose, planning the effort and tracking the effects of the effort are paramount. Process improvement must be planned and tracked as if it were a project. If not, slippage will occur, and focus and momentum will be lost.

Chapter 13

People, Roles, and Responsibilities

This chapter discusses the major players involved with a process improvement effort. Group and individual responsibilities are highlighted. However, your organization may require more — or fewer — groups. Also note that one person can fulfill many of these roles simultaneously or serially, depending on the size of your organization and the complexity of your process improvement (PI) effort.

Process Improvement Champions, Sponsors, and Groups

Process improvement efforts generally require the following individuals and groups:

- *PI Sponsor:* The person from the organization responsible for overseeing the entire PI effort. This person generally has the power to allocate funds and personnel. This person is usually at the directorate level or above.
- *PI Champion:* This is the public relations person for the PI effort. This person may or may not also serve as the EPG Lead. This person markets the idea, approach, and results of PI.

- *Engineering Process Group (EPG) Lead:* This person leads the group that reviews processes. This person assigns tasks to the EPG members, monitors their efforts, and plans the daily duties of the EPG.

- *EPG Members:* These individuals serve on the EPG as committee members. They are responsible for ensuring that process improvement documentation is written and followed. They are also responsible for generating metrics to track the process improvement process. They lead the PATs.

- *Process Action Teams (PATs):* These teams generate the process improvement documentation — policies, processes, procedures, charters, and Action Plans.

- *Transition Partner:* Usually one or two individuals who are outside consultants brought in to help set up, plan, lead, and monitor progress in organizational process improvement. These individuals bring experience doing process improvement from several other organizations and industries.

Engineering Process Group (EPG)

Previously, under the CMM®, the group responsible for establishing the process improvement structure, and directing and monitoring its activities was called the SEPG — Software Engineering Process Group. Now that group is referred to as the EPG — Engineering Process Group — as "Engineering" takes in more than just software efforts. Remember: CMMI no longer focuses only on software — it was designed to include the many areas of your organization needed to produce a product. Exhibit 1 depicts a typical structure that has proven useful to us when we have instituted process improvement in other organizations. Notice that the Transition Partner and EPG Lead need to interact at multiple levels in the organization.

The primary role of the EPG is to improve processes within the organization. This group needs to understand the current process (As-Is), develop a vision of the desired process (To-Be), establish and prioritize process improvement actions, produce a plan to accomplish actions, and commit resources to execute the plan. The EPG is formed from individuals within the organization. The head of the EPG — the EPG Lead — reports on process improvement activities to the Steering Committee. The Steering Committee is responsible for allocating resources, budget, and time to the EPG. The Executive Steering Committee is responsible for providing the

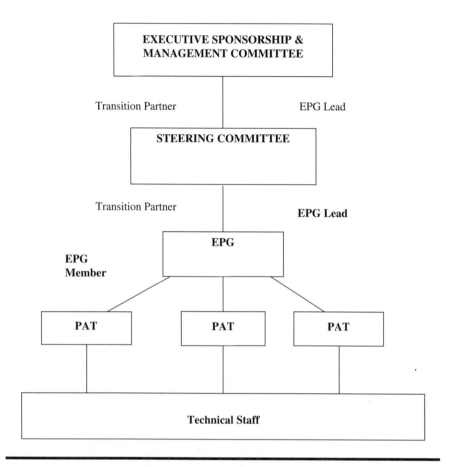

Exhibit 1. Implementing a Virtual PI Organization

initial funding, vision, and directives for process improvement. The Process Action Teams (PATs) are individual teams created to address specific process improvement concerns or process areas. Generally speaking, they focus on the areas of weakness found during assessments. The PATs are the "worker bees." They write the procedures, pilot them, and update them as needed. Members of the PATs are pulled from the technical staff from many projects throughout the organization. The technical staff may also include project managers, and we recommend that they also serve on PATs. Sometimes, a Transition Partner is hired to help the organization structure, create, and track process improvement activities. This transition partner is usually an outside consultant with process improvement experience performed at several other organizations. An organization may have several EPGs in existence at the same time, as well as several layers of EPGs. It all depends on size and complexity.

When establishing a process improvement (PI) organization, you need to identify a PI champion. Usually, the champion will be responsible for gaining staff and resources to generate the PI program, and "push" the concept to all layers of the organization. The PI champion may also serve as the EPG Lead, or may appoint someone else for this duty. The EPG Lead is tasked with reporting to the Executive Steering Committee, and with overseeing and directing the efforts of the EPG and the various Process Action Teams (PATs) created to develop and implement change. The EPG Lead may also develop and maintain PI management plans. The plans need to document PI tasks, EPG schedules, resource utilization, and risks. Results are reported to senior management. The EPG Lead, before establishing the rest of the EPG, may need to work with senior management to address fundamental infrastructure needs. Typical infrastructure needs that might be addressed by the EPG Lead include:

- Setting up or stabilizing communication mechanisms throughout the organization
- Establishing and staffing the EPG, Steering Committee, and Executive Boards
- Establishing and maintaining a Configuration Control Board (CCB)
- Developing CCB control of PI documentation
- Creating mechanisms to present ideas and requests for improvement to the EPG and PATs
- Developing organizational policies for each process area
- Creating a measurement framework to assess success and progress made
- Providing appropriate training and support
- Evaluating and providing appropriate support tools

The EPG will be responsible for developing and implementing Action Plans that address the deficiencies discovered during the assessment process. Action Plans are written by the Process Action Teams (PATs) and reviewed by the EPG to address the deficiencies found during the assessment. Action Plans must be reviewed to determine their thoroughness, completeness, and ability to be effectively implemented within the organization's environment. Action Plans are written and updated based on current assessment results and in conjunction with site business objectives. While the EPG is responsible for these tasks, they can be performed by, or in conjunction with, other individuals within the organization.

One way to create Action Plans and to devise processes (and their associated procedures) is to institute process discovery and definition workshops. These workshops are where the steps necessary to document current "As-Is" processes and generate preliminary "To-Be" processes can occur. The participants of this effort generally include the EPG members, the members of the PATs, and any other respected subject matter experts. The EPG monitors the results of the PATs' activities. If necessary, the Action Plans are updated to refine the approach taken or to address new issues.

The organization should conduct an EPG-led process review that is performed at all project initiations (to get validation and buy-in of tailoring and process compliance), during major project reviews and milestones (to gather preplanned collection of process measurement data), and at project completion (for lessons learned collection and plan versus actual analyses). The EPG should also review current organizational methods in use for process and product measurement, determine if the right measurement data are being collected, and make necessary adjustments to the collection and analysis process. This step ensures that metric reporting and follow-up actions are in place.

Every six months, we recommend that assessments or mini-assessments be performed to determine the extent to which the deficiencies discovered during the baseline assessment have been resolved. When it appears that most of the deficiencies have been addressed, a new, formal assessment of all the process areas (PAs) in the desired maturity or capability levels should be performed to establish a new baseline and prioritize follow-on activities.

Sounds like the EPG has a lot to do. Yes, it does. Most organizations find that being a member of the EPG is a full-time job. Those organizations that allow an individual to only charge this effort as part-time has usually started the process improvement death march. This death march is well-known. It is caused by a general misunderstanding of what process improvement is about and why it is being undertaken. The death march usually begins by senior management announcing that a certain level of the CMMI® will be achieved by a specific date. That date may be two years in advance, but is generally only one year in advance. Unless you have been doing process improvement using the CMMI for at least two years, we would not recommend setting this date so close. Generally speaking, it took organizations at least 18 to 24 months to achieve Level 2 using the CMM. And most organizations reported a much longer timeframe. If management is browbeating its workers into achieving a level in a shortened timeframe, it is totally missing the boat. This sort of mentality shows that this organization does not understand process improvement, is not really dedicated to it, and will not reap lasting benefits from it. They just want the rating. The death-march approach has failed for many,

many organizations. Even organizations that have successfully "passed" an appraisal have slipped back because of lack of a solid foundation and true institutionalization.

Process Action Teams (PATs)

How do the PATs work? An EPG member leads a specific PAT. The PATs are conducted like the EPG (charters, agendas, behaviors, tracking action items, etc.). No one sits on a PAT without receiving training in the process area under development; otherwise, the PAT member does not really know what is expected, what he is supposed to do, and so he makes it up as he goes along, straying from the CMMI. PAT member qualifications are the same as for the EPG, that is, qualified and motivated individuals.

If the EPG has not developed templates, before beginning this effort, a PAT might be created to do just that — so that all of the PATs follow the same structure, reducing the need to rewrite documentation. Search Web sites to get several examples of everything, including blank templates for procedures. It is OK to use a DoD-based Web site and examples, even if you are not working in a DoD-based organization. The CMMI brings structure to an organization. The DoD thrives on structure. It has good stuff and it is free — take a look! Start with the Software Engineering Institute's (SEI) two Web sites: www.sei.cmu.edu and seir.sei.cmu.edu. The latter Web site requires a password and log-on ID; it contains a bulletin board and recent articles.

The PATs need to generate PAT Charters, PAT Plans, and a CMMI compliance matrix that tracks back to the practices for each process area they are developing. This matrix ties activities to practices and specific people and dates. The matrix is used for status tracking, and to check on the extent of the documentation produced. PATs generally write the procedures and processes for the organization.

If I am on a PAT, how do I determine where to start? The EPG will determine which process areas to focus on first, based on the results of the SCAMPI. The PAT Lead (an EPG member) will determine which practices and associated findings to attack in which sequence, by reviewing complexity, available staff, skillsets of staff, etc. The PAT Lead works with his group, determining work assignments and the sequence of the work. The PAT Lead, working with the PAT members and the EPG, will ask the following questions:

- Can a practice be combined with another practice or practices into one document instead of several?
- What are the dependencies between the other practices in that process area and with other process areas?

- How do these activities tie in with activities of other PATs?
- Do we need to write procedures for all of the practices in the process area?
- Are we going to have a separate Metrics PAT that focuses on the Directing Implementation common feature?

Here is an example. Each process area has some sort of requirement for "objectively evaluating adherence." Are you going to have each PAT write a procedure documenting how this will be done, or will you try to write one overall, generic procedure for how to perform this function for all of the process areas, and a checklist for those items to review per process area? You can do this in whatever way makes sense for your organization, as long as the practices for each process area are covered.

Consider having each PAT initially write procedures for evaluating adherence reviews and for Directing Implementation. Then stop, gather what has been written, and keep the best and discard the rest. Start writing a generic tailoring procedure that can be used when deciding which procedures and which part of the procedures to use for which parts of your organization. This approach helps sell the procedures to the organization. You might define a large, medium, and small project, and what tailoring can be done based on this definition. Include a tailoring section in each procedure. However, little tailoring will be necessary if you write your procedures for the most common business practices. For example, if you are a large company that writes automobile insurance policies for millions of customers, and the programs that support this effort were written in the 1970s in COBOL, do not try to write procedures for tracking customer complaints via your brand-new intranet Web site. You are not in the Web site business — you are in the automobile insurance business. And the procedures you write must be specific enough to be followed. That means they must be detailed. You cannot write detailed procedures for Web site customer service that can be used by the rest of the automobile insurance departments. Another example: if you are building weapons systems using nuclear missiles, do not think you can use the same procedures written for tracking financial accounts payable.

So, get the PATs working. After they get some experience with the CMMI, get all the PATs together. Discuss who is doing what. Draw a chart on how the work is fitting together. Draw a chart on what needs to be done, and where the connections are. Don't get too detailed; and don't get too excited when you find duplication of effort or work deferred to other PATs.

Whatever you choose will be wrong and you will have to backtrack. The PATs love deferring work to another PAT. It is not always fair or workable to have one PAT write documentation for all of the PATs to implement. Remember: you should just choose an approach, start out doing it one way or another, and then stop and see what you have and whether it is working.

Training for PI Members

Train the EPG in the three-day Introduction to CMMI, Process Improvement Planning, and the SCAMPI method. Before starting each PAT, get training in the process area or area the PAT is to focus on. Initial training for the rest of the organization can consist of receiving an overview of the CMMI. Be prepared for questions. If there are no questions, either the audience does not understand your presentation, they do not care about your presentation, or they care very much but feel that they are being dragged into this effort and have no voice.

To avoid such a scenario, have a well-respected member of your EPG give an overview of why they have started doing PI, what the organization can expect the EPG to do, why it is important, and what the organization (each individual) needs to do to support this effort. And concentrate on WIFM — What's In It For Me? Make sure to relate the benefits to something relevant for the people in your organization. Setting up a common drive where the staff can view what is being written, and share information as it is being written, will also aid in making individuals feel that they are part of this process.

EPG and PAT Member Qualifications

The members of these groups need to be motivated. We do not want lazy, dead-weight individuals who are just waiting for retirement to come; neither do we want "BSers." A BSer is a person full of himself who talks a good game but cannot deliver on his promises. An EPG or PAT needs imaginative self-starters with a wide-range of experience. Experience can include working in different jobs within the organization (which shows how such things as roles, duties, and other organizational departments fit together) and also working at other companies. This diversity provides other perspectives that may prove useful in your organization. Because writing will be such a large part of this effort, people who are able to write and like to write should be approached. Another big selling point for implementing the procedures written is if they were written by respected members of the organization (technically respected, as well as the movers and shakers).

How many people should be on an EPG? The SEI has published 1 to 3 percent of your organization. If you are in a large organization, that may be too many. If you are in a small organization, that may be too few. We find that between five and ten motivated people usually work well. However, they have to be prepared to write procedures and do work — not just review and comment on the work other people have produced.

Sometimes, to get buy-in, the director of this effort will recommend EPG and PAT members for political reasons. If you must, you must. However, buy-in does not come from politics; it comes from doing something good that makes life easier in the workplace. If forced to choose, choose quality over quantity, and talent over politics. Remember: you will never get total, 100 percent buy-in.

Conducting Meetings

This section holds true for both the PATs and the EPG. Hold meetings at least weekly, require attendance, and require timeliness. Take notes and publish the notes, but rotate who actually takes the notes — you do not need a secretary but you do want each person to contribute equally — not just have someone whose only role is to take notes. Send out an agenda at least one day before the meeting. Try to get the sponsor and executives to attend a meeting here and there. They are busy, but their attendance proves to the members that their efforts are being noticed. It also shows buy-in from the executives. The EPG meetings should consist primarily of reviewing the status of what is occurring on the PATs and planning how to resolve issues that occur on the PATs. Discuss any problems, issues, or concerns. Allow for questions back and forth. Document and track action items. Store the meeting minutes in an online common drive (include dates of meetings).

There needs to be a simple and easy mechanism for the organization to present ideas and issues to the EPG. Whether this is done via your intranet or whether you have Engineering Change Proposals or Process Improvement Proposals, it does not matter. What matters is that the people in your organizations feel that they are part of the process of process improvement. They need to be able to introduce ideas, as well as to challenge the ideas currently under development produced by the EPG. Also necessary is a mechanism to communicate to the organization what the EPG is doing. See the discussion in Chapter 15 concerning a communication plan for ideas. Remember: you have to communicate things at least seven times and three ways just to be heard.

Quality Assurance (QA) and the EPG

What is the difference between Quality Assurance (QA) and the EPG? Can we not have QA do process improvement too? Can we not just structure the organization so that process improvement becomes another QA initiative? No, that is a recipe for disaster. If you set up your process improvement effort as part of QA's duties, process improvement will be seen as just another QA task. It will not receive the attention from management — and from the organization as a whole — that it requires. Can QA people serve as part of the EPG? Of course! However, the EPG should be representative of your entire organization — not just the QA department.

In addition, QA and the EPG serve different functions. QA reviews both the *products* built and the *activities* that occur on a *project*. The EPG is responsible for reviewing *processes* that occur across the *organization*. Therefore, there is some overlap; however, QA's primary role focuses on the *projects* while the EPG focuses on *processes* throughout the *organization*. The EPG does not concentrate on products — that is QA's job.

What about standards? Does QA not review products to see if they conform to standards? Yes. However, one of the flaws of both the CMM and the CMMI is that the authors of both models assumed that organizations had standards in place and were using them. While some of the older, larger, more mature organizations did have standards, the smaller, younger ones did not. So before they could focus on process, they had to back up and devise some product standards. In their search for standards, they often just usurped the standards written for DoD (MIL-STD-2167A, MIL-STD-498, IEEE, NIST, FipsPub) or they just copied standards from a previous workplace. This is also not a good idea. Standards must fit the type of work done and the culture of the organization. Standards should be tailored to work for everybody mandated to use them. Otherwise, they will not be used.

Summary

The organization needs to devise a method to assign resources, schedule the work, decompose activities to a manageable size, trace requirements and contractual obligations, and measure success. We suggest that individuals be given certain roles to play to carry out these assignments. We suggest that a sponsor designate a champion, and that an EPG Lead be appointed to work with personnel from the organization to establish the process improvement infrastructure. The CMMI is tremendously interconnected. Your organization will want to know how everything fits together. Do not attempt to flowchart the CMMI. This exercise goes in one ear and out the other because people have little experience with the CMMI and cannot equate it with anything relevant to them.

Try to do most of what the CMMI suggests. If it does not fit, document why and devise an alternative practice. Tailor your approach to your organization. For example, when writing procedures, DoD likes books; commercial organizations do not. Keep it simple and to the point.

Process improvement is continuous. Once you start, you will uncover more and more areas to be improved and issues to be resolved.

Chapter 14

Documentation Guidelines

This chapter presents our approach for generating the piles of documentation necessary for process improvement. The thing to remember is that this documentation is *necessary* documentation. You do not write just to get credit for finishing your assignment to write a particular piece of documentation. The old CMM® tenet still applies: "If it isn't used, it doesn't exist." Process improvement is not a documentation drill. Generally speaking, if your procedures are not used throughout the organization, then you have no procedures! The whole purpose of the CMMI® is to use what you have developed. Your documentation is not "for show."

Introduction

Why is documentation necessary? Consider this example. Suppose you are stuck at work one evening. You think you can get home in time to fix dinner, but doing some shopping beforehand is definitely out. So you call your teenage son and ask him to go to the store and buy some food for dinner. Would you leave it at that? Those of you that have teenagers know the answer is a resounding "No." You decide that you will fix macaroni and cheese for dinner, and you tell him this over the phone. Consider all of the different options someone would have with only that requirement. Do you get the boxed stuff? If yes, do you get the name brand or the store generic? If you are fixing it from scratch, what kind of cheese do you get? How much? What kind of macaroni? How much? Do you need anything else, like maybe milk? Regular, skim, condensed, evaporated? Now, back to the teenager. If you tell him all this over the phone, what else do you tell him? That is right — write it down! Why? Because you know he is more likely to get it right if he writes it down than if he just tries to remember it, unless your teenager is some kind of genius.

Well, process improvement is the same way. If you want someone to do it right, and have everyone doing a task consistently, then write it down. And write it in enough detail that it is not open to interpretation. Understanding this concept is the heart of this chapter.

When writing documentation, or making writing assignments, remember that people hate it, people are not good at it, they think they can do it until they try and then they cannot, but they can be taught. When writing documentation, don't use documentation from your previous organization. You will get to check off the Designing procedures part of your plan, but...

- You will not get buy-in from the organization.
- Your wonderful procedures will never be implemented across the organization.
- You will fail the SCAMPI.

Does the CMMI not tell me how to do stuff? Can I not just copy what it says and reword it a little bit? No! The CMMI documents best practices from other organizations. It describes *what* to do, not *how* to do it. The organization's job is to document *how* to do things.

I know what you are thinking: "This is gonna be hard..." Your organization will figure out that this effort is more than they originally thought. They will start justifying why they cannot or will not do something. Usually it boils down to it is too hard, they do not know how, it is a hassle, they do not want to do it. That is not a strong justification!

Do not worry — we provide some templates and guidelines as examples in Chapters 15 and 16.

Definitions

We are often asked to interpret the words in the CMMI. Part of that interpretation includes defining the different types of documentation required to implement an effective process improvement strategy.

What is a standard? What is a process? What is a procedure? What is the difference? A *standard* is a structure serving as a foundation to be used as a model for later development. It is recognized as an acceptable example and has been officially authorized for use. Its purpose is to promote uniformity and consistency of results, leading to a quality *product*. The IEEE defines a *process* as a sequence of steps performed for a given purpose. The CMMI definition is much more convoluted and is discussed elsewhere in this book. What is the difference?

Standards are generally thought of as pertaining to products, specifically formats for deliverables. This is *what* the *product* should *look* like. Examples are a template for a System Requirements Specification, a Test Results Report format, a System Implementation Plan boilerplate, and Coding standards (program layout and data naming conventions).

Processes consist of actual steps of *what* to do to build the product. *Procedures* consist of step-by-step instructions of *how* to perform the process. The following example relates to a Risk Management Process. In a Risk Management Process, we might simply list the steps as:

1. Identify the risk.
2. Prioritize the risk.
3. Mitigate the risk.

Well, that is alright as far as it goes; but if you proudly handed these three steps to your project managers of several different projects, do you really think they would all follow this process the same way? Do you think they would all identify risks in the same manner? Would they prioritize them at the same level of criticality? Would they choose the same approaches for controlling the risks? No. That is why we need procedures to support the processes — processes are at too high a level to be consistently applied. An example of a supporting risk management procedure might be something like:

- If the risk affects safety of human beings, categorize it as level 1.
- If the risk will cause the site to shut down and all processing to stop, categorize the risk as Level 2.
- If the risk will allow processing to continue, or consists of a simple fix, categorize it as Level 3.

In addition, there would be examples and definitions to help flesh out the information listed in the steps (such as how to identify a Level 1, 2, or 3 risk and what to do about it). It is just a simple example for this discussion.

The point is that the CMMI requires processes to be *documented in enough detail to be followed*. A process is not just a high-level flowchart of "whats." It needs supporting procedures to be effective.

In addition to processes, procedures, and standards, there are policies, charters, and plans. A *policy* is a high-level document, generated under senior management sponsorship, that directs the organization to perform. It is a high-level statement of what is to be done, and who is responsible to do it, and maybe even why it is to be done. A *plan* is a document specific to achieving a goal, objective, or producing a product. There can be many levels of plans, from high-level strategic vision plans, to lower-level project plans that describe how the project will be run, to very detailed and specific Action Plans to address specific weaknesses found during a process assessment. Plans should discuss estimates for the size of the endeavor, number of personnel needed to be assigned, skillsets needed from those individuals, tasks divided into milestones, deliverables, training required, time the task is scheduled to take, general approach, risks, money, and assumptions. A *charter* is a document that describes why a group was formed and how a group intends to act. It discusses prescribed behaviors, when the group will meet, the time of the meetings, rules of conduct, scope of the group, resolution of issues, and purpose.

Process Definition Approaches

This section describes our approach to supporting the Process Action Teams (PATs) that are charged with developing processes and procedures to be implemented throughout the organization.

One way to develop processes and the rest of the documentation necessary is to begin with writing workshops. Those individuals tasked with creating documentation should attend these workshops where ideas concerning the area of documentation are discussed. Then, after the workshop, the individuals tasked with the assignment go back to their desks and begin writing. *The documentation itself is not produced during the workshop.* That would take forever. However, the workshops are very useful in giving people ideas. Also consider assigning two people to write the document. However, make sure that each is writing the document — or that they have worked a deal wherein one writes it, and the other reviews it and makes changes. Do not just assume that they are writing the document. We have found that sometimes when this dual approach is used, one person assumes (or wishes) that the other person is writing the document, and vice versa, and the document does not get written. And do not think that this documentation will be perfect — or good — or even usable. Make sure you plan for re-writes and re-reviews.

All workshops should be facilitated by someone who knows how to facilitate a workshop. A key to conducting an effective workshop is preparation. The workshop facilitator (who can be the EPG Lead, an EPG member, or an outside consultant) should begin working with the workshop sponsor to:

- Define the purpose of the workshop.
- Develop a logical agenda and write a comprehensive outline.
- Identify measurable objectives.
- Identify potentially hot topics and controversial agenda items.
- Review current policies, procedures, and processes.

The general steps that occur in facilitating a workshop are described below.

Identify Workshop Parameters

The first step is to work with the EPG to define the objective(s) of the workshop and gain an understanding of the expected participants; for example, their technical sophistication and relative interest in the issues at hand. Then determine the most suitable scope of activities and material contents to be prepared for the workshop stakeholders as well as the appropriate level of detail to be presented.

Prepare Workshop Activities and Materials

Prepare and publish a workshop agenda along with instructions to the anticipated participants. If the purpose of the workshop is to share information, prepare presentation slides. If the purpose is to collect information, construct exercises and data-gathering templates. If the purpose is to make decisions, then establish preliminary criteria, trade-offs, and scoring/ranking methodologies. Present the draft workshop materials for EPG review and approval. Make sure to have plenty of flipcharts and markers available. Some organizations prefer to do this via computer or groupware, using a package such as Lotus Notes.

Manage Workshop Logistics

Work closely with staff to ensure the timely distribution of any read-ahead packets that outline the workshop's purpose and scheduled activities. Verify that adequate meeting space is reserved and properly set up in advance, all necessary materials and supplies are available, and equipment is in working order.

Facilitate Workshops

Facilitation support begins by making any necessary introductions, reiterating the purpose of the workshop, and reviewing the ground rules for an orderly, productive exchange of information. Then proceed to initiate and focus discussions on the planned topics while making ad hoc adjustments to allow issues requiring additional attention to be fully addressed. Always maintain control of the workshop at all times, taking the steps necessary to keep it on target and moving at an appropriate pace.

Document Workshop Outcomes

Consolidate all information discussed and collected during the workshop, and document major outcomes and decisions made. In coordination with organizational staff, distribute the resulting documentation to the workshop participants for their review and comment so that there is no misunderstanding with respect to workshop proceedings. Updates and clarifications are made as appropriate.

Analyze Workshop Findings

Conduct a thorough analysis of the workshop findings in conjunction with key organizational representatives. Analyze this information to determine its significance and implications, as well as to identify any constraints and opportunities for improvement. Supportable conclusions are drawn and rational, justifiable recommendations are forwarded.

Plan for any schedule changes by developing contingency plans for workshop dates and facilitators. The EPG, when reviewing any materials, should ensure that any workshop deliverables are CMMI-compliant.

Some organizations find the preceding workshops too lengthy, too formal, too time-consuming, and too costly. If the organization does not desire to follow the above approach, there is another way. Identify knowledgeable people in the organization; interview them about how they do their jobs; write it down; compare what they do and how they do it to the CMMI; identify gaps; and fill in the gaps with your ideas on *how* to do things. Then present this to the EPG for approval and piloting. The EPG cannot really predict whether the procedures will work. Pilots have proved very helpful in this area. Another way to write procedures is to assign them to one individual, and have him go back to his desk and write them. While this may get you off the hook, and while it looks like something is being done, this method generally does not work. It is too much work for one individual. Even if you have several individuals writing procedures, they still will need help reconciling how *they* perform a function versus how *the rest of the organization* does it versus what the *CMMI* is recommending.

Summary

When writing any of the documentation discussed, remember to focus your efforts on what is:

- Practical
- Practicable
- Tied to the CMMI
- Tied to SCAMPI results

Make sure the people writing the procedures understand that they will also have to follow them. One of my client organizations calls this "Eat your own dog food." It is easy to write bad procedures if you think they will not pertain to you.

Chapter 15

Planning and Tracking the Effort

This chapter discusses the various plans needed to guide the process improvement effort, and a few approaches to tracking the tasks involved. While the CMMI® considers process descriptions and procedures to be part of the "plan" needed for each process area, this chapter defines a plan as the strategy necessary to prepare the organization for process improvement. Processes and procedures are discussed in Chapter 16.

Defining Plans

CMMI requires a "plan" for every process area (PA). However, these plans incorporate not only what one would normally expect in a plan (activities, timeframes, general approach and strategy, estimated resource expenditures), but also what used to be called "procedures" (see Chapter 14 for a discussion of procedures). To add greater value to your Process Improvement (PI) program, we have separated these concepts. In reality, it does not matter whether you call these documents "plans," "procedures," "George," or "Shirley," as long as you generate some documentation that covers these concepts.

A plan is not a schedule. It is the documented strategy necessary to perform work. It generally includes a definition of the scope of the work, the resources needed, why the work is to be done, how the work will be tracked, how it will be reviewed, schedules, and costs. It also includes an explanation of why the work was planned the way it was, so that if

181

errors occur or project managers change, the plan can be understood and updated to promote project continuation.

There are three types of plans in process improvement that must be addressed:

1. *Process Improvement (PI) Plan:* Overall Strategic Plan used for funding, resources, justifying the PI program, and defining goals.
2. *Implementation/Operations Plan:* Tactical Plan, or more detailed plan, that defines the effort for the entire organization into manageable tasks based on the results of the SCAMPI; also called a PI Action Plan.
3. *Action Plans:* Very detailed plans created by the PATs (Process Action Teams) that focus on what the PAT is supposed to do and how and when it will be done. PATs focus on one PA or one problem area noted as a weakness from the SCAMPI assessment.

A Communication Plan is also popular. We discuss that plan at the end of the section on plans.

The PI Plan

Executives need a PI Plan. Its purpose is to get executive buy-in, generate a written contract for PI, and get money allocated for PI. Sometimes, the sponsor will generate the plan, sometimes the EPG Lead will generate the plan, and sometimes the Transition Partner (outside consultant) will generate the plan. Whoever creates the plan must remember that PI must be managed like any other well-managed project: do a schedule, track against the schedule, assign staff, identify and track deliverables, etc. Process Improvement must be planned and tracked just like any other project. The PI Plan should address and schedule the following activities:

■ Using a SCAMPI to baseline current processes
■ Establishing the EPG and PAT structure
■ Providing training in the CMMI and PAs
■ Measuring progress through mini-assessments
■ Designing — Piloting — Implementing processes
■ Conducting full-blown SCAMPI for certification

The PI Plan defines the problem, the purpose of PI for this organization, and the purpose of this plan. This plan is used to sell the CMMI and process improvement to the organization — its executives, its managers, and its lower-level staff. The PI Plan must document the benefits and costs, and define the business goals and objectives linked to business issues confronting the enterprise.

The plan also defines the scope of the work and how to manage changes to scope. It documents project resources and other support needed. Assumptions and risks are also addressed (most common — pulling staff away from PI to do "real work," emergent work, production emergencies, etc.).

As for tracking and controlling the effort, the PI Plan documents how you will track, control, measure, and report the status of the work. In the plan, present your schedule with milestones included at the lowest level of detail that you feel you can realistically accomplish, and that you feel are necessary to track at a level that keeps the effort focused. Discuss rewards and include a "Miscellaneous" category for anything else that fits your organization, or will politically motivate individuals who might prove to be obstacles in this effort.

We do not include an example PI Plan because these plans can be very different, depending on why an organization is undertaking process improvement, the culture of the organization, and the different levels of planning required. The PI Plan is often written by a Transition Partner (outside consultant) in conjunction with the proposed PI Champion and PI Sponsor. Because budgets and schedules are a large part of this plan, financial statistics for this program can be found on the SEI (Software Engineering Institute) Web site — www.sei.cmu.edu. Also check with the budget or financial area of the enterprise for data on past improvement, quality, and measurement programs, as well as any major expenditures forecast for upcoming projects and organizational endeavors.

Implementation/Operations Plan

The Implementation/Operations Plan comes after the shock of the baseline SCAMPI has worn off. It is now time to get real. The PI Plan is a high-level, strategic vision type of plan. It makes a case for process improvement and calculates the initial, overall budget. The Implementation/Operations Plan is more detailed. It is based on the results of the SCAMPI appraisal that documented how close an organization is to a maturity or capability level, which process areas are satisfied or not satisfied or nowhere near to being satisfied, and the weaknesses found in how the organization implements the PAs. Therefore, this plan is based much more on reality and real issues. This plan may contradict the original PI Plan. Document any deviations from the original PI Plan.

This plan discusses how to address and implement the results of the SCAMPI. Take those results, review and analyze them, and prioritize the PAs, issues, and concerns. Determine how to set up the EPG/PAT/CCB infrastructure, which individuals to assign to these activities, the training required, and an initial pilot strategy.

The PAs should be prioritized based on complexity, difficulty implementing or performing within this organization, amount of documentation needed, how close to attainment based on the SCAMPI, "bang for the buck," and where an early success might be achieved.

Format your plan based on the four phases of process improvement: Set Up, Design, Pilot, and Implementation (see Exhibit 1).

The last section of the Implementation Plan discusses controlling the effort. Basic tracking mechanisms should initially focus on the following areas. As learning and sophistication increase within the organization, more metrics can be added. Basic metrics to track include:

- Actual size of deliverables
- Actual effort (staff hours) expended for major activities
- Start and end dates for major activities
- Completion dates for identified milestones
- Number and type of changes to this plan

Action Plans

Action Plans (see Exhibit 2) are usually produced by the PATs assigned to address the weaknesses found during the SCAMPI. PATs are usually set up according to process areas (RM, PP, IPM). Action Plans should be based on the SCAMPI results. They also must be *measurable*. Tie them directly to the CMMI PAs and practices to maintain focus on the CMMI itself, and to make tracking progress easier. Where the organization decides to deviate from the CMMI, build and document a strong case for doing so. Alternative practices can be substituted for the practices, when justified appropriately and strongly. Action Plans will focus on how to generate processes and procedures, and how to introduce them into the organization once produced. Tracking and measuring the effectiveness of the Action Plans and the processes and procedures is usually a function of the EPG.

Communications Plans

Achieving success in process improvement programs requires more than good policies and procedures. The organization must "buy in" to the effort, and support must be maintained throughout the implementation program, especially early on when costs are highly visible but benefits are not. An effective communications plan may prove critical to PI program success. Whether your organization is small or large, whether your organization requires a formal or informal approach, you must determine a

Exhibit 1. Implementation/Operations Plan Template

1.0 Set Up
    1.1 SCAMPI Results
    1.2 Areas of Focus
    1.3 EPG Structure
    1.4 Process Action Team (PAT) Structure
    1.5 Configuration Control Boards
    1.6 Quality Assurance
    1.7 Schedule
    1.8 Tools
    1.9 Risks
    1.10 Reviews and Approvals

2.0 Design Phase
    2.1 Generate PAT Charter
    2.2 Review, modify, approve charter
    2.3 Generate Action Plan
    2.4 Review, modify, approve plan
    2.5 Assign work per Action Plan
    2.6 Do the work (policies/procedures/standards)
    2.7 Develop metrics and measurement techniques
    2.8 Develop required training material
    2.9 Track status
    2.10 Review/recommend tools
    2.11 Facilitate/review/monitor work
    2.12 Update Action Plans
    2.13 Attend meetings/Support EPG

3.0 Pilot Phase
    3.1 Select pilot projects
    3.2 Document success criteria and measurement techniques
    3.3 Orient and train project members in CMMI concepts
    3.4 Orient and train members in processes and procedures
    3.5 Perform the pilots
    3.6 Monitor the pilots
    3.7 Analyze results from the pilots
    3.8 Measure success
    3.9 Provide lessons learned
    3.10 Update procedures and OSSP as needed

4.0 Implementation Phase
    4.1 Select one or more true projects
    4.2 Document success criteria and measurement techniques
    4.3 Orient and train project members in CMMI concepts
    4.4 Orient and train members in procedures
    4.5 Assist in implementation as needed
    4.6 Monitor and measure success
    4.7 Provide lessons learned
    4.8 Update procedures and OSSP as needed
    4.9 Implement across more projects as needed
    4.10 Sign off completion of PATs

5.0 Control and Monitoring

Exhibit 2. Sample Action Plan Template

EXECUTIVE OVERVIEW
1 Objective/Scope
    1.1 Problem Statement
    1.2 Vision after Success
    1.3 Goal Statement
2 Entry Criteria
    2.1 Management Sponsor(s)
3 Major Inputs
    3.1 Relevant Assessment Information (Results/Deficiencies)
    3.2 Relevant Existing Work (Projects/Tasks/Pilots/PA Improvements and Results)
4 Summary of Approach
    4.1 Steps/Tasks for PA (based on practices)
    4.2 Short-Term Scenario (Schedule for Implementation)
5 Major Outputs
6 Exit Criteria

DETAILED PLAN
7 Programmatic Issues
    7.1 Constraints/Limitations
    7.2 Assumptions/Dependencies
    7.3 Risks
    7.4 Alternatives
8 Schedule
    8.1 Steps
    8.2 Process Improvement Project (PERT/GANTT)
9 Required Resources
    9.1 People (who/how much of their time)
    9.2 Training
    9.3 Computer/Technological Resources
    9.4 Other

MANAGEMENT OF PLAN
10 Reviews
    10.1 Peer Reviews
    10.2 Management Reviews
    10.3 Other Reviews
    10.4 Measurement Criteria
11 "Roll Out"/Implementation/Training Plan

---

method for keeping everyone informed. A communications plan has four key objectives:

1. Achieve and maintain an enterprise awareness of the CMMI and the PI Program
2. Maintain the PI Program focus and momentum
3. Facilitate process implementation activities
4. Provide a vehicle for rewards and recognition

There are numerous target audiences in any organization. Each audience is impacted differently and may have a different role to play. Communications need to be targeted to the various audiences. In addition, communications should utilize multiple vehicles for delivering the message to facilitate reaching a broader audience. Our experience shows that things need to be communicated at least seven times and three ways before people even hear the message. Communications mechanisms used include:

- Articles in monthly newsletters
- Articles by participants from the various divisions or departments, PAT members, Transition partners, and EPG staff
- Intranet Web pages containing information on PI activities, such as workshops and pilot projects, and which may include the Process Asset Library of procedures and best practices that may be of value to personnel
- Briefing to senior management at yearly management retreats
- Presentations at "all hands" meetings

Tracking the Documentation

Monitoring the process improvement effort is critical to stay focused and ensure that progress is being made. To track the activities of the PATs, we provide a sample compliance matrix in Exhibit 3. This matrix is based on tracking the activities performed during the Design phase. Piles of documentation will be written. This exhibit may help you track this effort. However, do not be fooled into thinking that once you have your procedures written, you are finished. Remember: you still have to train the pilot participants, pilot the procedures, re-write them based on the pilot results, train the organization in the procedures, roll out the procedures for implementation, and track adherence and changes. There is still a lot of work to be done. The Action Plans can track PAT efforts, and the PI Plan and Implementation/Operations Plan can be used to track EPG and organizational-level tasks.

In Exhibit 3, only the practices for a specific process area (RM, Requirements Management) are listed. It should be noted that, to fully understand and implement the practice, the *subpractice* must usually be analyzed and incorporated into the procedure. This template can also be used for tracking infrastructure documentation such as plans, charters, and standards preparation, as well as any other activities performed throughout the PI effort.

Another example is shown in Exhibit 4 using the CMM for Software as the model. This example also depicts Requirements Management, as

Exhibit 3. Sample CMMI Compliance Matrix

No.	Practice or Activity	Associated Procedure/Document	Assigned To	Date Due	Date Reviewed	Status
	Process Area: RM					
	Process Area: GG2: Institutionalize a Managed Process					
1	GP2.1 (CO1): Establish an organizational policy	Policy			03/02/02	Approved
2	GP2.2 (AB1): Plan the process	1. Plan 2. Process description 3. Schedule 4. Estimates			03/02/02	Complete
3	GP2.3 (AB2): Provide resources	See Plan				Complete
4	GP2.4 (AB3): Assign responsibility	See Plan				Complete
5	GP2.5 (AB4): Train people	See Plan and training materials				In progress
6	GP2.6 (DI1): Manage configurations	TBD				In progress
7	GP2.7 (DI2): Identify and involve relevant stakeholders	See Implementation Plan				Complete

#						Status
8	GP2.8 (DI3): Monitor and control the process	TBD				Deferred
9	GP2.9 (VE1): Objectively evaluate adherence	Procedure PI5 Procedure PI7				Complete
10	GP2.10 (VE2): Review status with higher-level management	Procedure PI6				Complete
	Process Area: SG1: Manage Requirements					
11	SP1.1: Obtain an understanding of requirements	Procedure RM1				EPG review
12	SP1.2: Obtain commitment to requirements	Procedure RM2				EPG review
13	SP1.3: Manage requirements changes	Procedure RM3, RM4 Procedure CM4				Pending
14	SP1.4: Maintain bi-directional traceability of requirements	Procedure RM4				Rejected
15	SP1.5: Identify inconsistencies between project work and requirements	Procedure RM5				Pending

Exhibit 4. Sample CMM Compliance Matrix

No.	Process Area	CMM Reference	Document	Assigned To	Date Due/Reviewed	Status
1	Infrastructure		SPI Plan			
2	Infrastructure		Implementation Plan			
3	Infrastructure		Organization's Standard Software Process (OSSP)			
4	Infrastructure		SEPG Charter			
5	Infrastructure		SEPG Presentation Template			
6	Infrastructure		Procedure Template			
7	Infrastructure		Training Packet Guidelines for Pilots			
8	Requirements Management		RM Charter			
9	Requirements Management		RM Action Plan			
10	Requirements Management		RM WBS			
11	Requirements Management		RM Schedule			
12	Requirements Management	CO1, AB1, AB3, AB4	Policy for managing system requirements allocated to software: includes establishing responsibility, providing adequate resources, and required RM training			

13	Requirements Management	AB2, AC1	Procedure for Requirements Specification and Review						
14	Requirements Management	AB2, AC2	Procedure for completing Requirements Traceability Matrix (RTM): includes use as basis for SDP and work products.						
15	Requirements Management	AC3	Procedure for SRS and RTM changes						
16	Requirements Management	ME1	Procedure for RM metrics						
17	Requirements Management	VE1, VE2	Procedure for Project and Senior Management reviews						
18	Software Project Planning		SPP Charter						
19	Software Project Planning		SPP Action Plan						
20	Software Project Planning		SPP WBS						
21	Software Project Planning		SPP Schedule						
22	Software Project Planning		SPP Process Overview Document						
23	Software Project Planning	Com-1	Software PM designated in Policy for SDP and commitments						

Exhibit 4. Sample CMM Compliance Matrix (continued)

No.	Process Area	CMM Reference	Document	Assigned To	Date Due/Reviewed	Status
24	Software Project Planning	Com-2	Policy for planning a software project			
25	Software Project Planning	Abil-1	Statement of Work for each software project			
26	Software Project Planning	Act-6	Procedure for developing a Software Development Plan			
27	Software Project Planning	Act-7	Software Development Plan for each software project (*Note:* may be contained in several "documents" of different names)			
28	Software Project Planning	Act-9	Procedure for estimating size of software work products			
29	Software Project Planning	Act-10	Procedure for estimating effort and cost for the software project.			
30	Software Project Planning	Act-11	Procedure for estimating critical computer resources			
31	Software Project Planning	Act-12	Procedure for deriving software project schedule			
32	Software Project Planning	Act-13	Risk identification and assessment document for each software project			
33	Software Project Planning	Act-14	Plans for software facilities and tools for each software project			

34	Software Project Planning	Act-15	Estimates and basis for estimates data are recorded for each software project			
35	Software Project Planning	ME 1	Measurements are made to determine status of software planning activities (rationale for measurements and how to collect and analyze them)			
36	Software Project Planning	VE1, VE2	The activities of SW project planning are reviewed with Senior Management and Project Management — procedures for both			
37	Software Project Planning	VE3	SQA audit of PP Activities — procedures for quality reviews — may be found in SQA KPA			

well as some infrastructure documentation and Project Planning. Note that all of the practices are not mentioned: this is only an example. We feel that most practices should be covered in some way by documentation — either a single document per practice or, more likely, several documents that describe how to do several practices.

It is also necessary to track how the procedures are being used in the projects, and to what extent they are being used. For this task, we suggest talking to people to find out. If people will not talk, and do not voice their displeasure, it does not mean they are happy campers. It means they have concerns but feel that voicing the concerns will be of no use. They feel they have not been part of the process and their opinions are worthless. So, no news is not good news. If people do not feel part of the process, they will not buy into it. And ultimately, they might sabotage the effort. So try to find out what is happening.

The opposite also holds true. People will complain ad nauseum about the procedures because:

- They have to read them. No one likes to read anymore: we wait for the movie or the video game to become available.
- They have to follow them.
- They have to change the way they work.
- Someone is monitoring how they do their jobs.

We will not go into changing the culture — there are already several books on the market about that. Suffice it to say, people do not like to change. So reward them for their efforts and praise them.

In addition to simply talking (and listening) to people, we suggest a report card. Simply create a checklist that can be e-mailed to each project manager and have him (or her) fill it out and return it to the EPG. It should track whether each project is using the procedures, which ones are used or not used, and why or why not.

You may have to take a stand to stop the complaints. But before you do, you had better check to see whether these folks are justified in their complaints. Are these procedures really a good fit for them, or are they forced to use them just because the procedures took a long time to write and you need to get the Maturity Level to bid on contracts? Is the appraisal team on its way to conduct a SCAMPI for a rating? Is that why you have not changed the procedures? Or is it because it took blood to write the procedures, so there is no way they will ever be changed? Was the organization forced to cut the time it took to produce the procedures? Was the Pilot phase skipped? Were people pulled from the PATs to do "real work"?

This brings us to management commitment. We usually have to set up a special one- to three-hour executive briefing for management because they are not willing to take the time to attend the full-blown class. True management commitment is shown by providing adequate resources and funding. That means enough of the right people, enough time, and enough money to do the job. While management might send out memos promoting the greater glory of the organization and why the organization should adhere to process improvement, real management commitment does not really happen — especially at first. Management (and we mean very senior management — the executive levels that decide process improvement must be done to garner future business) does not understand what process improvement really means and what it takes. We have taught over 150 Introduction classes; and in all that time, we have had only one executive in the class. The remaining students were usually process improvement people or developers. Management will *say* they are committed. It is up to you to make them prove it by following the concepts expressed in this book.

Summary

The CMMI combines procedures, process descriptions, and approaches into a document called a "plan." Chapter 16 discusses processes and procedures. This chapter broke out the parts of the CMMI plan into three major documents, or strategies. While there are many plans that can be written, the following plans are normally needed to promote a successful process improvement effort:

- A plan that documents why process improvement is being initiated, and what it will cost
- A plan that specifies the areas of the organization and the issues to focus on, and assigns personnel
- A plan that addresses each weakness found and builds a schedule with associated deliverables

Chapter 16

Defining Processes, Procedures, Policies, and Charters

This chapter is the "meat and potatoes" chapter. It provides guidelines for creating process improvement documentation and presents templates. You do not have to use these templates; they are simply provided to help you get started. Find something that fits your organization's culture and use it.

Defining Processes

A process consists of:

- Roles and responsibilities of the people assigned to do the work
- Appropriate tools and equipment to support individuals in doing their jobs
- Procedures and methods defining *how* to do the tasks and the relationships between the tasks

A process is *not* just a high-level flowchart. A life-cycle standard (e.g., DOD-MIL-STD-498 or 2167a) is not a process. A tool is not a process. A process consists of sequential steps of *what* needs to be done, plus the procedures detailing *how* to do the *whats*.

The CMMI® definition of a process is found in Chapter 3 of the staged representation. It states that "A process as used in the CMMI product suite consists of activities that can be recognized as implementations of practices in a CMMI model. These activities can be mapped to one or more practices in CMMI process areas to allow a model to be useful for process improvement and process appraisal." Although this definition does focus on implementing the practices of the CMMI, we find the definition unsatisfactory. We prefer to look at the definition in the CMMI for process description. A process description is "a documented expression of a set of activities performed to achieve a given purpose that provides an operational definition of the major components of a process. The documentation specifies, in a complete, precise, and verifiable manner, the requirements, design, behavior, or other characteristics of a process. It also may include procedures for determining whether these provisions have been satisfied. Process descriptions may be found at the activity, project, or organizational level." This definition seems to allude to the fact that processes must be detailed enough to be followed, and that procedures can lead to that effect.

More about procedures later. Let us now concentrate on how to define a process. With a defined process, you can see where to improve quality, productivity, cost, and schedule. A defined process is the prerequisite for process improvement. Without defining processes in an orderly fashion, sustained improvement is impossible. Defined processes improve communication and understanding of both the currently existing "As Is" processes used in the organization, and the "To Be" processes that constitute the desired end result. Defined processes aid in planning and execution of the plans, provide the ability to capture Lessons Learned, and help facilitate the analysis and improvement of organizationwide and enterprisewide processes.

When is a process defined? When it is documented, training is provided in the process, and it is practiced on a day-to-day basis. To create process documentation, the writers of the process at hand must understand the current process (As Is) and must have developed a shared vision of the desired process (To Be).

Where to start? Translate your products and services into outcomes. That is, if you build B1 Bombers, your outcome would be the fully constructed bomber. However, you would also have to break down this outcome into its constituent parts: the body, the software, the hardware, etc. Then break those parts down into their parts, etc. You will need a documented process (actually documented process*es*) for the work to be performed to develop each outcome. Now take one outcome and divide it by all of the activities it takes to produce that outcome. Be sure to include organizational units and support areas. This involves figuring out the *tasks* associated with the work to be performed, the *inputs and outputs, dependencies,* and *roles and responsibilities.*

Yes, it is a lot of work and, yes, it is difficult work.

Most templates for defining processes include the following entities:

- Activity Entry Criteria
- Activity Exit Criteria
- Activity Input
- Activity Output
- Activity Performed By
- What Activity Is Next

This is called the ETVX format, and was created by IBM and used by the SEI (Software Engineering Institute) as part of its process framework. This generic method of transcribing activities, ETVX, stands for: Entry Criteria, Tasks, Verification, and eXit Criteria. Terms used include:

- *Work Product/Work Outcome:* any product, service, or result
- *Activity:* the action taken to create or achieve the product, service, or result; this can also be the Task part of ETVX.
- *Agent:* the person who accomplishes or performs the action to achieve or create the product, service, or result

Examples of Work Outcomes are the results or products of a process, such as a Project Plan, a project schedule, allocated requirements, management approval, management sign-off, or trained employees. The following paragraphs demonstrate a sequence to be used when defining processes, as well as questions to ask and examples.

Activity Entry Criteria

Question: When can this activity begin?

Entry criteria describe the conditions under which the activity can be started.

Answer: Jot down a verb describing the state of an activity.

Examples: Approved Statement of Work, responsibilities for creating the Project Plan, an approved Test Plan.

Activity Exit Criteria

Question: When is this activity completed?

Describe the conditions under which an activity can be declared complete and may determine the next activity.

Answer: Verb about the state of the product, the person performing the activity, or the activity itself.

Examples: The Project Plan is ready for review, customer commitments are approved and incorporated into the project schedule, control mechanisms are in place for changes to the schedule.

Activity Input Criteria

Question: What interim work products are used by this activity?

Input is a relationship or link between an activity and a work result. Inputs are the results of a prior activity and used by the activity being described.

Answer: The name of the resultant work product.

Examples: Statement of Work, approved allocated requirements.

Activity Output Criteria

Question: What work results or products are produced by this activity?

Output is a relationship or link between an activity and a work result. Outputs are the results produced by the activity being described.

Answer: The name of the resultant work product.

Examples: A piece of code, a test procedure, a design specification, an approved Statement of Work.

Activity Performed By

Question: Who performs this activity?

"Activity performed by" is a relationship or link between an activity and an agent (the person performing the activity). It is the organizational unit, role, or automated agent responsible for performing the activity.

Answer: A list of the organizational units, roles, or automated agents that participate or are affected by the work.

Examples: The Quality Assurance (QA) group, a Project Manager, a Lead Software Engineer.

What Activity Is Next?

Question: What activity is next?

Activity flow is a conditional relationship or link between activities. Activity flow defines the ordering of activities and is generally dependent on exit criteria.

Answer: The result produced.

Examples: Final product OR product leading to the next set of ETVX activities.

Sometimes, Entry criteria and Inputs are combined, and Exit criteria and Outputs are combined. They are not really the same, as Entry and Exit criteria are *triggers*. Inputs and outputs are *products*. It is up to you how to do it. Most organizations currently combine the concepts.

Sometimes the previous ETVX information is presented as a flowchart with accompanying verbiage describing what goes on; sometimes it is presented as a list of sequenced steps; and sometimes it is presented as pages and pages of text. Whatever format fits the culture of the organization should be used.

After documenting the processes, the supporting procedures would be written, based on the process steps just documented. The procedures describe in detail *how* to perform the steps in the process.

Exhibit 1 shows an example of a process for Requirements Management. This template was created by an organization that did not depend on a lot of verbiage in its documentation. The organization wanted just the facts — short and sweet. Although the information looks short, if there are many steps to a process, this can get quite complicated.

Exhibit 2 shows another example of the same process by the same organization when it decided to add more text to explain the above process. Included in the text were the supporting procedures. The exhibit is simply the Table of Contents for the process. The complete process was 20 pages long. Although it was called the "Requirements Management Process," it only concentrated on creating the Requirements Specification, the Requirements Traceability Matrix, and changes to the requirements document itself.

Defining Procedures

What are Procedures? Procedures are step-by-step instructions on *how* to perform a task (see Exhibit 3). To be repeatable, the steps need to be broken down to a level that anyone who needs to perform the task, with a general understanding of the work to be done, can perform the work adequately by following the instructions. Procedures are a subset of processes. The process is *what* to do; the procedures are *how* to do the steps in the process.

Exhibit 1. Process for Requirements Management

Action	Responsibility
Obtain Work Request from the customer	SM, PM
Review Work Request	PM
Create initial budget/estimates/schedule	PM
Initial planning	PM, project team
High-level requirements	PM, project team, customer
Risk identification and documentation	PM
Requirements Spec Draft	PM, project team
Technical review	PM, project team, QA
Customer review	Customer
Refine requirements	PM, project team, customer
Create Requirements Traceability Matrix (RTM)	PM, project team
Review requirements and RTM	PM, customer, project team, QA
Review/update risks	PM
Update estimates and schedules	PM
Review requirements, schedules, and estimates	PM, project team, QA, customer
Requirements Spec Final	PM, analysts
Approvals and sign-offs	Customer, QA, PM, SM, EPG
Baseline Requirements Spec	PM, CCB, EPG
Assess, track, and incorporate changes	PM, CCB, QA, EPG, customer, project team

Note:

PM = Project Manager
SM = Senior Management
CCB = Configuration Control Board
QA = Quality Assurance
EPG = Engineering Process Group

Procedures are step-by-step instructions of how your processes are performed. They include:

- Sequence of activities
- Deliverables
- Controls
- Inspections/Reviews
- Guidelines and standards used

Exhibit 2. Requirements Management (RM) Process

TABLE OF CONTENTS

Procedures are created the same way as processes. Once you have generated a process, the process becomes the major tasks or steps. Break down each process step into its constituent parts. Those activities become the steps in the procedure. Then consider roles, agents, products, outcomes. Two things I might add to the above procedure template are measurements to be taken (and then refer to the procedure that details how to take the measurements) and verification that the procedure has

Exhibit 3. Procedure Template

Document Number:	Date:
	Revision Number
Description:	
This procedure involves... The activity's primary aim is to...	
Entry Criteria/Inputs:	Exit Criteria/Outputs:
Roles: Role Name: What does s/he do?	
Assets: Standards, reference material, deliverables, previous process descriptions...	

Summary of Tasks (list major tasks/process steps):
Task 1
Task 2
Task 3
Task 4

Procedure Steps:
Task 1
      Detail Step 1
      Detail Step 2
      Detail Step 3
      Detail Step 4
Task 2
      Detail Step 1
      Detail Step 2
      Detail Step 3
      Detail Step 4

Continue...

been followed (and refer to the verification procedure). When it comes to measurements and verifications, most organizations write one overall measurement process and procedure and one overall verification process and procedure, as everything must be measured and verified. Measurement and verification are global activities that cross all process areas in the CMMI and all maturity and capability levels.

You do not have to use the previous format for procedures. Some organizations prefer to be more wordy.

Defining Policies

Policies are high-level "whats." They contain *who* is responsible for doing work, usually by position title, not by the specific name of the individual. Most organizations using the CMM for Software simply copied the Commitment and Ability to Perform common features word-for-word, and assigned personnel to accomplish this function. Other organizations live and die by policies — if there is no policy to do work, then it will not be done. So, once again, it depends on your organizational culture as to how in-depth the policies should be. U.S. federal government organizations usually substitute their official directives to cover the policy requirement in the CMMI. Just make sure the documents substituted cover the guidelines offered by the CMMI. Policies are addressed in the first generic goal in the CMMI.

Exhibit 4 shows an example of a policy used in an organization. Notice that it summarizes the goals for Requirements Management as listed in the CMMI.

Charters

Charters are usually generated for the EPG (Exhibit 5) and PATs (Exhibit 6), and are often very similar in format — their scope is different, depending on the roles and responsibilities of each group. Charters contain statements addressing the following:

- *Customer*: Who are the customers?
- *Sponsor*: Who is sponsoring this effort?
- *Start date*: When does this PAT begin? If this is the EPG, how long will this EPG focus on the goals and objectives defined?
- *End date*: See previous.
- *Purpose*: Why are we here? What problem are we to address?
- *Scope*: How long, what results are expected, what is included and not included, and why/why not?
- *Deliverables*: Action Plans, processes, charters, other plans, training materials, procedures, policies.
- *Members*: Who are the members? (by name and title)
- *Percentage of their time*: This is mandatory. Use this measure to track if anyone is over-allocated. As a member of this team, can you really devote this much time to your task? Is the EPG full-time? PAT activities are usually part-time. The rest of the time, the PAT members work on their normal tasks.
- *Role of each team member*: What position do they fill? What deliverables are they expected to write?
- *Authority of the PAT/EPG*: Define problem resolution here. Does this PAT have the right to overrule another project manager?

Exhibit 4.   Requirements Management (RM) Policy

1.0 Purpose

The purpose of Requirements Management (RM) is to manage the requirements of the project's products and product components and to identify inconsistencies between those requirements and the project's plans and work products.

2.0 Scope

This policy applies to software projects within the XXX Division of the XXX organization. The term "project," as used in this policy, includes system and software engineering, maintenance, conversion, enhancements, and procurement projects.

3.0 Responsibilities

The project manager shall ensure that the RM process is followed. Each project will follow a process that ensures that requirements will be documented, managed, and traced.

4.0 Verification

RM activities will be reviewed with higher-level management, and the process will be objectively evaluated for adherence by the Quality Assurance (QA) staff.

5.0 Sign-offs

The following shall review and approve this policy:

Associate Director
Quality Assurance
EPG Chairman

- *Assumptions*: All members will attend and actively participate in all meetings.
- *Ground rules*: On-time attendance.
- *Attendance*. Is 100 percent attendance required, or can someone attend in your place? Will quorums be used? What constitutes a quorum?
- *Decision process*: Usually done through consensus. Consensus is that all members agree with the decision and can publicly support it. If you don't choose consensus, what constitutes a majority?
- Expected behaviors.
- Unacceptable behaviors.

Exhibit 5.   Example EPG Charter

Rev B, 3/7/03

This document describes the mission, objectives, and preliminary tasks necessary to establish the Engineering Process Group (EPG) at the XXX organization. This charter will apply to all members of the EPG.

Mission
The mission of the EPG is to implement process improvement (PI) at xxx. PI activities include fostering an understanding of the Software Engineering Institute's (SEI) Software Capability Maturity Model Integration (CMMI); conducting a baseline SCAMPI; generating Action Plans based on the results of the SCAMPI; implementing the activities documented in the Action Plans; and monitoring results.

Objectives
The objectives of PI are to achieve all goals of the Process Areas (PAs) for Levels 2 and 3. Level 2 achievement is projected for xxx date. Level 3 achievement is projected for xxx date. These objectives will be accomplished by reviewing and augmenting existing documentation; conducting periodic assessments; performing training and orientation as needed for personnel; participating on teams established to institute PI; incorporating planned activities into existing practices; and monitoring and measuring results.

EPG Membership and Operating Procedures
The EPG will consist of senior members of the systems and software development staff, will be managed by the PI project leader, and will be facilitated by an on-site PI consultant. The EPG will meet once a week. This weekly meeting will serve as the focal point for reporting the status of the Process Action Team (PAT) tasks. The EPG will serve as a forum to discuss and resolve issues occurring during PI project activities, to introduce information and new technologies or methods into xxx, and to review material generated during project process improvement activities.

PI Structure
The PI reporting structure is as follows. Each member of the EPG (except for the PI project leader and consultant) will serve as the chairman (or lead) of each PAT. This structure allows for an effective flow of information from the EPG to each PAT, from each PAT to the EPG, and for sharing information among the different PATs. Each PAT will exist only on a temporary basis. As the activities detailed in the Action Plan for each PAT are accomplished, that PAT will be dissolved. The members of that PAT will then be assigned other PI tasks. PAT teams will consist of the EPG representative (as PAT lead) plus other members of the organization, as necessary. For example, if one of the tasks in the Action Plan is to generate Configuration Management standards,

Exhibit 5. Example EPG Charter (continued)

a PAT will be established for that purpose. The PAT lead may request help in this area from other organizational individuals knowledgeable in configuration management standards used both at xxx and across the industry. Those individuals may be temporarily drafted on a part-time basis to assist in generating those standards. After the standards have been documented and approved by the EPG, those individuals will no longer be needed, the PAT will be disbanded, and the PAT lead will be used either on another PAT or as needed elsewhere for PI duties.

Steering Committee Obligations
The EPG chairman (the PI project leader) will in turn report EPG activities to management and an Executive Steering Committee. Senior management determines the budget and is responsible and accountable for the ultimate direction of PI at xxx.

EPG Tasks
Initial EPG tasks will include training in the CMMI and the SCAMPI process, generating business meeting rules, setting up PATs, developing detailed Action Plans on a PA-by-PA basis, and instituting a PI infrastructure.

As a result of the SCAMPI presented to management on February 6, 2003, the following tasks were generated:

Generate an OSSP to structure further PI efforts.
Search for standards, where a standard will provide organizational focus and support, enforced by our QA personnel.
Implement Requirements Management (RM) and Configuration Management (CM) by establishing PATs to generate policies, procedures, with the EPG monitoring the results.
Implement a Configuration Control Board (CCB) with the EPG performing this function until resources become available to perform this function separately from the EPG.

Project Planning (PP) and Project Tracking and Oversight (PTO) will be planned and acted upon once the results of the pilots for the preceding PAs (RM, CM) have been reviewed.

Level 2 PAs should be the primary focus at this time. All efforts must be supported by training. Training must be received, not only in the CMMI, but also in the PA assigned to the various PAT members. PATs cannot be expected to write procedures for performing a PA if they have not been trained in what the CMMI requires and what the PA consists of.

Pilot projects need to be selected to pilot the CMMI procedures and instructions. The monitoring of CMMI-related activities will be performed by the EPG.

Exhibit 6.   PAT Charter Template

Customer:
Sponsor:
Start: **End:**
Purpose of the PAT:

Linkage to Business Objectives:
(from strategic or business plan if we have it)

Scope:

Deliverables:

PAT Members:

Name	% of Time	Role
1.		
2.		
3.		
4.		

PAT Authority:

Assumptions

Ground Rules:
Attendance

Decisions

Behaviors

Sign-offs:

Summary

Process Improvement is continuous. You will never get the perfect procedure written, so try for something workable. Communicate that you do not want something awful but that perfection is out of reach. Get something and pilot it. The pilots will show where the gaps are more effective than yet another EPG review. This does not mean that you do not have EPG reviews! It means that do not have to keep re-reviewing and re-reviewing. Let the organization show you what works and what does not.

Chapter 17

A Boatload of Metrics

This chapter offers some guidelines for metrics to use in your organization. It presents some metrics that are commonly collected in organizations, some tips on how to devise metrics, and some advice on structuring your metrics process.

We could not possibly discuss everything necessary to set up and administer a top-notch metrics program in one small chapter. To that end, we have listed several books on the subject in the Summary section of this chapter.

For a discussion on the importance of collecting consistent data, and when and how to collect that data, read Chapter 18 ("Statistical Process Control") and Chapter 19 ("A High Maturity Perspective"). By the way, you will find that we use the terms "measurement" and "metric" interchangeably. We apologize if this offends you, but we decided that we really do not want to weigh in on the war of words around measurement. We expect our readers to be smart enough to make the translation from the word "metric" to "measure," if they prefer.

Background

When beginning a process improvement effort in an organization, invariably a project manager or the executive in charge will pull one of us aside and ask, "What metrics should we collect?" We hate that question. We hate it because it shows that the person asking the question has no clue about what process improvement is and generally only wants a "quick fix" for his organization. "Just tell us what to collect, we'll do it, and then we're done." We do not think so. Now, true, this judgment is harsh; after all, these people are only beginning the process improvement journey. However, one of the first deliverables requested by management from us for any organization is a list of metrics to collect. The managers then mull over the metrics and decide not to collect them anyway because by collecting the metrics, we can really track and report on what is going on in the projects; and heaven knows, we just cannot have that! So, much moaning and groaning takes place — "We don't have the people to do this; we don't collect these numbers; we don't need these numbers; the staff won't stand for it"; and so on. And then, after discussing the pros and cons of each metric, we begin with a very small list. After seeing that metrics really do help an organization (after several very difficult months), the managers are glad that we collect those metrics. Then we begin to suggest that there are more metrics that will help them, and we must begin the battle all over again.

The purpose of metrics is not to drive everybody crazy; rather, it is to look at the numbers as indicators of how your project is doing and how all of the projects are doing. If the numbers are not what you expected, is there a problem? Where did the problem occur? Where was that problem injected originally? Understanding the metrics and what they mean are critical elements for successfully running an organization.

Selecting Metrics for Your Organization

One place to begin looking for metrics to collect that will benefit your organization is the CMMI®. In the CMMI, an entire process area is devoted to metrics, that is: Measurement and Analysis. It resides at Maturity Level 2 in the staged representation, and in the Support Process category in the continuous representation. In addition, one of the Common Features — Directing Implementation — also addresses measurement. Just like the CMMI pre-supposes that you have standards and are using them, the CMMI also pre-supposes that you are collecting appropriate metrics about your project (e.g., schedule and cost overruns, people turnover on your project, number of errors in deliverables submitted and returned from the client, etc.). This is often not the case. In fact, in some organizations just beginning the process improvement journey, no metrics are kept. While that may shock some of you, there are large state and local agencies that have no timekeeping systems; there are some publicly held companies that do not track dollars spent on projects that are contracted out; and also the reverse, companies that only track contractor work, not their own, internal commitments.

The CMMI specifically relates its metrics to the process area (PA) activities; for example, how long it took you to arrange your planning activities (in the Project Planning PA), how long it took to write the Quality Assurance Plan (in the Product and Process Assurance PA), etc. So, what good is tracking how long you took to write a project plan if you do not also track late delivery of products and late milestones? So use the metrics mentioned in the CMMI only as a guideline when deciding which metrics might be appropriate for your organization.

We also recommend the metrics listed in the Measurement and Analysis Common feature of the original CMM for Software. We find that these metrics make sense, are directly tied to each key process area, are commonly collected and used in organizations, and are straightforward. Although it is called the CMM for Software (actually, its real name is the Capability Maturity Model — CMM — and most people have just added the "for Software" appellation), if you go through the book and take the word "software" out, you will find that most of the concepts and metrics described can be used in almost any organization, software-based or not.

There is another way to determine which metrics might be the most beneficial to your organization. It is called the Goal-Question-Metric (GQM) technique. We discussed this approach previously when discussing tying process improvement efforts to business goals. We basically said that this approach sounds good, but is difficult to successfully implement in low-maturity organizations because their business objectives are generally not documented in sufficient detail to really tie directly to the CMMI (their business objectives are basically described as "to make money"). However, when it comes to metrics, once an organization has seen the list of measurements it can collect, it will become apprehensive and overwhelmed. So, using a list of possible measures, and using the GQM technique to decide which metrics to select, if facilitated correctly, can be useful.

The basic G-Q-M approach is to:

- *Determine the goal.* What business goal are you trying to support? Why are you collecting these numbers? What will they do for you? Why is it important to collect metrics?
- *Determine the question* that is most closely associated with achieving the goal.
- *Determine the measurements* that help answer the question, or metrics that would provide you with the response to the question.

So, a simple example of using the GQM technique is the following:

- Goal: Reduce the time it takes for our requirements definition process (while maintaining quality).
- Question: Where is the most time spent?

- Metric(s): Refer to our list below. Some suggested metrics are:
  - Number of requirements changes proposed versus number approved and number implemented
  - Time it takes for the different phases of our requirements process
  - Number of users interviewed per job function and category
  - Number of errors traced back to the Requirements phase
  - Time it takes for requirements sign-off
  - Quality of the delivered product

Obviously, more refinement of the question and metrics is needed. For example, what metric (number) can you use to quantitatively define "quality"? What part of the requirements process is broken? Do we really need to reduce the time it takes to gather, refine, document, and manage changes to our requirements? Or would it be better to reduce the time spent somewhere else in the life cycle?

Be sure to clearly define what is being measured. For example, if you are measuring the time it takes to perform the requirements process, does that only include the time to write and review requirements, or does that also include the time to attend status meetings to discuss the requirements process?

It is also critical that the purpose of each metric be explained *and* understood. Everyone should understand:

- Why the metrics are being collected
- How the metrics will be used
- What is expected from each person as to gathering, reporting, interpreting, and using the metrics

After selecting the metrics, pilot them in your organization. When selecting pilot projects, make sure the projects selected are already following whatever "best practices" your organization has. If not, then this project is probably not going to be successful at piloting anything. In fact, some organizations will deliberately choose a dysfunctional project to pilot improvement efforts because:

- They vainly hope that trying anything on these projects will somehow automatically improve the projects.
- They really do not want the improvement efforts to work so they can go back to doing things the way they used to.

Also make sure that these projects are not piloting everything in your organization, and that they are not going to be overburdened by collecting and piloting the metrics. There are more recommendations for planning and tracking pilots in previous chapters, as well as in the Appendices section.

Another reminder: metrics should not be collected and used to judge anyone's work on a personal basis. That is, metrics should not be used to justify a person's salary or motivate individual performance. Metrics are used to determine how your project- or organizational-level processes are working — not whether your people are "good" or "bad." Dysfunctional behavior is often the result when people feel they are being measured.

List of Metrics

Every organization we have ever assisted with process improvement efforts has always asked: "What metrics should we collect?" Well, once again, define your metrics to your business needs and the problems you face. Having said that, most executives and managers still want and need examples. So here they are.

The metrics listed are arranged according to the Maturity Levels and Process Areas (PAs) in the CMMI. We have tried to present metrics that might be found more commonly, and used more effectively, at certain stages of organizational sophistication. However, just because a metric appears in a process area at Level 3, and you are just trying to reach Level 2, if that metric will help you, then use it. This list is arranged somewhat arbitrarily. Some readers will say, "Hey, that metric goes better in a different process area (process area X)." That is OK because this list is just to get you thinking about measurements that can be of help to you and your organization.

These metrics are by no means the only measurements to collect in an organization. They are simply representative of those measures we have found collected the most frequently. We used the Directing Implementation Common Feature of the CMMI as the basis for these metrics, supplemented by metrics our clients have used in their own organizations. You should also note that most of the organizations we have assisted in their process improvement efforts and in their metrics programs began by reviewing the metrics documented in the CMM and CMMI, and then decided whether or not these metrics would work for them.

For the most part, this list represents base measures to collect. Base measures are simple values of some attribute; for example, the size of a document in pages or the effort to produce a document in hours. To get value from your measurement, you will most likely want to compare actuals to planned, and to produce derived measures from your base measures. Derived measures are a function of two or more base measures; for example, productivity in hours per page to produce a document.

Level 2

Requirements Management

1. Requirements volatility (percentage of requirements changes)
2. Number of requirements by type or status (defined, reviewed, approved, and implemented)
3. Cumulative number of changes to the allocated requirements, including total number of changes proposed, open, approved, and incorporated into the system baseline
4. Number of change requests per month, compared to the original number of requirements for the project
5. Amount of time spent, effort spent, cost of implementing change requests
6. Number and size of change requests after the Requirements phase is completed
7. Cost of implementing a change request
8. Number of change requests versus the total number of change requests during the life of the project
9. Number of change requests accepted but not implemented
10. Number of requirements (changes and additions to the baseline)

Project Planning

11. Completion of milestones for the project planning activities compared to the plan (estimates versus actuals)
12. Work completed, effort and funds expended in the project planning activities compared to the plan
13. Number of revisions to the project plans
14. Cost, schedule, and effort variance per plan revision
15. Replanning effort due to change requests
16. Effort expended over time to manage the project compared to the plan
17. Frequency, causes, and magnitude of the replanning effort

Project Monitoring and Control

18. Effort and other resources expended in performing monitoring and oversight activities
19. Change activity for the project plan, which includes changes to size estimates of the work products, cost/resource estimates, and schedule
20. Number of open and closed corrective actions or action items
21. Project milestone dates (planned versus actual)

22. Number of project milestone dates made on time
23. Number and types of reviews performed
24. Schedule, budget, and size variance between planned and actual reviews
25. Comparison of actuals versus estimates for all planning and tracking items

Measurement and Analysis

26. Number of projects using progress and performance measures
27. Number of measurement objectives addressed

Supplier Agreement Management

28. Cost of the COTS (commercial off-the-shelf) products
29. Cost and effort to incorporate the COTS products into the project
30. Number of changes made to the supplier requirements
31. Cost and schedule variance per supplier agreement
32. Costs of the activities for managing the contract compared to the plan
33. Actual delivery dates for contracted products compared to the plan
34. Actual dates of prime contractor deliveries to the subcontractor compared to the plan
35. Number of on-time deliveries from the vendor, compared with the contract
36. Number and severity of errors found after delivery
37. Number of exceptions to the contract to ensure schedule adherence
38. Number of quality audits compared to the plan
39. Number of Senior Management reviews to ensure adherence to budget and schedule versus the plan
40. Number of contract violations by supplier or vendor

Process and Product Quality Assurance (QA)

41. Completions of milestones for the QA activities compared to the plan
42. Work completed, effort expended in the QA activities compared to the plan
43. Number of product audits and activity reviews compared to the plan
44. Number of process audits and activities versus those planned
45. Number of defects per release and/or build
46. Amount of time/effort spent in rework

47. Amount of QA time/effort spent in each phase of the life cycle
48. Number of reviews and audits versus number of defects found
49. Total number of defects found in internal reviews and testing versus those found by the customer or end user after delivery
50. Number of defects found in each phase of the life cycle
51. Number of defects injected during each phase of the life cycle
52. Number of noncompliances written versus the number resolved
53. Number of noncompliances elevated to senior management
54. Complexity of module or component (McCabe, McClure, and Halstead metrics)

Configuration Management (CM)

55. Number of change requests or change board requests processed per unit of time
56. Completions of milestones for the CM activities compared to the plan
57. Work completed, effort expended, and funds expended in the CM activities
58. Number of changes to configuration items
59. Number of configuration audits conducted
60. Number of fixes returned as "Not Yet Fixed"
61. Number of fixes returned as "Could Not Reproduce Error"
62. Number of violations of CM procedures (noncompliance found in audits)
63. Number of outstanding problem reports versus rate of repair
64. Number of times changes are overwritten by someone else (or number of times people have the wrong initial version or baseline)
65. Number of engineering change proposals proposed, approved, rejected, implemented
66. Number of changes by category to code source, and to supporting documentation
67. Number of changes by category, type, and severity
68. Source lines of code stored in libraries placed under configuration control

Level 3

Requirements Development

69. Cost, schedule, and effort expended for rework
70. Defect density of requirements specifications

71. Number of requirements approved for build (versus the total number of requirements)
72. Actual number of requirements documented (versus the total number of estimated requirements)
73. Staff hours (total and by Requirements Development activity)
74. Requirements status (percentage of defined specifications out of the total approved and proposed; number of requirements defined)
75. Estimates of total requirements, total requirements definition effort, requirements analysis effort, and schedule
76. Number and type of requirements changes

Technical Solution

77. Cost, schedule, and effort expended for rework
78. Number of requirements addressed in the product or product-component design
79. Size and complexity of the product, product components, interfaces, and documentation
80. Defect density of technical solutions work products (number of defects per page)
81. Number of requirements by status or type throughout the life of the project (for example, number defined, approved, documented, implemented, tested, and signed-off by phase)
82. Problem reports by severity and length of time they are open
83. Number of requirements changed during implementation and test
84. Effort to analyze proposed changes for each proposed change and cumulative totals
85. Number of changes incorporated into the baseline by category (e.g., interface, security, system configuration, performance, and useability)
86. Size and cost to implement and test incorporated changes, including initial estimate and actual size and cost
87. Estimates and actuals of system size, reuse, effort, and schedule
88. The total estimated and actual staff hours needed to develop the system by job category and activity
89. Estimated dates and actuals for the start and end of each phase of the life cycle
90. Number of diagrams completed versus the estimated total diagrams
91. Number of design modules/units proposed
92. Number of design modules/units delivered
93. Estimates and actuals of total lines of code — new, modified, and reused
94. Estimates and actuals of total design and code modules and units

95. Estimates and actuals for total CPU hours used to date
96. The number of units coded and tested versus the number planned
97. Errors by category, phase discovered, phase injected, type, and severity
98. Estimates of total units, total effort, and schedule
99. System tests planned, executed, passed, or failed
100. Test discrepancies reported, resolved, or not resolved
101. Source code growth by percentage of planned versus actual

Product Integration

102. Product-component integration profile (i.e., product-component assemblies planned and performed, and number of exceptions found)
103. Integration evaluation problem report trends (e.g., number written and number closed)
104. Integration evaluation problem report aging (i.e., how long each problem report has been open)

Verification

105. Verification profile (e.g., the number of verifications planned and performed, and the defects found; perhaps categorized by verification method or type)
106. Number of defects detected by defect category
107. Verification problem report trends (e.g., number written and number closed)
108. Verification problem report status (i.e., how long each problem report has been open)
109. Number of peer reviews performed compared to the plan
110. Overall effort expended on peer reviews compared to the plan
111. Number of work products reviewed compared to the plan

Validation

112. Number of validation activities completed (planned versus actual)
113. Validation problem reports trends (e.g., number written and number closed)
114. Validation problem report aging (i.e., how long each problem report has been open)

Organizational Process Focus

115. Number of process improvement proposals submitted, accepted, or implemented
116. CMMI maturity or capability level
117. Work completed, effort and funds expended in the organization's activities for process assessment, development, and improvement compared to the plans for these activities
118. Results of each process assessment, compared to the results and recommendations of previous assessments

Organizational Process Definition

119. Percentage of projects using the process architectures and process elements of the organization's set of standard processes
120. Defect density of each process element of the organization's set of standard processes
121. Number of on-schedule milestones for process development and maintenance
122. Costs for the process definition activities

Organizational Training

123. Number of training courses delivered (e.g., planned versus actual)
124. Post-training evaluation ratings
125. Training program quality surveys
126. Actual attendance at each training course compared to the projected attendance
127. Progress in improving training courses compared to the organization's and projects' training plans
128. Number of training waivers approved over time

Integrated Project Management for IPPD

129. Number of changes to the project's defined process
130. Effort to tailor the organization's set of standard processes
131. Interface coordination issue trends (e.g., number identified and closed)

Risk Management

132. Number of risks identified, managed, tracked, and controlled
133. Risk exposure and changes to the risk exposure for each assessed risk, and as a summary percentage of management reserve
134. Change activity for the risk mitigation plans (e.g., processes, schedules, funding)
135. Number of occurrences of unanticipated risks
136. Risk categorization volatility
137. Estimated versus actual risk mitigation effort
138. Estimated versus actual risk impact
139. The amount of effort and time spent on risk management activities versus the number of actual risks
140. The cost of risk management versus the cost of actual risks
141. For each identified risk, the realized adverse impact compared to the estimated impact

Integrated Teaming

142. Performance according to plans, commitments, and procedures for the integrated team, and deviations from expectations
143. Number of times team objectives were not achieved
144. Actual effort and other resources expended by one group to support another group or groups, and vice versa
145. Actual completion of specific tasks and milestones by one group to support the activities of other groups, and vice versa

Integrated Supplier Management

146. Effort expended to manage the evaluation of sources and selection of suppliers
147. Number of changes to the requirements in the supplier agreement
148. Number of documented commitments between the project and the supplier
149. Interface coordination issue trends (e.g., number identified and number closed)
150. Number of defects detected in supplied products (during integration and after delivery)

Decision Analysis and Resolution

151. Cost-to-benefit ratio of using formal evaluation processes

Organizational Environment for Integration

152. Parameters for key operating characteristics of the work environment

Level 4

Organizational Process Performance

153. Trends in the organization's process performance with respect to changes in work products and task attributes (e.g., size growth, effort, schedule, and quality)

Quantitative Project Management

154. Time between failures
155. Critical resource utilization
156. Number and severity of defects in the released product
157. Number and severity of customer complaints concerning the provided service
158. Number of defects removed by product verification activities (perhaps by type of verification, such as peer reviews and testing)
159. Defect escape rates
160. Number and density of defects by severity found during the first year following product delivery or start of service
161. Cycle time
162. Amount of rework time
163. Requirements volatility (i.e., number of requirements changes per phase)
164. Ratios of estimated to measured values of the planning parameters (e.g., size, cost, and schedule)
165. Coverage and efficiency of peer reviews (i.e., number/amount of products reviewed compared to total number, and number of defects found per hour)
166. Test coverage and efficiency (i.e., number/amount of products tested compared to total number, and number of defects found per hour)
167. Effectiveness of training (i.e., percent of planned training completed and test scores)
168. Reliability (i.e., mean time-to-failure usually measured during integration and systems test)
169. Percentage of the total defects inserted or found in the different phases of the project life cycle

170. Percentage of the total effort expended in the different phases of the project life cycle
171. Profile of subprocesses under statistical management (i.e., number planned to be under statistical management, number currently being statistically managed, and number that are statistically stable)
172. Number of special causes of variation identified
173. The cost over time for the quantitative process management activities compared to the plan
174. The accomplishment of schedule milestones for quantitative process management activities compared to the approved plan (i.e., establishing the process measurements to be used on the project, determining how the process data will be collected, and collecting the process data)
175. The cost of poor quality (e.g., amount of rework, re-reviews and re-testing)
176. The costs for achieving quality goals (e.g., amount of initial reviews, audits, and testing)

Level 5

Organizational Innovation and Deployment

177. Change in quality after improvements (e.g., number of reduced defects)
178. Change in process performance after improvements (e.g., change in baselines)
179. The overall technology change activity, including number, type, and size of changes
180. The effect of implementing the technology change compared to the goals (e.g., actual cost saving to projected)
181. The number of process improvement proposals submitted and implemented for each process area
182. The number of process improvement proposals submitted by each project, group, and department
183. The number and types of awards and recognitions received by each of the projects, groups, and departments
184. The response time for handling process improvement proposals
185. Number of process improvement proposals accepted per reporting period
186. The overall change activity including number, type, and size of changes
187. The effect of implementing each process improvement compared to its defined goals

188. Overall performance of the organization's and projects' processes, including effectiveness, quality, and productivity compared to their defined goals
189. Overall productivity and quality trends for each project
190. Process measurements that relate to the indicators of the customers' satisfaction (e.g., surveys results, number of customer complaints, and number of customer compliments)

Causal Analysis and Resolution

191. Defect data (problem reports, defects reported by the customer, defects reported by the user, defects found in peer reviews, defects found in testing, process capability problems, time and cost for identifying the defect and fixing it, estimated cost of not fixing the problem)
192. Number of root causes removed
193. Change in quality or process performance per instance of the causal analysis and resolution process (e.g., number of defects and changes in baseline)
194. The costs of defect prevention activities (e.g., holding causal analysis meetings and implementing action items), cumulatively
195. The time and cost for identifying the defects and correcting them compared to the estimated cost of not correcting the defects
196. Profiles measuring the number of action items proposed, open, and completed
197. The number of defects injected in each stage, cumulatively, and over-releases of similar products
198. The number of defects

Another comparison of base versus derived measures follows. The base measure we have listed is "Cumulative number of changes to the allocated requirements, including total number of changes proposed, open, approved, and incorporated into the system baseline." The derived measure that can be produced from this base measure is "the percentage of changes incorporated compared to the total number of changes proposed." Most organizations also want to compare actuals to benchmarked industry data.

Remember: this list is just a start. With a little creativity, we are sure you can come up with even more.

OK, there it is. I'm glad that's over.

Questions to Ask When Generating and Reviewing Metrics

Most organizations collect some sort of measurements, even if they are only when projects start and finish, or how much money has been spent so far. When structuring a metrics process, you should consider asking the following questions of your project managers:

- What metrics do you collect?
- How do they track to the cost-effort-schedule metrics needed by senior management or other corporate activities?
- Do you use and understand "Earned Value"?
- Do you track the time it takes to enter, track, and report metrics?
- Do you use any graphs or automated tools?
- Which metrics work for you, and which ones do not work for you? Why and why not?
- How have you used the metrics?
- What problems do you see in entering, collecting, analyzing, and reporting the metrics?
- How do you use the WBS? Does it tie back to the activities tracked by the metrics?
- How are the metrics you collect tied to business goals and the business problems in this organization?
- How do you analyze the metrics data?
- How do you verify that the data are correct and accurate?
- As for trends, what problems does your project have? Do the metrics reflect this finding? Did using the metrics help you identify this problem?
- In which phase of the life cycle did these problems occur?
- Do the metrics collected reflect or help you identify the phase of the life cycle in which the problem occurred, or the cause of the problem?

Selection of the metrics to be used on the projects should take into consideration the size of the project (both in dollars, personnel, and product size); project classification (Development, Enhancements, or Maintenance); and the complexity of the system being built. In addition, the metrics should reflect the needs of the projects that represent the main functional areas in your organization. This approach will help to ensure coverage of representative projects of the organization.

Planning the Metrics Process

Metrics programs must also be planned. A simple Measurement Plan Outline is shown in Exhibit 1. This is admittedly, a very simple outline for your metrics planning. Be sure to discuss how each metric will be collected, why, how it ties back to business objectives or problems, the format to be used to define and document each metric, and why everything

Exhibit 1. Measurement Plan Outline

I. Introduction (Purpose, Scope)
II. Organizational and Project Issues
III. Overall Measurement Approach
IV. Approach for Project Management Metrics
V. Approach for Technical Metrics
VI. Approach for Introducing Metrics into the Organization
VII. How Metrics Will Be Collected and Used
VIII. Roles and Responsibilities
IX. Communication/Feedback Plan
X. List of Measurements

discussed is relevant to the reader. The List of Measurements in the Measurement Plan needs to include your project's and organization's definition of each measure. Do not assume that because you know what a "defect" is that everyone else has the same definition in mind. Be sure to keep your definition practical. Defining metrics is not an academic exercise.

Some Problems You May Encounter

The following is a list of problems we have encountered in metrics programs found in organizations. This list can be used as a checklist for any metrics or metrics programs you have implemented in your organization.

■ Metrics are collected but not used.
■ No mechanism exists to distribute project performance metrics for review, comparison, and use.
■ Project-level metrics do not appear to be used to help project managers manage their projects.
■ There is no understanding of the value of metrics or how to use them.
■ No formal feedback loop is found on the quality of the metrics, questions about them, etc.
■ Metrics reports are difficult to review for trends.
■ Metrics data are inconsistent.
■ Personnel collect and input data that they think are right but are unsure.
■ A standard WBS (a basic building block for management activities) is not followed consistently, and metrics cannot be traced back to WBS activities.

- No one reviews the metrics data in the various databases for data integrity.
- Training and communication are not occurring throughout the organization.
- Procedures need to be devised to document metrics generation, collection, review, and use.
- Existing procedures need to be updated to reflect changes.
- Automated tools are not used; the wrong automated tool is used; or the automated tool is used incorrectly.
- The metrics reports are difficult to read and understand.
- Procedures are not well-defined or consistently followed (e.g., usage of "may ... if desired ... at PM's discretion").
- The time it takes to identify, track, collect, and report the metrics is not measured.
- Redundant data entry is rampant.

Recommendations

Recommendations fall into two main categories:

1. Recommendations to improve the metrics identification and collection process itself
2. Recommendations to improve actual performance on projects

Recommendations to Improve the Metrics Identification and Collection Process Itself

The number-one, overall recommendation is to *automate the process and make it seamless and simple.* If it's too hard, people won't do it. Other recommendations include:

- Involve your project managers and process owners in designing the metrics to be collected. Help them understand why metrics are collected and how to use them to help run their projects.
- Collect metrics that the project managers need. Other metrics (i.e., corporate-level metrics used for executive reviews) can be generated automatically, based on the project-level data, and rolled up into a corporate report.
- Metrics should not be used punitively. They should be used to help assist the project managers in running their projects more effectively, and to help improve estimating and tracking techniques.

- Facilitate workshops to derive meaningful metrics. Involve the project managers, directors, supervisors, metrics team, quality assurance personnel, process improvement specialists, technicians, budget and finance representatives, and any other interested individuals. Try to map your project-level and senior management-level metrics to the business objectives and problems the organization faces.
- Provide feedback to the project managers and staff on the metrics collected so that they can see how they are doing compared to other projects in the organization and to other projects throughout the different business units.

Recommendations to Improve Actual Performance on Projects

Train the project managers and anyone else who generates, collects, reviews, or uses the metrics. First of all, make sure your project managers (PMs) have received detailed, effective training in basic project management. Some managers simply do not have the skillsets required for the increasingly sophisticated tasks that their jobs require. For example, it is not uncommon to find PMs who are not really administrative-type managers concerned with costs and budgets. They more closely resemble technical leads. These PMs do not focus their energies on administrative tasks such as documentation, planning, tracking, and reporting. They mostly concentrate on the technical fixes required for design and coding. Therefore, training on Earned Value — what it is, how to use it, how it can work for them — must be undertaken, as well as true training in how to do the job in your organization.

Metrics must be used. Instruct your staff (especially the PMs) in how the metrics can be used to help them manage their projects. Basically answer the following question: "What's in it for me?" Just mandating that the metrics be used, and to follow the procedures, will not work.

Summary

Generating metrics is not really that difficult — just look at the list presented herein. However, generating *meaningful* metrics that can be *used* in your organization is somewhat more complicated. Getting buy-in for the metrics effort will take some time and persuasion, and collecting and understanding the metrics will also present a challenge.

Do not give up; most process improvement books (the CMMI among them) do not expect you to get it right the first time. In fact, the one thing that you will find is that as you use the metrics, you will need to update them and make changes as your business needs change and as your staff becomes more knowledgeable.

Make sure you understand each metric selected for use, why it was selected, how it will be used, and how and when it will be collected. If not — ask. Maybe someone who generated the metrics decided that because these numbers worked at his previous place of employment, they should work here. Or maybe the metrics were designed for some other department or type of work or level in the corporation that does not meet your needs.

There are many, many books on metrics, and metrics programs available. Although we make no recommendations, the ones our customers have used most frequently include:

> *Measuring the Software Process,* William Florac and Anita Carleton, Addison-Wesley, Reading, Massachusetts, 1999
>
> *Practical Software Measurement,* John McGarry, David Card, Cheryl Jones, Beth Layman, Elizabeth Clark, Joseph Dean, and Fred Hall, Addison-Wesley, Reading, Massachusetts, 2002
>
> *Metrics and Models in Software Quality Engineering,* Stephen Kan, Addison-Wesley, Reading, Massachusetts,1995

Chapter 18

Statistical Process Control

This chapter is entitled "Statistical Process Control," or SPC. This topic is often the most dreaded of all subjects when discussing process improvement. Why? Because it involves numbers, and then scrutinizing the numbers to determine whether the numbers are correctly collected, reported, and used throughout the organization. Many organizations will collect metrics "because the book says we have to in order to get our rating." Well, I have to admit that is a good reason, but it is not the best reason. When used correctly, metrics can help decision makers make good decisions. When used incorrectly, they can help decision makers justify their mistakes. Metrics can also be used by managers to abuse their people. So, this chapter spends a lot of time discussing metrics and the data that go into them.

It would be absurd to think that one small chapter in this book could teach you all about SPC. What we have tried to do in this book is to distill the knowledge you need to implement process improvement activities in your organization. So, this chapter also tries to do that; that is, to summarize what can sometimes be difficult concepts into something you can use right away. We have tried to summarize the information we have learned over the years and to summarize the best practices we have found in other organizations.

This chapter introduces different types of charts and discusses reasons for using the charts and reasons for collecting data. You will not be an expert in SPC once you have read this chapter. You will, however, have a very basic understanding of what SPC is about and where your organization might start.

Those of you who are experts at SPC can skip this chapter. However, for those of you who are experts who decide to read this chapter, we ask a little leeway. Everyone has a different approach to SPC — what should be used, what works best, definitions. We also have our own opinions, which may differ from yours. This chapter is also written to be understood, not to impress anyone with high-faluting terminology or inscrutable examples, so the terminology used may be somewhat irritating to a few of you.

One more thing. "Data" are plural. Although most people generally say that "the data *is* not yet available," proper grammar is to say that "the data *are* not yet available." So it may sound a little funny when you read it.

Background Information

What is statistical process control? SPC consists of some techniques used to help individuals understand, analyze, and interpret numerical information. SPC is used to identify and track variation in processes. All processes will have some natural variation. Think about it this way: suppose you get into your car and drive to work every weekday. What can vary about that? Well, assuming that you do not change the route you take, the natural variation can be the number of stoplights you hit (that means the lights you must stop at — not that you hit them with your car), the number of cars waiting at the stoplight, the number of cars that are making turns at the stoplight, etc. It can also include the number of accidents (if accidents are a normal part of your drive into work), the number of school buses you get behind, and, on a really good day when everything seems to irritate you, the number of trash trucks you follow that you just cannot seem to pass. All of these frustrations are those that you currently, normally encounter on your way to work. While the number of trash trucks may change, and the number of cars turning may change, the basic process of driving to work has not changed. Those variations are *normal* variations. The *exceptional* variation would be when you decide to drive into work on a weekday that just happens to have a holiday fall on that day. Suppose that, due to a crushing workload, you decide to drive into work on Labor Day (which for those of you not familiar with U.S. holidays, always falls on the first Monday in September). Hopefully, you do not always go to work on a holiday, so this is an exception. You follow the same route, but it does not take as long, you do not hit as many stoplights, and the number of cars in front of you is lessened.

Due to the normal variation in any process, the numbers (in this example, the number of cars waiting at the stoplight, the number of accidents that may occur) can change when the process really has not. So, we need to understand both the *numbers* relating to our processes and the *changes* that occur in our processes so that we may respond appropriately.

Other terms that you may see are *common causes* of variation and *special causes* of variation, as well as *common cause systems* and *special cause systems.* Common causes of variation result from such things as system design decisions and the use of one development tool over another. This variation will occur predictably across the entire process associated with it and is considered normal variation. Special causes of variation are those that arise from such things as inconsistent process execution and lack of resources. This variation is exceptional variation and is also known as assignable causes of variation. We will use both terms. Other terms you will hear are *in control* for predictable processes or steady-state; and *out of control* for unpredictable processes that are "outside the natural limits."

When a process is predictable, it exhibits routine variation as a result of common causes. When a process is unpredictable, it exhibits exceptional variation as a result of assignable causes. It is our job to be able to tell the difference and to find the assignable cause. When a process is *predictable*, it is performing as consistently as it can (either for better or for worse). It will not be performing perfectly; there will always be some normal, routine variation. Looking for assignable causes for processes that are running predictably is a waste of time because you will not find any. Work instead on improving the process itself. When a process is *unpredictable,* that means it is not operating consistently. It is a waste of time to try to improve the process itself. In this case, you must find out why it is not operating predictably and detail the "whys" as specifically as possible. To do that, you must find and fix the assignable cause(s); that is, the activity that is causing the process to behave erratically.

An example of fixing an assignable or special cause of variation in the driving to work example would be if your car breaks down on the way to work. If this happens once, you might not take any action. However, if your car is old and breakdowns occur frequently, you might decide to remove this special cause by buying a newer car.

In contrast to the predictability of a process, we may want to consider if a process is capable of delivering what is needed by the customer. Capable processes perform within the specification limits set by the customer. So, a process may be *predictable,* but not *capable.*

Exhibit 1. Check Sheet Used for Counting and Accumulating Data

Student Name	In Class This Week?
Jane	√ √ √ √ √
Robert	√ √ √ √ √
Jennifer	√ √ √
Puff Daddy	

Seven Common Tools

SPC takes numbers and presents the numbers pictorially to tell a story. The story that is told demonstrates what is happening within the process. That story is often called "the voice of the process." The pictures produced must be explained and must be accurate. To that end, there are seven commonly recognized tools for statistical process control:

1. Check sheet
2. Run chart
3. Histogram
4. Pareto chart
5. Scatter diagram/chart
6. Cause and effect or fishbone diagram
7. Control chart

Some basic examples are shown in Exhibits 1 through 7. These examples are for illustration only — we do not go into how to derive the values for each chart and then how to translate the values into meaningful representations.

Check Sheet

The check sheet (Exhibit 1) is used for counting and accumulating data.

Run Chart

The run chart (Exhibit 2) tracks trends over a period of time. Points are tracked in the order in which they occur. Each point represents an observation. You can often see interesting trends in the data by simply plotting data on a run chart. A danger in using run charts is that you might overreact to normal variations, but it is often useful to put your data on a run chart to get a feel for process behavior.

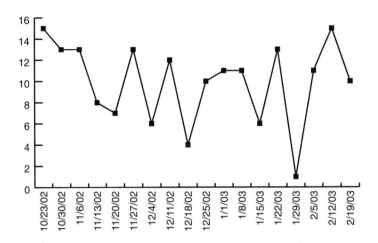

Exhibit 2. Run Chart

Histogram

The histogram (Exhibit 3) is a bar chart that presents data that have been collected over a period of time, and graphically presents these data by frequency. Each bar represents the number of observations that fit within the indicated range. Histograms are useful because they can be used to see the amount of variation in a process. The data in this histogram are the same data as in the run chart in Exhibit 2. Using the histogram, you get a different perspective on the data. You see how often similar values occur and get a quick idea of how the data are distributed.

Pareto Chart

The Pareto chart (Exhibit 4) is a bar chart that presents data prioritized in some fashion, usually either by descending or ascending order of importance. Pareto diagrams are used to show attribute data. Attributes are qualitative data that can be counted for recording and analysis; for example, counting the number of each type of defect. Pareto charts are often used to analyze the most often occurring type of something.

Scatter Diagram/Chart

The scatter diagram (Exhibit 5) is a diagram that plots data points, allowing trends to be observed between one variable and another. The scatter diagram is used to test for possible cause-and-effect relationships. A danger

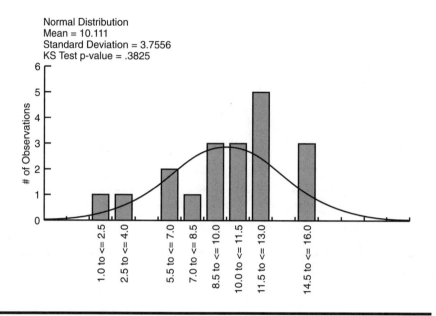

Exhibit 3. Histogram

is that a scatter diagram does not prove the cause-and-effect relationship and can be misused. A common error in statistical analysis is seeing a relationship and concluding cause-and-effect without additional analysis.

Cause-and-Effect/Fishbone Diagram

The cause-and-effect/fishbone diagram (Exhibit 6) is a graphical display of problems and causes. This is a good way to capture team input from a brainstorming meeting, from a set of defect data, or from a check sheet.

Control Chart

The control chart (Exhibit 7) is basically a run chart with upper and lower limits that allows an organization to track process performance variation. Control charts are also called process behavior charts.

Some of you may have reviewed the charts above and said, "Wait a minute! That's not a Pareto diagram; that's a bar chart!" or "That's not a control chart; that's a run chart!" Your organization may call these charts and graphs something totally different. Just make sure you use the right calculations for the charts, know where the data come from, know what the data represent, and how to interpret the charts.

	Number of Defects by Type
Requirements	19
Design	13
Timing	6
Hardware	6
Logic	5
Interface	3
Secuity	3
Data	1

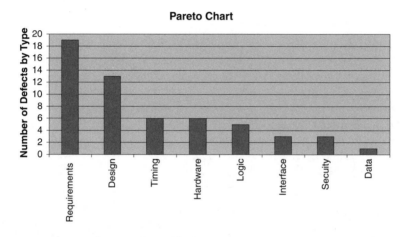

Exhibit 4. Pareto Chart

While some people include the fishbone diagram as a "statistical" tool, others do not because the fishbone does not necessarily focus on quantitative data. We have included it because we often use it during data gathering workshops.

Why are pie charts not listed? Pie charts are the most commonly found charts in organizations, and are used frequently in newspapers and articles across this country. Why are they not included as statistical tools? I believe it is because pie charts simply take counts of data that could be (or actually are) listed in tables, either just by raw count or by percentages, and display these data as parts of the pie. I like pie charts — they are easy to understand. However, I do not believe that they allow the viewer to understand the "voice of the process" better than other types of charts.

These seven graphical displays can be used together or separately to help gather data, accumulate data, and present the data for different functions associated with SPC. For example, I like to use the fishbone diagram when conducting brainstorming sessions with my clients. We select a problem that has occurred in the organization and brainstorm the

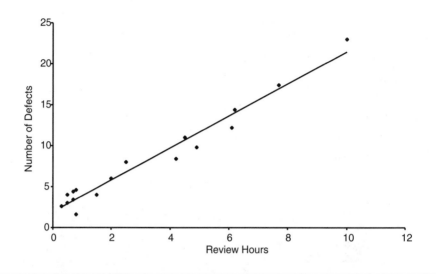

Exhibit 5.   Scatter Diagram/Chart

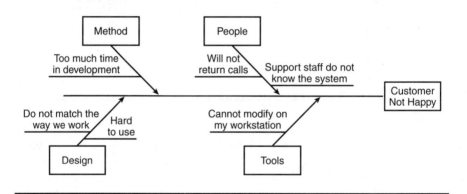

Exhibit 6.   Cause and Effect/Fishbone Diagram

causes and effects of the problem. We then draw a scatter diagram to spot trends in the gathered data. In any event, most people prefer to review data represented pictorially than by data listed in endless tables. While tables can list the values or results found, they cannot show the relationships between the values and between each table, or illustrate areas that are not performing in a statistically predictable way.

Representing and Reporting Data

Charts are based on data. To produce accurate charts, the data must be at the level of detail needed for process control. Those of you operating

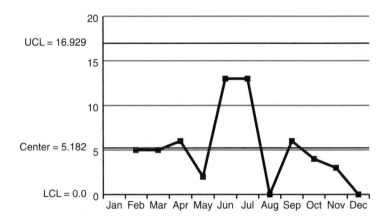

Exhibit 7. Control Chart

in low-maturity organizations (Maturity Levels 1 or 2) will not be able to produce accurate charts. Why not? Because, at your current level of functioning, your processes are not yet stable enough to produce consistently accurate data at the level of detail needed for process control. That is why SPC is not broached in the CMMI® until Maturity Level 4. So do not jump right into producing statistical charts and graphs when initiating a process improvement effort — you are not ready for it — yet.

Data must be consistent. What does that mean? It means that the data were collected at the same time in the process and in the same manner. I once assessed an organization that had proclaimed itself to be a Level 4 organization — that means that they were able to quantitatively predict their quality, productivity, and schedule ability in statistically accurate terms, and manage with the data. The data I found were in no way, shape, or form statistically accurate. Yes, the organization had been collecting data for 15 years. But what did the data say? What did they look like? For the first 14 years, the organization had collected data on all of their projects for "When the Project Started" and "When the Project Ended." That was it. Each project lasted from five to eight years. These data tell you just about nothing. Because the customer had requested an outside, external assessment, the organization for the last (one) year had collected data according to their system development life cycle. So they collected data relating to when each project started the Requirements phase and when each project ended that phase. Then they collected start and end dates for the Design phase, the Construction phase, the Testing phase, and the Implementation/Delivery phase. They mixed all this data in with the previous data from the previous 14 years. This is not an example of consistent data.

Another example of inconsistent data that we run across quite often is that collected from peer reviews. It is a good idea to collect data from peer reviews. If these data are collected during peer reviews for, say, code, these data can be used to show trends in programming errors found that might be solved via increased training in coding techniques or in improving the processes used for eliciting and documenting requirements, and then designing systems. But once again, the data must be consistent. For example, suppose a peer review is done on a program comprising 8000 lines of code, and eight errors are found. Another peer review is done on a program comprising eight lines of code, and six errors are found. The second peer review found fewer errors. Does that mean that the person who coded the second program is a better coder than the person who coded the first program? Of course not. You also need to consider the complexity of the programs, the length of the programs, the type of language, etc. Just collecting data for the sake of collecting data and populating your brand-new database with numbers is not a good enough reason to jumble all of these numbers together.

What questions should you ask yourselves when reviewing the data for your charts? The following seven questions are a start:

1. Who collected these data? (Hopefully the same people who are trained in proper data collection techniques.)
2. How were the data collected? (Hopefully by automated means and at the same part of the process.)
3. When were the data collected? (Hopefully all at the same time on the same day or at the same time in the process — very important for accounting data dealing with month-end or year-end closings.)
4. What do the values presented mean? (Have you changed the process recently? Do these values really tell me what I want or need to know?)
5. How were these values computed from raw inputs? (Have you computed the data to arrive at the results you want, or to accurately depict the true voice of the process?)
6. What formulas were used? (Are they measuring what we need to measure? Are they working? Are they still relevant?)

... and the most important question of all:

7. Are we collecting the right data, and are we collecting the data right? (The data collected should be consistent, and the way data are collected should also be consistent. Do the data contain the correct information for analysis? In our peer review example, this information would be size, complexity, and programming language.)

Much of the data reported to senior management is contained in some sort of report, usually produced and presented monthly. These data are usually aggregated data; that is, data that have been collected from various processes and various parts of the processes. These data are then summarized and combined into percentages of something or other. Do not trust these data. They are just that — data (numbers), not meaningful information. While on the surface these data may seem logical and accurate, they really are not. For example, most financial/budget/cost data are collected at "month-end closing." However, month-end closing within several departments often follows inconsistent processes. Each department follows processes that vary at least somewhat throughout the organization. Each department is collecting different data that measure *their* work and the cost of the work done in *that* department. The "month-end" process therefore varies. It varies in the processes used to collect the data, the data collected, the persons collecting the data, and the time when the books are actually closed and the accounts reconciled. These data from all of the departments are then aggregated and summed, making them look accurate. The point is that the data cannot be used as a basis of any sort of reasonable predictions because they consist of a mixture of apples and oranges. A control chart, based on this aggregated data, would be of no value. If you really wanted to improve your month-end closing process, you would need to chart the process for each individual department and then determine where improvements are needed.

Know your data. Make sure they represent actual activities that occur, and not just counts of how many times something or other happened.

The Tyranny of Control Charts

Every organization I have ever worked for or appraised ends up using control charts. At first, I did not understand why. The reason for my not understanding was because the charts were not generated correctly and the numbers were never explained. It was simply enough to draw pretty pictures that made management happy. One organization I worked for produced 127 control charts. I was called in to help them reduce the number of charts produced. My analysis of the charts revealed one stunning conclusion: although 127 charts were produced, there were really only three charts produced many times over. The charts produced tracked productivity of contractor labor, cost of contractor labor, and CPU uptime versus downtime. The reason so many charts were produced was that some managers wanted them in color; some managers wanted them for the month ending on the 15th of the month; other managers wanted them ending on the 30th of the month; others wanted them produced weekly;

and others wanted them produced monthly and quarterly. But they were basically the same charts! Once this observation was reported to senior management, the lower-level managers were told to only view the charts for data reported at the end of the month, and no more color representations.

Another organization that I appraised did the following "dog and pony show" for the appraisal team. We were given a presentation by the Metrics Team of the metrics and control charts used in this organization. Several members of the Metrics Team stood up, presented their charts on the overhead projector, and then sat down. After the presentations were over, the appraisal team had a chance to ask questions. My team members were silent. They had been suitably impressed by the length and depth of the metrics collection and reporting. The charts were pretty, in color, and seemed sophisticated. I was not impressed. My job was to help my team determine whether the metrics collected were appropriate enough to use to measure the stability and predictability of the processes used in this organization. So I began asking questions of the leader of the Metrics Team. My first question was, "How did you collect the data?" He told me the data were collected using an automated tool. I asked for a demo of the tool. During the demo, I asked, "What data were collected? How was it determined to collect these data? How were the charts used in the organization? What did all the charts show? Where were the data that could back up the information on the charts? What story were the charts really telling?" He could not answer my questions. Instead, he had me talk to the programmer who had coded the program used to collect the data. The programmer could not tell me why the programs used the formulas to collect and calculate data values. He only knew that he was responsible for updating the program. When was the last time he did that? Well, he had been there 12 years and had never updated the program. He told me to talk to the Strategic Planning Manager who was responsible for creating the Master Schedule. So I did. She also could not tell me why these data were selected and what the charts showed. She told me to talk to the Contracting Officer who was in charge of the budget, and billing the clients. She also could not tell me the answers, nor could she explain how the budget was derived or how the billing was calculated. She referred me back to the Strategic Planning Manager. She referred me back to the Metrics Team. Basically, no one in this organization really knew where the data came from, how they were collected, and whether or not they were still relevant. No one had bothered to ask. They were happy producing pretty pictures. No decisions were being made based on these charts.

The two organizations discussed above used control charts to display their data. I soon learned that control charts are a wonderful means of displaying data to use to identify information, *when people understand what the data mean and how to interpret the charts*. So, while I have titled this section The *Tyranny* of Control Charts, that is really a misnomer. We will discuss control charts at length.

Control charts are used to identify process variation over time. All processes vary. The degree of variance, and the causes of the variance, can be determined using control charting techniques. While there are many types of control charts, the ones we have seen the most often are the:

- *c-chart.* This chart uses a constant sample size of attribute data, where the average sample size is greater than five. It is used to chart the number of defects (such as "12" or "15" defects per thousand lines of code). c stands for the number of nonconformities within a constant sample size.

- *u-chart.* This chart uses a variable sample size of attribute data. This chart is used to chart the number of defects in a sample or set of samples (such as "20 out of 50" design flaws were a result of requirements errors). u stands for the number of nonconformities with varying sample sizes.

- *np-chart.* This chart uses a constant sample size of attribute data, usually greater than or equal to 50. This chart is used to chart the number defective in a group. For example, a hardware component might be considered defective, regardless of the total number of defects in it. np stands for the number defective.

- *p-chart.* This chart uses a variable sample size of attribute data, usually greater than or equal to 50. This chart is used to chart the fraction defective found in a group. p stands for the proportion defective.

- *X and mR charts.* These charts use variable data where the sample size is one (1).

- *X-bar and R charts.* These charts use variable data where the sample size is small. They can also be based on a large sample size greater than or equal to ten (10). X-bar stands for the average of the data collected. R stands for the range (distribution) of the data collected.

- *X-bar and s charts.* These charts use variable data where the sample size is large, usually greater than or equal to ten (10).

So, as you can see, you can sometimes use several of the charts, based on type of data and on the size of the sample — and the size of the sample may change. While some folks will quote hard and fast rules for the use of these charts, we have found that organizations often modify when they are used and how they are used, based on the preferences of someone influential in the organization. In any case, when using these charts, look for trends or patterns in the data collected. Try to collect 20 to 25 groups of samples to be statistically correct, although five or six may prove useful in detecting initial trends.

The above definitions use the terms "attribute" data and "variable" data. *Attribute* data are data counted as discrete events or occurrences. For example, Yes/No, Good/Bad, Is/Is Not Defective. These data are usually counts of something. For our purposes, examples are number of CMMI Process Area goals attained, percent of defects found per month, number of trained people on a project team, percent of projects using function points to calculate size. *Variable* data are data that vary and must be measured on a continuous scale. These measurements are usually quantitative measures. Examples are length, time, volume, height, effort expended, memory utilization, and cost of rework.

Control charts help detect and differentiate between *noise* (normal variation of the process) and *signals* (exceptional variation that warrants further investigation). An everyday example of noise in a process is the "white lab coat effect." This effect is what happens when you go to the doctor to get your blood pressure checked. Anyone who has a tendency to high blood pressure will generally become a little nervous during this procedure. Therefore, the blood pressure reading taken by the medical professional (in the white lab coat) has been known to skew higher than if the reading had been taken in the comfortable surroundings of your own home. Another example is for those of us trying to maintain our weight. Even those persons who are successfully maintaining their weight notice fluctuations throughout the month — especially women. By tracking our weight over the period of a year, we will find that the average stays about the same. Unless we start super-sizing our meals and indulging ourselves in ice cream or key lime pie. In fact, if we do indulge ourselves several days (or months) in a row, we know that we will gain weight. That indulgence is therefore a signal to watch our intake of food, exercise more, and do all that other stuff we know we should do.

The Moving Range Control Chart

Which chart should I use? Although others may disagree, we recommend that you use the Average Moving Range (XmR) chart for most situations because:

- It is easy to use.
- It is easy to understand.
- It is easy to implement.
- It is most often the most appropriate for use in an organization.
- It is the most-often found and most-often used chart in high-maturity organizations.

Exhibit 8. Moving Ranges for Calendar Year 2002

Month	Jan	Feb	Mar	Apr	May	Jun	Jul	Aug	Sep	Oct	Nov	Dec
2002	10	15	20	14	12	25	12	12	18	22	25	25
mR Values		5	5	6	2	13	13	0	6	4	3	0

There are automated tools that can support building and displaying these charts. But remember: a tool does not do the thinking for you. It is up to you to collect the data correctly, to collect the correct data, and to interpret the results correctly.

Another suggested reason for using the XmR chart: Do you understand the terms "binomial probability" and "Poisson probability"? Do you know how to verify these probability models? If the answer is "No" or "What kind of language are you speaking?," then stick with the XmR . Life is complicated enough.

The task we need to undertake is to figure out how to tell the difference between noise and signals. Properly generated control charts, specifically the XmR chart, can help us in this task. Past data (historical data) are critical for generating accurate control charts and for correct SPC analyses. To determine whether the results found are normal noise or true signals, comparisons of past data limits must be made, and moving ranges determined. What is a moving range? Variation between successive values. For example, Exhibit 8 shows the count for each month of the year 2002. The mR values (moving range) show the difference between the counts for the various months.

We can then average the moving ranges (Exhibit 9). Add up all of the moving ranges and divide by the number of months differentiated (11), and we come up with 5.18 for our average moving range. The centerline shows the average moving range for Exhibit 8. The upper limit is 16.93.

Moving ranges for calendar year 2001 are shown in Exhibit 10. We then average the moving ranges. Add up all of the moving ranges and divide by the number of months differentiated (11), and we come up with 4.27 for our average moving range. The centerline in Exhibit 11 shows the average moving range for Exhibit 10. The upper limit is 13.96.

Moving ranges for calendar year 2000 are shown in Exhibit 12. We then average the moving ranges. Add up all of the moving ranges and divide by the number of months differentiated (11), and we come up with 2.64 for our average moving range. The centerline in Exhibit 13 shows the average moving range for Exhibit 12. The upper limit is 8.61.

While these charts are clear and easy to understand, they do not tell us enough of the story. To make these charts more relevant, we need to include a corresponding chart for the individual values represented by

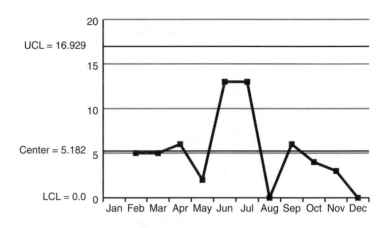

Exhibit 9. 2002 Moving R Chart

Exhibit 10. Moving Ranges for Calendar Year 2001

Month	Jan	Feb	Mar	Apr	May	Jun	Jul	Aug	Sep	Oct	Nov	Dec
2001	10	12	20	18	11	22	15	18	20	22	25	25
mR values		2	8	2	7	11	7	3	2	2	3	3

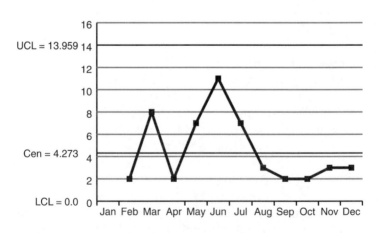

Exhibit 11. 2001 Moving R Chart

the individual months for each year in order to show a correlation or relationship between the values displayed. Are these good numbers or bad numbers? The charts will help us decide.

Exhibit 12. Moving Ranges for Calendar Year 2000

Month	Jan	Feb	Mar	Apr	May	Jun	Jul	Aug	Sep	Oct	Nov	Dec
2000	8	10	12	14	15	18	12	15	18	22	25	25
mR values		2	2	2	1	3	6	3	3	4	3	3

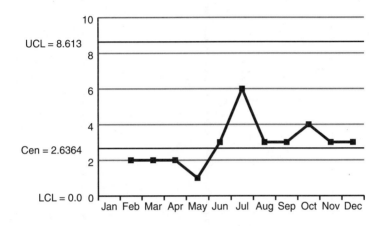

Exhibit 13. 2000 Moving R Chart

Exhibit 14. Individual Values for Calendar Year 2002

Month	Jan	Feb	Mar	Apr	May	Jun	Jul	Aug	Sep	Oct	Nov	Dec
2002	10	15	20	14	12	25	12	12	18	22	25	25
mR values		5	5	6	2	13	13	0	6	4	3	0

The centerline shows the average of the individual values (the sum of the values for the individual months divided by 12). Please review Exhibits 14 through 19.

Using the information in Exhibit 14, we produce the chart shown in Exhibit 15. The centerline is 17.5. The upper limit is 31.28 and the lower limit is 3.72.

Using the information in Exhibit 16, we produce the chart shown in Exhibit 17. The centerline is 18.17. The upper limit is 29.53 and the lower limit is 6.8.

Using the information in Exhibit 18, we produce the chart shown in Exhibit 19. The centerline is 16.17. The upper limit is 23.18 and the lower limit is 9.15.

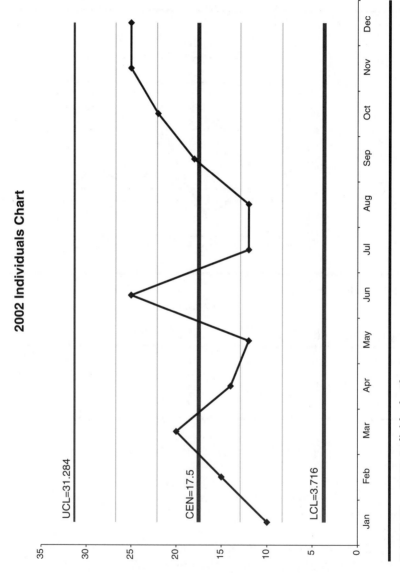

Exhibit 15. 2002 Individuals Chart

Exhibit 16.   Individual Values for Calendar Year 2001

Month	Jan	Feb	Mar	Apr	May	Jun	Jul	Aug	Sep	Oct	Nov	Dec
2001	10	12	20	18	11	22	15	18	20	22	25	25
mR values		2	8	2	7	11	7	3	2	2	3	3

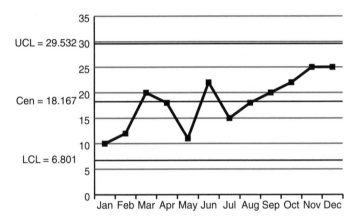

Exhibit 17.   2001 Individuals Chart

Exhibit 18.   Individual Values for Calendar Year 2000

Month	Jan	Feb	Mar	Apr	May	Jun	Jul	Aug	Sep	Oct	Nov	Dec
2000	8	10	12	14	15	18	12	15	18	22	25	25
mR values		2	2	2	1	3	6	3	3	4	3	3

Now we can combine the values for all of the charts for all of the years into two charts: one for Individual Values for all three years (Exhibit 20), and one for the Average Moving Ranges for all three years (Exhibit 21) — and compare the two.

In Exhibit 20, the centerline is 4.66. The upper limit is 15.21. Notice that lower limits are not calculated for Average Moving Range charts. This is because the calculation would result in a negative value and a range cannot be negative.

In Exhibit 21, the centerline is 17.28. The upper limit is 29.67. The lower limit is 4.89. You can clearly see cycles in this chart. The line for December to January shows a precipitous drop that appears to occur

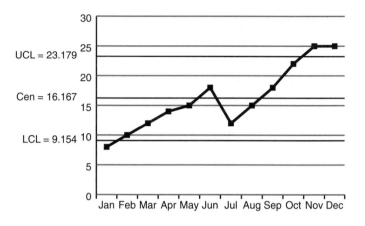

Exhibit 19.   2000 Individuals Chart

every year. The line for February begins a climb back up. The line for March to April goes downward. The line for May goes back up. June and July are down. July to December is up. The chart does not tell us why, but we can clearly see that *something* is happening. We need to investigate that *something* to determine what is going on.

Computing Limits for the XmR Chart

We know that the values for the centerlines for each chart were computed by simply taking the average of the values displayed (i.e., by adding up the values for each month and then dividing by the number of months/values to compute the average). How were the upper and lower limits calculated for the charts shown above? We can calculate the limits for both the X (Individual Values) chart and the Average Moving Range (mR) chart as follows:

- *For the mR (moving range) chart.* The upper range (or upper control limit, or upper natural limit) is computed by multiplying the average moving range (the centerline of the mR chart) by 3.27.
- *For the X chart (individual values chart).* The upper range for the X chart is computed by multiplying the average moving range of the associated chart by 2.66 and then adding the value for the centerline of the X chart. The lower range for the X chart is computed by multiplying the average moving range by 2.66 and then subtracting the value for the centerline of the X chart.

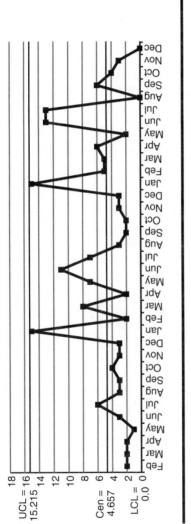

Exhibit 20. Average Moving Ranges for Years 2000, 2001, and 2002

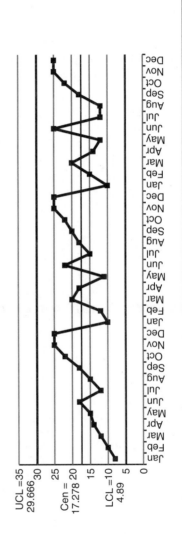

Exhibit 21. Individual Values for Years 2000, 2001, and 2002

Notice that values for both representations (individual values and average moving range values) must be gathered and computed. The upper and lower limits for the individual values chart (X chart) depend on the average variations calculated for the centerline of the average moving range chart. Therefore, these charts are interdependent and can be used to show relationships between the two types of charts and the two types of data.

When you present these charts to management, they may decide that the variation looks a little too big for their comfort. So, they may suggest moving the limits to plus or minus some value. No! The only way to change the limits is to change the process itself. Remember: the charts show the "voice of the process." So, if management desires to improve the limits, they must improve the process. The numbers shown in the charts reflect the results of the process. Our job is to find what caused these results. When analyzing the causes, and adjusting the process, remember that the inputs and outputs of the process may be affected, as well as any other processes that depend on the original process under review. So, focusing on one or two causes will have downstream ramifications and will probably affect parts of your process, as well as other processes.

We have also seen the limits for the XmR charts calculated using median ranges instead of average ranges. The median moving range is often more sensitive to assigned causes when the values used contain some very high range values that inflate the average. Remember that the median range is that range of numbers that hover around the middle of a list sequenced in ascending or descending order: thus, the median range chart will automatically "throw out" the very high- or low-end values. Use of the median moving range approach is valid; however, the formulas (constants) change. The constant value 2.66 changes to 3.14, and the constant value 3.27 changes to 3.87. If you decide to use both methods on your data, you will find some slight differences in the limits, but not much. Try it and see.

Do not panic over computing these numbers. Most of the automated tools out there will do it for you, and draw the charts. While we make no recommendations, the tool we used to generate the charts in this chapter is an add-on to Microsoft Excel.

Hints on How to Read the Charts

The most obvious interpretation is when one or more data points fall outside your control limits (either upper or lower). Those values should be investigated for assignable causes, and the assignable causes should be fixed. If your control chart shows three out of four consecutive points hovering closer to the limits than to the centerline, this pattern may signal a shift or trend, and should be investigated (because predictable processes generally show 85 to 90 percent of the data closer to the centerline than to the limits). Remember: useful limits can be constructed with as few as five or six consecutive values. However, the more data used to compute the limits, the greater the certainty of the results.

Another way to spot trends is to look at the data points along the centerline. If eight or more consecutive data points are clustered on the same side of the centerline, a shift in the original baseline or performance of the process has probably occurred, even without a data point falling outside the limits. This is a signal to be investigated.

Also look for six consecutive points, either increasing or decreasing in value. These points could signal a trend. Other points to notice are 14 points in a row alternating up and down, up and down; or 15 points clustered around the center line, with some of the points immediately above the line, and some immediately below the line.

Notice that we do not say that "this is a problem." We do not know yet. However, we do know that something has happened that needs more focus.

c-CHARTS

While XmR charts are the most often applied in organizations, and are the most appropriate charts to use most often, they are not infallible. Sometimes, an event will occur that "skews the norm;" that is, a rare event way outside of the average has occurred. When this happens, a c-chart is better used. A c-chart is used for rare events that are independent of each other.

The formulas for c-charts are different from XmR charts. First, calculate the average count of the rare occurrence over the total time period that the occurrence happened. That number becomes the centerline. The upper limit is calculated by adding the average count to three times the square root of the average count. The lower limit is calculated by subtracting the average count from three times the square root of the average count.

The question to ask yourself is: "Why am I charting rare events? What do I hope to discover?" Charting the number of times a rare event occurs is pretty useless. However, charting the time periods between recurring rare events can be used to help predict when another rare event will occur. To do this, count the number of times the rare event occurs (usually per day per year) and determine the intervals between the rare events. Convert these numbers into the average moving ranges and, voilà, you can build an XmR chart.

u-CHARTS

The u-chart is based on the assumption that your data are based on a count of discrete events occurring within well-defined, finite regions/areas, and that these events are independent. The u-chart assumes a Poisson process. You may want to consider a u-chart when dealing with defects (counts) within a group of pages (region/area); for example, number of errors per page or the number of defects per 1000 lines of code.

The u-chart differs from the XmR chart in that the upper and lower control limits of the u-chart change over time. The $\bar{u}$ in u-chart is the weighted average of the count ($\bar{u}$ = Σcountj/Σsizej). The upper control limit is calculated by adding $\bar{u}$ to three times the square root of the $\bar{u}$ divided by the last size (sizej). The lower control limit is calculated by subtracting $\bar{u}$ from three times the square root of the $\bar{u}$ divided by the last size (sizej).

Now go back and look at our example of inconsistent data gathered from peer reviews. We said, "Suppose a peer review is done on a program comprising 8000 lines of code, and eight errors are found. Another peer review is done on a program comprising eight lines of code, and six errors are found. The second peer review found fewer errors. Does that mean that the person who coded the second program is a better coder than the person who coded the first program? Of course not. You also need to consider the complexity of the programs, the length of the programs, the type of language, etc." A u-chart is sometimes used for just this example because it takes into consideration the size of the program reviewed by charting the defect density and not just the number of defects. However, we still do not recommend using a u-chart in this case. It is too easy to misinterpret the results, and too easy to use the wrong data to construct the charts.

OK, so if this all sounds too complicated and you do not like the idea of your limits changing with each observation, then just go ahead and use the XmR chart with your count-based data. The XmR chart's behavior will resemble the c-chart and the u-chart because these are special cases of the individual chart.

Summary

Keep it simple. If collecting and analyzing data is difficult, it will not be done. Do not try to chart every metric you have. Start by identifying where the problems are in your organization, and devise metrics to track and monitor your current processes and improvement efforts. Or, you can start with a list of metrics that you currently collect and use, and decide which ones (two or three) might relate to the problems your organization faces.

SPC depends on historical data. It also depends on accurate, consistent process data. If you are just beginning the process improvement journey, do not jump into SPC. You (your data) are not yet ready for it. That is why the CMMI waits until Maturity Level 4 in the staged representation to suggest the application of SPC techniques. At Level 2, processes are still evolving. At Level 3, they are more consistent. Level 4 takes process information from Level 3, and analyzes and structures both the data and their collection. Level 5 takes predictable and unpredictable processes, and improves them.

Do not just show pretty pictures. Know what they mean and where the data come from. Use the information provided in the charts to identify areas of improvement and measure whether improvements are really taking place.

Chapter 19

A High-Maturity Perspective

This chapter discusses several concepts associated with high-maturity organizations and offers some suggestions on how to transition to a high-maturity organization. We define a high-maturity organization as an organization operating at CMMI® Maturity Level 4 or 5 or Capability Level 4 or 5. While there are many high-maturity concepts we could tackle, we focus on those concepts that most people consider confusing.

The most fundamental high-maturity concept is how measurements are handled at high maturity. Measures in this chapter refer to both base measures and derived measures. Base measures are simple values of some attribute of interest; for example, the size of a document in pages, or the effort to produce a document in hours. Derived measures are defined to be a function of two or more base measures. An example of a derived measure is productivity. Productivity is a function of the size of a produced work product divided by the time to produce it (i.e., design document productivity in pages per hour is the number of pages in the document divided by the hours to produce the document).

The high-maturity measurement concepts that we are going to cover are event level measurement, process performance baselines, and process performance models. Event level measures are best used to build process performance baselines. Process performance baselines are used to build process performance models. The process performance baselines and process performance models rely on the predictable and stable processes that we described in Chapter 18, "Statistical Process Control."

Exhibit 1. Example Process Performance Baseline for Productivity for New Development

PPB Elements	Upper Limit	Mean	Lower Limit	Unit of Measure
Requirements Definition	50.8	35	31.6	Hours/Complex Requirement
	29.2	21	15.8	Hours/Nominal Requirement
	13.4	8.6	5.2	Hours/Simple Requirement
Design	81.4	49.8	43.6	Hours/Complex Requirement
	44.4	31.7	21.2	Hours/Nominal Requirement
	19.6	13.3	5.5	Hours/Simple Requirement
Implementation	13.4	8.6	5.4	Hours/Interface
	35.4	17.7	10.3	Hours/Design Page
	6.54	4.31	3.21	Hours/Object
Integration	301.5	153.5	23.5	Hours/Subsystem
	32.5	16.8	7.8	Hours/Component
Systems Test	19.52	12.4	8.3	Hours/Test Scenario

Event Level Measurement

One of the things that people often overlook in high-maturity measurement is the level of detail they want in their measures. Relating measures to events will give them this detail. An *event level measure* is a measure taken at the completion of an event; for example, the definition of a requirement, implementation of an interface, performance of an inspection, or execution of a test. Most organizations initially collect total hours at the phase level, that is, total hours in the Requirements phase, and therefore can only monitor and control at the phase level. This means that only at the end of the requirements phase can they see how they have done. With measures taken at the event level, more detailed monitoring and controlling can be done, and data can be used to manage throughout the phase. One does not have to wait until the end of the phase. One can adjust predictions within a phase at the completion of each event, in some cases, and take corrective actions, as appropriate. In addition, event level measures can be used within different life cycles. For example, the event of defining a requirement is the same within a waterfall life cycle or within most iterative life cycles.

Examples of event level measures are shown in Exhibit 2. The table is divided into three potential objectives that an organization may consider

Exhibit 2. Example Event Level Measures

Objective	Event	Measures
Productivity	Requirement (defined)	Hours, complexity
	Requirement (designed)	Hours, complexity
	Interface Implemented	Hours
	Object Coded	Hours
	Subsystem Integrated	Hours
	Test Scenario Executed	Hours
Product Quality	Design Review (completed)	Defects, pages, hours
	Inspection (completed)	Defects, lines, hours
	Test Scenario Executed	Defects, Hours, Coverage
Schedule	Task Completion	Days (number late or early)

important to meet its business goals. Those objectives are productivity, product quality, and schedule. The second column identifies some potential events of interest; for example, Requirement (defined), which would indicate that an individual requirement was defined. The third column identifies measures that would be collected and identified that relate to the event. In the case of Requirement (defined), the hours for the task and the complexity of the requirement (complex, nominal, or simple) are noted.

Process Performance Baseline

A *process performance baseline* (PPB) documents the historical results achieved by following a process. Once a PPB is developed, it is then used as a benchmark for comparing actual process performance in a project against expected process performance.

Exhibit 1 shows an example of a PPB containing the historical productivity results from executing the process used for new development within an organization. There are PPB elements for each of the five phases that this organization has in its life cycle: Requirements Definition, Design, Implementation, Integration, and Systems Test. Implementation for the example organization includes both the classic code and unit test of a software system, plus implementation of individual non-software components. The first line under Requirements Definition is the number of hours to define a complex requirement. There are elements for complex requirements, nominal requirements, and simple requirements with values for the upper limit, mean, and lower limit for each. The Design PPB elements are based on requirements and follow the same structure. Implementation,

Integration, and Systems Test PPB elements are based on the work products most important to those phases.

In addition to productivity for new development, an organization would want to develop additional PPBs covering other processes, for example, productivity for maintenance. In addition to productivity, other important organizational goals (e.g., product quality and schedule) would be covered in separate PPBs.

This example PPB points out one of the most important issues with using measures, particularly with using measures at higher maturity levels — that is, the need for clear definitions of measures. In this case, what the organization means by a complex requirement, a nominal requirement, and a simple requirement must be clearly defined so that the people collecting the data can tell how to count them. Most organizations start with a working definition and refine the definitions over time. In addition to defining what a requirement is, you also need to define what is included in the number of hours — is it only hours sitting at your desk writing a requirement? Does it include hours for attending status meetings to discuss your work? How do you count time for review of requirements? These are questions that need to be answered in your organization to ensure that the data are collected consistently.

So how do you use a PPB with your projects? New projects could use the example PPB for estimating their effort based on estimates of the number of requirements, number of interfaces, number of design pages, etc. The range of values (upper, mean, and lower) allows the estimators to determine the most likely, worst-case, and best-case estimates of not only productivity, but also the staffing levels that are needed.

We have personally witnessed the positive change in organizations when they have PPBs that people believe. The estimation and planning process becomes much more of a professional activity and less emotional. Project managers armed with PPBs based on historical process performance are less likely to fall victim to unfounded pressure to lower estimates and reduce schedules.

After planning, the PPB can also be used to monitor and control the project's work by comparing the actual number of hours to perform the work against expected range of values for the PPB element. Remember: if the actual number of hours is outside the expected range, it is only meaningful if your process is already stable. Stabilizing your process takes time. Look for the cause but do not overreact. Your process may have a lot of variation, and the tendency early on is to shoot the messenger. If people believe that bad things happen to people when the data are not what is expected, the people will find ways (devious and nefarious ways) to make the data acceptable. This is not what you want.

Process Performance Model

A closely related concept to the PPB is the *process performance model* (PPM). The PPM describes the relationships among attributes of a process and its work products, and is used to estimate or predict a critical value that cannot be measured until later in the project's life — for example, predicting the number of delivered defects or predicting the total effort. Attributes of a *process* include productivity, effort, defects produced, defects detected, and rework. Attributes of a *product* include size, stability, defects contained, response time, and mean time between failures. PPMs are built on historical data and are often built from PPBs. PPMs can be developed for a wide range of project objectives. Example PPMs include reliability models, defect models, and productivity models.

Exhibit 3 shows an example PPM for predicting effort based on both the PPB shown in Exhibit 1 and organization historical effort distribution. The PPB elements at the top of the second column (e.g., Number of Complex Reqs, Number of Design Pages, Number of Components, etc.) come from the Unit of Measure column in Exhibit 1. The Estimated Number of Elements column in Exhibit 3 is derived from project information gathered and from the organization's metrics database. The mean value for each PPB element by phase comes from the Mean column in Exhibit 1. The Historical Effort Distribution on line 12 of Exhibit 3 comes from project actuals stored in the organization's metrics database.

The purpose of the example PPM for effort shown in Exhibit 3 is to predict the total effort for the new development project. This model is designed to predict the total project effort throughout the life cycle, using more and better estimates and data as they become available. The example is divided into the following five sections

PPB Elements (Lines 1 through 10)

For each of the PPB elements the model contains an estimated number of elements and the mean effort in hours for each applicable phase from the example PPB shown in Exhibit 1. For example, line 2 shows that 75 complex requirements are estimated, that the mean number of effort hours in requirements phase for a complex requirement is 35, and that the mean number of effort hours in the design phase for a complex requirement is 49.8. At this time, only the number of complex, nominal, and simple requirement elements have been estimated; therefore, lines 5 through 10 show the remaining estimated number of elements as TBD (to be determined). Later in the project's life cycle, as estimates for these other elements become available, they would be added to the model.

Exhibit 3. Example Process Performance Model for Effort (New Development)

Line Number		Estimated Number of Elements	Req Phase	Design Phase	Implement Phase	Integration Phase	System Test Phase	Total Effort
1	PPB Elements:		Mean	Mean	Mean	Mean	Mean	
2	Number of Complex Reqs	75	35	49.8				
3	Number of Nominal Reqs	100	21	31.7				
4	Number of Simple Reqs	200	8.6	13.3				
5	Number of Interfaces	TBD			8.6			
6	Number of Design Pages	TBD			17.7			
7	Number of Objects	TBD			4.31			
8	Number of Subsystems	TBD				153.5		
9	Number of Components	TBD				16.8		
10	Number of Test Scenarios	TBD					12.4	
11								
12	Historical Effort Distribution (percent)		20	30	20	15	15	100
13								
14	Estimates:							
15	Based on PPB Elements		6445	9565	0	0	0	0
16	Based on Effort Distribution		6445	9668	6445	4834	4834	32,225
17								
18	Actuals by Phase		6752	0	0	0	0	0
19								
20	Prediction Based on Actual When Available or Best Estimate		6752	9565	6445	4834	4834	32,430

Historical Effort Distribution (Line 12)

This shows that, historically, projects have taken 20 percent of total staff effort in the requirements phase, 30 percent in the design phase, 20 percent in the implementation phase, 15 percent in the integration phase, and 15 percent in the Systems Test phase. (We have simplified the effort distribution percentages to make the example easier to follow.)

Estimates

The model has two estimates:

1. The first estimate on line 15 is based on the estimated number of PPB elements that most affect each phase. You can see how this is computed by looking at the value under the requirement phase. This value is computed by multiplying the estimated number of requirements by the mean number of effort hours for that type of requirement:
   - Number of complex reqs × mean effort req phase for complex reqs = 75 × 35 = 2625
   - Number of nominal reqs × mean effort req phase for nominal reqs = 100 × 21 = 2100
   - Number of simple reqs × mean effort req phase for simple reqs = 200 × 8.6 = 1720
   - Summing those three values, we obtain 6445.

   The total estimate based on PPB elements is calculated by summing the value for all phases. (Because only the first two phases are estimated, we do not have a total effort estimate on line 15.)

2. The second estimate on line 16 is based on the requirements phase estimate (6445 from line 15) proportionally propagated across the life cycle. We use the ratio of historical distribution for requirement effort to the historical distribution for effort of the other phases. Using the historical effort distribution from line 12 results in the following values:
   - Design effort = 6445 × (0.30/0.20) = 9668
   - Implementation effort = 6445 × (0.20/0.20) = 6445
   - Integration effort = 6445 × (0.15/0.20) = 4834
   - System test phase effort = 6445 × (0.15/0.20) = 4834
   - Total effort is then the sum of all phases = 32,225

Actuals by Phase (Line 18)

This captures the actual hours per phase. This example is shown at the completion of the Requirements phase where 6752 actual hours were used. No other actuals are yet available.

Prediction Based on Actual When Available or Best Estimate (Line 20)

This is the real purpose of this model. The values on this line are selected from Actuals by Phase (line 18) if available. If Actuals by Phase is not available, then the value from Estimate Based on PPB Element (line 15) is used, if available. Use the Estimate Based on Historical Effort Distribution (line 16) if no other values are available. The prediction is then 32,430, which is the sum of all phases. (Not to be confused with the *Sum of All Fears,* which is a book by Tom Clancy.)

So how do you use a PPM with your projects? You use PPMs to estimate or predict a critical value that cannot be measured until later in the project's life. Our example showed a model to predict total effort throughout the project life cycle. No one really knows what the total effort will be until the project is finished.

We have seen a model similar to our example used to accurately predict total effort. The PPM used came within 5 percent of the total effort following the completion of the Requirements phase. We have also seen models built that successfully predict the number of delivered defects, mean time between failures, and number of system failures during integration testing. The exciting thing about the use of the models is that the focus of project management is on trying to find defects and trying to accurately measure performance, and not on dysfunctional interoffice politics.

Transitioning to Level 4

Level 4, either Capability Level or Maturity Level, is about managing quantitatively. It includes both organizational- and project-level quantitative management. When reading the CMMI, you realize that it is written from the perspective of an organization and its projects executing at a steady state. The Organizational Process Performance process area describes an organization that has in place both the PPBs and PPMs that will be useful to the projects. The Quantitative Project Management process area describes projects that have selected processes that will satisfy the project's objectives, that are executing stable processes, and that are managing process performance to best satisfy the project's quality and process-performance objectives using PPBs and PPMs.

OK, so how do you transition to Level 4? Here are some steps that we recommend. You will most likely need to perform multiple iterations through these steps as you become more experienced and your data become better.

Select Measures that Will be the Basis for Your PPBs and PPMs

An organization needs to develop the PPBs and PPMs that will be used by the projects. These baselines and models are built around what is important to the goals of the organization and the projects. We mentioned in previous chapters that the only goals some organizations have are "to make money." *And so why is this a bad thing, you say?* Well it is not, but we need to decompose that goal into something that the engineering, product development, and support groups can directly contribute to. Identify the critical components and attributes, and identify measures of the standard processes and their work products. Measures related to product quality, cost, and schedule are often your best bet.

In Chapter 17, "A Boatload of Metrics," we identified a list of nearly 200 measurements. We are not advocating that you collect anywhere near that number for your baselines and models, but you can use that list as a resource.

An example of using a single measure to build a PPM occurred in an organization we worked with that was able to do some impressive forecasting work based on only one measurement (the number of defects expected per thousand lines of code based on a similar project). The organization used that single number, its project's rate of defects found, and its project's rate of defects closed over the past four weeks to build an initial prediction model of when it would finish testing. The organization improved the model over the project's life cycle and got real customer buy-in and support. Its simple prediction model allowed the organization to better manage both the project schedule and customer expectations, turning a "problem project" into a "success story." Before you ask, No — we are not saying that this one success story makes the organization Level 4; However, it did create an initial success that the organization was able to build upon and demonstrate the value of Quantitative Management to the organization.

Be sure to select measures that cover the life cycle for the types of projects that you want to quantitatively manage. For example, if you have maintenance projects, do not just measure the new product development life cycle. You might measure the number of problem reports, time to review problem reports, time to implement problem reports, time to test, number of retests, etc.

You need to consider both "breadth and depth." "Breadth" means the measures across the entire life cycle (e.g., cost, schedule, defects, and effort), and "depth" means the details in areas that are critical to your organization (i.e., the number of customer returns by release and the number of subcontractor failures by vendor).

Collect the Measures Identified from the Projects

Often, the most difficult part of measurement is to get good data. Again, do not be disheartened if you find problems with the data. Even if your standard process requires that your projects collect certain metrics, you may find that the data are missing or are incorrect. You may need to "mine the data" — this means dig them up. The data may be in lots of different forms — in paper records, Excel spreadsheets, Word documents, or PowerPoint slides. They may only be in project status reports. They may be in many separate systems in many separate departments — finance, engineering, human resources, etc. Do not be surprised if you need to invest a lot of time and money to uncover old data.

Work with the projects early and often to make the data better. You may decide to take more time to collect new and better data.

Analyze the Data from the Projects

Chapter 18, "Statistical Process Control," shows a number of tools that you can use to analyze the data. In some organizations, this will be the first time anyone outside the project has really looked closely at the data. You are most likely going to find missing, incorrect, or dirty data; and the data are likely to show that not all projects are really following the standard process. Your analysis activities should include the following steps:

1. *Review and fix the data.* Investigate and correct missing data, zeros (for things such as the number of hours to perform a task), and really large or really small numbers.
2. *Look for ways to normalize data across projects.* For example, use "defects by size," not just "defects."
3. *Plot the data.* Use a histogram to see if you have a normal or Poisson distribution. Use a scatter diagram to see any correlations. Use a run chart to view any trends. Use control charts once you find data that show promise.
4. *Investigate the out of control points for their root cause.* It is best to get project team members involved with this analysis because the recorded data are likely to be incomplete. Put corrective actions in place to address the root causes. (This is a good place to use the approach described in the Causal Analysis and Resolution process area.)

Establish Organizational PPBs and PPMs from the Project Data

Calculate the current and predicted process performance and capture that in a PPB. Be sure to establish baselines that cover the life cycle for the types of projects that you want to quantitatively manage. You will most likely want baselines that cover cost, schedule, and product quality. Be sure to identify the profile of the projects used to create the baseline; for example, large development projects using a waterfall life cycle and formal peer reviews, medium development projects using iterative life-cycle and informal peer reviews, or small maintenance projects using quality assurance-led reviews.

From the baselines, produce predictive models that will allow your projects to manage the goals that are important to your organization. You will most likely want models that predict productivity, defect insertion and detection, and schedule.

Derive Project Goals

The steps up until now have been organizational; and while that may be important, we need to remember that, as defined by the CMMI, the projects within the organization produce and deliver the products and services.

Thus, it is important to realize that the project has some goals to satisfy. These often include on-time delivery, implementing all the technical requirements of the project, and staying within cost and schedule. Goals can come from the customers; and goals may also come from your organization — if you are reading this book, it is likely that your organization wants to improve or at least wants to get a rating. Those are organizational goals.

You need to derive the project goals so that you know what to quantitatively manage to get to those goals.

Select Critical Subprocesses to be Managed by the Project

Ensure that you have a set of subprocesses that cover the life cycle (breadth) of the project, and ensure that the critical subprocesses go into enough detail (depth) on the things truly critical to the project.

Select the measures and define what needs to be done to collect and store the measures for the project. OK, here is where you might have a problem if the project goals are not covered as part of your organizational goals. Investigate adding these project goals to the organizational goals, but only if appropriate. Some projects truly are unique. You may need to identify unique measures, baselines, and models to satisfy these project goals. However, we have found that most projects are not truly unique from other projects; therefore, the goals of the projects should have been incorporated into organizational goals.

Select the Process Performance Baselines to be Used by the Project

You need to compare the profile of your project to the profile of projects used to create the baselines, and select a PPB or set of PPBs to use. Here is where you may have another problem if the projects used to create the PPB are nothing like your project. However, do not give up just because things appear different. Here is an example. We were recently working with a large enterprise with multiple groups throughout the United States. This company had been comparing the average number of hours to fix problem reports. It found maintenance data in three separate organizations of widely separated geographic locations, using different processes and separate collection activities. To the company's surprise, the values came back as 12 hours per problem report, 13 hours per problem report, and 15 hours per problem report, respectively. These organizations had not compared notes, yet they came within 20 percent of each other. While you may want much closer ranges, these data proved useful in initial quantitative management of the maintenance projects.

Select the Process Performance Model(s) to be Used by the Project

Having selected the project's goals, measures, subprocesses, and PPBs, you can select the PPMs to use on your project. These may include:

- Schedule and cost models
- Progress models
- Reliability models
- Defect models (defect identification and removal rates, defect removal effectiveness, latent defect estimation)
- Productivity models

You will need to calibrate the models to match your project's performance. For example, your project will have its own defect and identification and removal rates that may be different from what is in the defect model. Be sure you understand the basis of the models before you do any calibration.

Manage the Project Quantitatively

The project can now use the PPBs and PPMs to manage process performance and to work toward achieving the organization's and projects' goals. This work includes:

- Maintaining control charts of the subprocesses and identifying the root cause of out of control points
- Adding the actual performance data to the prediction models
- Taking corrective actions throughout all phases of the project's life cycle to best achieve the project's quality and process performance objectives

Start Early to Level 4

It takes some time for most organizations to collect the kind of data we have shown in the examples. If you do not have this much data, do not become disheartened. One of the things that we have found in working with organizations moving to high maturity is that even a little good data go a long way.

Transitioning to Level 5

The people we work with do not have as much of a problem with the concepts at Level 5 as we have seen with Level 4. However, there are a few points that need to be made with each of the process areas; that is, Organizational Innovation and Deployment (OID) and Causal Analysis and Resolution (CAR).

The OID process area contains a reasonable set of steps for a Level 5 process improvement function in the following seven specific practices as written:

SP1.1: Collect and analyze process- and technology-improvement proposals.

SP1.2: Identify and analyze innovative improvements that could increase the organization's quality and process performance.

SP1.3: Pilot process and technology improvements to select which ones to implement.

SP1.4: Select process- and technology-improvement proposals for deployment across the organization.

SP2.1: Establish and maintain the plans for deploying the selected process and technology improvements.

SP2.2: Manage the deployment of the selected process and technology improvements.

SP2.3: Measure the effects of the deployed process and technology improvements.

A key to the OID process area that does not come out at the specific practice (SP) level is the assumption that the organization's processes are quantitatively managed. This is a key assumption because stable processes and quantitative data are the basis for several of the practices.

Here are some steps that we recommend for implementing OID in your organization.

Create an Organizational Group Responsible for the Collection of Improvement Suggestions for Both Process and Technology

It is critical to the success of OID that you collect improvement proposals from across the organization and that these proposals are handled in a professional way. Establishing a group responsible for reviewing improvement proposals is not an explicit CMMI requirement (the CMMI's OID introductory notes refer to an infrastructure — not a group), but a responsible group is the only way we have seen OID work. People need feedback on their proposals. We go into a lot of organizations where the staff has given up making suggestions because "nobody listens anyway." You also need to make sure the group is not dysfunctional. We worked with one organization in which the primary author of the organization's standard process chaired the committee to review improvement suggestions. He saw all suggestions as a personal attack. The year after he was replaced as committee chair, the organization documented savings of more than $700,000 from implementing process improvement proposals.

Establish a Well-Defined Process for Improvement Proposals

The process or procedures for improvement proposals need to include details on the improvement proposal content, the routing, the analysis, the reviewing, the initial approval of proposals, the feedback, the piloting methods, measurement methods, the review of piloting results, and final approval to roll-out to the organization. The process or procedure should document the formats, the steps, and the authority. It should also identify the metrics to collect on the proposals, for example, number of proposals, how many from each group, time to respond, the number by status, etc. In addition, clear responsibility for independent process reviews and audits needs to be established to ensure that the process is followed.

The analysis of improvement suggestions needs to be based on the data collected as part of the Level 4 activities. Use your PPBs and PPMs to calculate the return on investment of the improvement proposals. To answer your question: no, we do not believe you can do real OID before you do Level 4.

Be sure to estimate a return on investment before running any pilot of the improvement. Update these estimates as the understanding of the improvement increases. Record historical data on all estimates. The pilot procedures and plans need to include evaluation techniques, for example, walkthroughs, prototypes, and human simulations, along with documented methods for measuring savings.

Establish Process Improvement Goals

Your organization should have improvement goals and manage to them. The organization needs to consider establishing three types of strategic process improvement goals:

1. Incremental improvements
2. Innovative improvement
3. Targeted improvements

Incremental improvements are stepwise improvements accomplished by making the current processes and tools a little better. A source of incremental improvement opportunities can be found by analyzing the organization's common defects from reviews and testing and other common causes of variation. The approach described in the Causal Analysis and Resolution process area works well for finding these kinds of improvements. These improvements are often the responsibility of the Process Improvement Group or a special team chartered to find incremental improvements.

Innovative improvements are major leaps in performance accomplished by bringing into the organization a significantly different process or technology. A good place to look for this type of improvement is from an external organization or specialists. These improvements are often the responsibility of a Process Action Team chartered to address a particular area or problem.

Targeted improvements are specific areas that have been identified as problematic. Senior management can establish an area of improvement as an organizational goal. For example, an organizational goal might be to reduce delivered defects by 20 percent. These goals are used to solicit improvement suggestions from across the organization.

The goal derivation, refinement, planning, and retirement process needs to be defined and understood by everyone involved in these activities. Be sure everyone participating is trained in goal derivation and process improvement, including senior management. Consider establishing a process action team(s) to create the process and create a draft set of goals. Use caution in defining the goals so that they do not belittle individuals or disciplines.

Clearly Communicate Process Improvement Activities and Goals to the Staff

Senior management is responsible for clear and positive communication to the staff of the goals, why the goals are important, and their personal commitment to improvement. This can be a very positive activity for the organization, but only when senior management takes the lead and describes the positive reasons for improving the process and technology.

Goals need to be considered part of the project commitment process. Imposing annual organizational goals on ongoing, preexisting projects is a change in requirements that needs to be managed as any other requirements change. Do not let your organization revert to Level 1 behavior by imposing uncommitted requirements on projects.

Remember to communicate "seven times and three ways." The three ways might be the company Web page or newsletter, staff meetings, and "all hands" meetings. We worked with one organization where the goal definition activity was not clearly communicated to the staff, and the rumor mill had decided that senior management was meeting with the project managers and technical leads to plan a massive layoff. The morale was turned around only after the Chief Technical Officer called a special engineering-wide meeting to communicate what was really going on.

The other process area described in Maturity Level 5 is Causal Analysis and Resolution (CAR). This process area is a high-level description of identifying causes of defects and other problems and taking action to prevent them from occurring. The steps identified in the five specific practices are:

SP1.1: Select the defects and other problems for analysis.
SP1.2: Perform causal analysis of selected defects and other problems and propose actions to address them.
SP2.1: Implement the selected action proposals that were developed in causal analysis.
SP2.2: Evaluate the effect of changes on process performance.
SP2.3: Record causal analysis and resolution data for use across the project and organization.

As discussed in Chapter 8, "Understanding Maturity Level 5," you can be doing these CAR activities much sooner than Level 5. However, from a high-maturity perspective, these activities become mandatory for a useful Level 5 implementation and very desirable for a successful Level 4.

When transitioning to Level 4, use the steps described as part of CAR to investigate special causes of variation for their root cause. As previously stated, it is best to get project team members involved with this analysis because the recorded data are likely to be incomplete. Put corrective actions in place across the organization to address the root causes, as appropriate.

At Level 5, use the steps in CAR when looking for incremental improvements. These steps can be the basis to investigate common causes of variation in your standard processes and technology usage, and to establish a plan to remove some of the undesirable common causes.

If you are looking for statistical techniques to use with CAR, consider the run sheet, Pareto chart, and cause and effect diagram from Chapter 18, "Statistical Process Control."

Summary

This chapter has described our perspectives and recommendations on high maturity. The high-maturity approaches described here take time and effort. We have seen the significant success that some organizations have experience with these approaches. We have also seen organizations attempt high-maturity behavior too soon before defining a solid set of organizational processes and working through the change management issues of Level 3. Those organizations have not been successful.

This chapter described both organizational- and project-level high-maturity activities. We have a special word of caution here: be careful that, in your organization, you do not build a wall between the projects and the organization. We have seen some companies where there is such a strong "we — they" approach to quantitative management that it has become dysfunctional. The projects point to the organizational group building the baselines and models and say it is their fault we cannot do QM because they have not given us what we need. And the organizational group points to the projects and says it is their fault because we do not have clean data. Do not let this happen in your organization. Work from the beginning to establish organizationwide cooperation.

Transitioning to high maturity can be overwhelming. When in doubt, an organization should hire outside, expert help. This assistance is offered in the form of classes, mentoring, supervising data collection and reviews, and building models. Of course, as consultants, we support this approach. However, some organizations are loathe to hire consultants. The most important thing to remember about *hiring* consultants is that you can always *fire* consultants if you are not happy with them. So if you need help, get it.

Chapter 20

Closing Thoughts

This chapter discusses the odds and ends that we have either skipped over or not discussed in much detail. The purpose of this chapter is to give you some things to think about, and to offer some final words of what we hope can be construed as wisdom.

Change Management

We have avoided talking about change management in this book. By "change management," we do not mean managing change as discussed in the CMMI® process areas (PAs). The CMMI talks about managing changes to requirements in the Requirements Management PA; about managing systemic changes in Configuration Management; and about managing changes to management plans in Project Planning and in Project Monitoring and Control. That is not the kind of change management we need to discuss.

The type of change management that needs to be addressed is that of changing the culture in your organization. There are many books on this subject, most of which will have you determine what type of organizational paradigm you match (e.g., open, closed, random, synchronous), the type of management style prevalent (e.g., dictator, collaborative, charismatic), and the category of change implementation you prefer (e.g., early adopter versus late adopter). Most of these books are written by social scientists, not by engineers. This is actually a good thing because most engineers prefer a carefully laid-out, step-by-step game plan that addresses technical problems in the organization, not people problems.

And people can be a problem. Just think how much easier it would be to make this process improvement stuff work if you did not have to bother with the people you run into every day in your workplace. Well, that is the same kind of thinking that suggests that systems would be a lot easier to build and deliver if it were not for all of those users out there.

The same holds true for process improvement. Process improvement is all about change. If you do not really want to change, then do not start this journey. Period. The Software Engineering Institute (SEI) has a line that goes, "If the level of discomfort is not high enough, then change will not occur." So, while people might complain about the way things are done, if the way things are done is not totally intolerable, you will have a fight on your hands to implement and institutionalize the changes that come with process improvement — because people hate change.

How can you overcome this resistance to change? Well, there are several approaches, but most boil down into two methods:

1. Force change (the hammer principle).
2. Reward change (the dangling carrot principle, using benefits and bonuses).

The first method, called the hammer technique, is where the head honcho in your place of work (the president, the CEO, your boss) says, "Either we get that level or you lose your job." Anyone found not following the newly written procedures (even if the procedures do not fit the organization) is punished. This technique, while draconian, has been known to work.

The second method, where change is rewarded, is where the organization comes up with awards, bonuses, promotions, positive attention, and proof that the new way of doing things creates a better work environment in which the person doing the work has more control over his day-to-day duties. This approach has also been known to work.

Wait a minute! Do both approaches work? Of course. As you will find with most anything in process improvement, every time you ask a question, the answer begins with, "It depends." While some of the people responding might be trying to give you a snow job, "it depends" is often the best answer. So what does "it depend" on?

■ The size of your organization
■ The culture
■ The budget
■ The type of work
■ The history of introducing and accepting new ideas
■ The type of people

- Personalities and egos
- Politics
- Consistent approach and commitment
- And many more issues

So, take into consideration the type of place in which you work, and tailor and customize your process improvement efforts to it. And then start over again, because you will be wrong. Expect missteps and stumbling blocks. There is no true step-by-step approach that works brilliantly each and every time. We have tried to summarize best practices that we have seen applied effectively in organizations with which we have worked. So take these lessons learned and try them on for size. As with anything you try on, you may need to go up or down a size, and maybe the color is not quite right for you. But at least it is a start.

If we had to pick one overall initial stumbling block that we have run into, it is that some people see their world through rose-colored glasses or prefer living in denial, to wit, "there are no problems in my organization/project." Well, guess what? It is called process *improvement.* If there are no problems, if everything is perfect, then you do not need to improve. But because you have already decided (or someone has decided for you) to do process improvement (probably for the mandated rating for business contract awards), then you will have to change. To prove it, do an appraisal using the CMMI as the reference model. That first appraisal is always an eye-opener. When you match your organization's practices against the CMMI practices, you will find that there are gaps. Those gaps can be considered *problems,* or *areas of improvement.* Start there.

It is great to talk about the need for change and accepting that change is part of process improvement. But how do we get from here to there?

This brings us to Dr. Phil. At the time that this book was written, Dr. Phil McGraw is an absolute phenomenon in the United States. Dr. Phil currently hosts his own television show, which, among other things, is about change. Now, Dr. Phil concentrates on changing people's personal lives; that is, losing weight, overcoming past slights, and becoming a better person overall. While we like Dr. Phil's no-nonsense approach (which seems to be what attracts most people to his show, as well as his folksy humor and country-boy ways of turning a phrase), we sometimes disagree with him on his solutions for problem resolution.

Dr. Phil makes no bones about the fact that he is not offering psychological counseling for the long term. He offers people what he calls "a wake-up call." This wake-up call is supposed to change your life, and apparently in most cases it does. However, he did one show in which he offered solutions. In this case, we do not think he really accomplished what he set out to do.

On this particular show, Dr. Phil interviewed a woman who was upset over her young daughter's weight. The mother, intending to motivate her daughter to lose weight, would call her daughter names such as fat and stupid. Did this inspire her daughter to lose weight? Of course not. Did the mother know she was not really helping? Yes. The reason the mother went on the show was for help in stopping her diatribes against her daughter, and for help in replacing her (the mother's) bad habits with good, new ones.

What did Dr. Phil do? He said he gave her *steps* to help. He basically had her review the tape to see how she was hurting her daughter and destroying any positive self-image the girl might have once had. The mother then said, "I know what I am doing is wrong, but I can't stop. What should I do?" Dr. Phil responded by asking if she had not heard him correctly. Did watching the tape and hearing the discussion between Dr. Phil, the mother, and the daughter not give her any insights?

Well, we guess it did for her, but we felt cheated. We did not hear any sequenced steps of how to change her behavior. We would have liked something like the following (and we are no psychologists — this is just an example):

- Take a deep breath, and let it out slowly when you feel like criticizing.
- Look at your daughter and try to see her as the beautiful, young girl she is.
- Tell her something nice, something that you like about her.
- If you cannot think of anything, lie. Come up with something. Use your imagination.

What does this have to do with process improvement? Everything.

What this woman had learned from her short time with Dr. Phil was the *process* of her actions. What she wanted was *procedures* detailing what to do, when, and how. If you want change to occur in your organization, you must not only give wake-up calls, but also follow through with instructions that support the changes needed.

Rewards and Punishment

Sociological and psychological studies have been done that conclude that the best way to ensure long-lasting change is through positive — not negative — reinforcement. To that end, your organization needs to devise a new reward system. Instead of rewarding the person who always stays late when a new system is going into production or is to be shipped to the customer, why not ask yourself, "Why is this person staying late? Is he incompetent? Does he purposely wait to start his duties until the last minute? Does he enjoy the attention he gets from 'saving the show'? Did he do anything to obstruct the system going in more smoothly that necessitated his staying late? Did he not plan his work correctly? Did I not plan the work correctly? Did we not adequately staff this job?" The point is that the reward system must change. Reward people for doing their jobs right the first time, not for acting like saviors and pulling all-nighters. Our motto is "Dare to Be Dull." Or another way to think of it is "No Surprises."

One of the best "rewards" to demonstrate to process improvement novices, and to your organization as a whole, is the WIFM effect; that is, What's In It For Me? If you can tie process improvement activities to potential benefits that people in your organization can realize and respond to, then more people will be able to overcome their fear of change and be co-opted into the process improvement challenge.

It is naïve to think that only positive reinforcement will promote process improvement. It would be wonderful if your organization hired only truly altruistic people who will put everyone else's needs and desires above their own so that process improvement can occur, the organization can get their ratings, business contracts will ensue, and everyone will live happily ever after in fairyland.

It does not happen that way. Yes, you should be open to changing your very hard-written procedures if they do not work. They will always need modification. However, if people are not following the procedures, and not contributing to improving them, then these people need to have what we have heard called a "come to Jesus meeting" with senior management and be told to "get with the program."

People need a way to clearly communicate when the procedures are not working. A well-managed improvement proposal process serves two primary purposes: (1) to capture real problems with the processes and procedures; and (2) it gives people a way to complain. Face it; change is difficult. We have worked with a lot of people that just need to voice their complaints and then they get on with the work. Do not overlook this human need to have their voices heard and to feel as if they are part of the process of process improvement.

Management Commitment

We were once at a conference where Watts Humphrey (who many people consider to be the father of process improvement using the CMM) was the featured speaker. At the end of his lecture, he asked for questions.

One brave soul stood up and launched into a dissertation about the lack of support his organization was getting from senior management. Senior management expected the organization to achieve a certain level rating by a specific date, yet they had not adequately staffed and funded the effort. Whenever there was a problem in production, the process improvement people were told to return to their old jobs and do "real work." Basically, there was no management commitment to this effort. The poor soul then asked Watts Humphrey, "What should I do?" Humphrey responded by saying, "Quit."

When we heard this response, we were furious. This poor man had bared his soul to the assembled crowd and was desperate for a plan of attack that would yield positive results and, quite probably, help him keep his job. And all he had received was a terse, one-word answer — "Quit." How arrogant of Watts Humphrey to respond in such an unhelpful manner.

Well, after thinking about it for awhile (and being placed in similar situations many times), we cannot help but agree. True management commitment is absolutely necessary. How can you measure true commitment? Easy — put your money where your mouth is. That is, ask your management and your sponsors the following questions:

- Have you given us enough time to do this?
- Have you given us enough money in the budget to do this?
- Have you given us enough people to do this?
- Have you given us the right people to do this?
- Have you given us authority to act, not just made us responsible?
- Have you really developed a vision of what the true problems are?
- Have you really developed a vision of what you want this organization to do?
- Have you made this effort *the* priority in your organization?
- Do you really understand what process improvement is and how it will affect everyone — including management — in the organization?
- Do you realize that *you* have to change, not just your people?
- Do you realize that *your* work will be scrutinized, as well as that of your lower-level managers?

If the answers are yes, then maybe you have a chance. One of the things that we have learned over the years is that an organization takes on the behavior characteristics of its leaders. We have seen this at all levels in the organization. If management will not change, then the organization cannot change. End of discussion.

Quality Assurance Is the Key

An independent and objective quality assurance (QA) department is the key to implementing and institutionalizing change management and process improvement. By independent and objective, we mean that the people performing the QA activities are not under undue influence to just let things slide. They also have a reporting chain that is separate from the managers and individuals whose work they are reviewing. Job performance and evaluation of QA personnel should also be independent of individuals associated with the work being reviewed.

This battle for establishing a separate QA office is one of our most frequent. Organizations simply do not want to budget for staff that does not *directly* contribute to building the product. Smaller organizations have difficulty budgeting for this duty, and those organizations that cannot shift the cost onto the customer also stall this effort. Some organizations decide that they will have the programmers from one team perform QA reviews on the work of programmers from another team. While this sounds OK at first, it often does not work out that way. Why not? Because people start making deals: "If you pass my stuff, I'll pass yours." Also, most of these people have not been trained in QA, do not understand what QA is really about, and do not realize the importance of QA activities. They would rather be programming, building, or testing things.

Let us talk about human nature. Most of us try to do a good job. But, when we know that someone will be looking at and reviewing what we do, and how we do it, we tend to pay a little more attention to the details, and maybe try a little bit harder to make sure everything works right. QA also enforces following procedures, and notifies the process group and management when the procedures do not work. Most organizations are under a lot of schedule pressure. Schedule often gets attention because it is easy to see; that is, the date is here and the product did not ship. Quality is more difficult to see.

Another advantage of having independent, objective QA staff is when things go wrong, or are about to go wrong. If your procedures say that the product cannot be delivered until certain defects have been fixed, and the tests show that these defects have not been fixed, QA can step in and notify/argue with senior management and delay shipment. If shipment is not delayed, QA can at least make sure that senior management signs off on the shipment with the understanding of all the defects and their ramifications. So, when customers receive products that do not work as expected, finger-pointing back to the "worker bees" can be reduced. (There are reasons why shipping a defective product may be a good idea and a wise executive decision, but we do not go into that here.)

In previous chapters, we discussed metrics and data collection. QA is a great place to report metrics that measure how things are working or not working in the projects, and then have QA report their findings to management. So, if one project manager tells senior management that this project is "on track," QA can dispute that by showing the milestones missed and expected project delays. QA can also report the metrics that track the results of peer reviews and testing that demonstrate the quality of the product (or lack thereof). The metrics collected as part of the normal QA activities cited in the Product and Process Assurance process area of the CMMI can be used to accurately measure progress and quality, and should be reported as part of management reviews.

A last point on QA. You need to staff QA with enough qualified people to get the work done. We have seen a lot of organizations that go through the motions and create a QA group out of the people that "can't do real work." And of course this approach fails. QA needs to be staffed by professionals that will be respected across the organization for their contributions. And the QA staff needs to be large enough to do the work. For most organizations, we recommend at least 5 percent of the development and maintenance budget be allocated to QA staffing and activities.

Summary

Process improvement and change go hand-in-hand. You cannot have one without the other. Everyone must change, including technicians, practitioners, management, quality assurance, engineers, process improvement personnel, and even users and customers. Change is painful. If the pain of how you currently do your job is not high enough, then you probably will not change the way you do your job.

We do not usually tell jokes, and most people do not understand our jokes, but we are reminded of one. It is the old joke about changing light bulbs. Question: How many psychiatrists does it take to change a light bulb? Answer: One. But the light bulb has to *really want* to change. The same goes for process improvement.

If you are not really going to do process improvement, burn this book. Good luck on your journey.

Appendix A

Comparison of CBA IPIs to SCEs to SCAMPI

There are different types of assessment techniques currently in use, including:

1. Software Capability Evaluations (SCEs, pronounced "skis")
2. CMM-Based Appraisals for Internal Process Improvement (CBA IPIs)
3. Standard CMMI® Assessment Method for Process Improvement (SCAMPI)

We discuss each in turn.

Introduction

There are three families of SCEs:

1. Acquisition
2. Contract Monitoring/Process Monitoring
3. Internal Evaluations

compared to only one type of CBA IPI:

1. Internal Process Improvement (IPI)

283

An Acquisition SCE can be used by the organization to evaluate the capabilities of vendors vying for contracts; a Contract Monitoring SCE can be used to monitor the performance of vendors or in-house units performing contracts; a Process Monitoring SCE can be used to baseline current performance, and then later to measure progress against that baseline; and an Internal Evaluation can be used to baseline practices internal to an organization, begin internal process improvement activities, and measure progress. This last usage of the SCE maps to the functionality provided by the CBA IPI, and corresponds to the Diagnosing phase of the IDEAL^{SM} model.

Historically, SCEs were first designed only for Acquisition SCEs, that is, for an organization or company to assess the capability of vendors vying for contracts to determine the risk associated with awarding the contract to the proposed vendors. This single application is no longer the case. SCEs are now used by organizations for software process improvement (*a la* CBA IPIs), as well as for acquisitions and contract monitoring. SCEs were originally designed to be applied against any of the existing CMMs, notably CMM for Software and Software Acquisition CMM.

Training

Some organizations will choose to do CBA IPIs because they think they are saving money on training. During a CBA IPI, a Lead Assessor may only train his team in the fundamentals of the CMM (approximately three days), the basic steps in the CBA IPI (approximately two to four days), and then conducts the CBA IPI (on from three to eight projects — this is tailorable). A team that has only been trained by the Lead Assessor may only be exposed to only the viewpoint and interpretation of that Lead Assessor. If they choose to go on and become Lead Assessors, no matter how many times they have done CBA IPIs and completed the training for that CBA IPI, they *must* attend the Introduction to the CMM class conducted by an SEI authorized vendor before beginning Lead Assessor training.

Previously for SCEs, the student needed to take the Introduction to the CMM from an SEI authorized vendor before SCE training. To qualify for the SCE training, the student must (in addition to having taken the CMM class) have had *at least*:

■ Seven (7) years of increasingly responsible software development experience (spread out among systems analysis, coding, testing, configuration management, quality assurance, systems programming, database administration and analysis, for example)

- Three (3) years of project management experience (costing, budgeting, tracking, scheduling)
- Two (2) years of acquisition experience (for federal acquisition/procurement SCEs only)

The 7–3–2 is no longer mandatory to receive the training. Neither is the authorized CMM course. However, those prerequisites are highly recommended for any individual planning to participate on an SCE as an SCE team member. When the student passes the Introduction to the CMM course, he receives an SEI certificate that entitles him to continue pursuing other SEI-authorized courses. This Introduction class is basically the prerequisite to other SEI courses. The student then takes the SCE course. The student does not have to repeat the two courses again to participate in more SCEs. By taking the courses before performing on the SCE team, he also receives the benefit of being instructed by several people who may have different interpretations of the CMM. The CMM is *not* prescriptive — it is open to interpretation.

Conduct

Both SCEs and IPIs are conducted by a "Lead" — either a Lead Evaluator (SCEs) or a Lead Assessor (IPIs). This lead must have participated in at least two previous SCEs (for the evaluator) or two previous IPIs (for the assessor) to qualify for training. (SCEs cannot be substituted for IPIs — IPIs cannot be substituted for SCEs.) The training is mandatory and can only be conducted by the SEI.

The SCE is then led by the SEI-authorized Lead Evaluator. The SCE may or may not include members of the organization on the team, depending on the type of SCE and depending on whether financial remuneration or contract award will be based on the outcome. For an internal evaluation, the team *must* include members internal to the organization under review.

The IPI is led by an SEI-authorized Lead Assessor. The Lead Assessor, as part of the method, *must* train the members of the team (even if they have already participated on an IPI). The team *must* consist of members of that organization being assessed.

Similarities and Differences

Both SCEs and IPIs seek to understand how an organization operates compared to the CMM. Both look for strengths, weaknesses, and consistency across the organization by reviewing project activities. Both can be used for software process improvement. Both conduct site visits and review existing documentation. Both can result in developing Action Plans (not for Acquisition SCEs. Action Planning is left to the vendor awarded the contract). For maturity level ratings, both assess organizations. Both methods have a trained leader, either an SEI-authorized Lead Assessor or an SEI-authorized Lead Evaluator.

Previously, SCEs only evaluated three to five projects in a five-day on-site visit, while CBA IPIs usually looked at four to eight projects in a five- to ten-day on-site period. Now, for SCEs, both the number of projects and the time spent on site are tailorable to the organization's needs. The two prevailing misconceptions about SCEs are that they are only used for acquisitions, not improvement activities, and that they only look at three projects within a five-day limitation.

One other difference does exist, depending on the type of SCE (SCE family). If the SCE is done with financial incentives as a possible result of the rating (such as award fees), or if it is an Acquisition SCE, members of the evaluated organization cannot participate on the SCE team (conflict of interest may apply and predispose the actions and results of the team). However, for improvement activities (the third SCE family listed), members of the organization are allowed to be part of the team, and are an essential part of the team.

The final difference is a big one. SCE results are protestable in a court of law. Big bucks are involved with contract awards based on SCE results. Therefore, because the SCE team may be sued, most SCEs are held to rigorous standards. The rigor of the SCE method is not tailorable, depending on the SCE family invoked. That is, the Internal SCE is conducted as rigorously as the Acquisition SCE. A side-by-side comparison is given in Exhibit 1.

SCAMPI and CMMI

The SEI has generated a new model — the CMMI — and a new appraisal methodology — SCAMPI. The SCAMPI method now incorporates a number of the principles of the SCE as documented in the SCE Method Description for SCE version 3.0. SCAMPI can be used for assessments on both the staged and continuous representations of the CMMI. SCAMPI is an appraisal method for organizations that want to evaluate their own or another organization's processes using the CMMI as their reference model. SCAMPI consists of a structured set of team activities that include conducting interviews, reviewing documents, receiving and giving presentations, and analyzing surveys and questionnaires. SCAMPI results are ratings

Exhibit 1. Comparison of SCEs to CBA IPIs

	Software Capability Evaluation	*CMM-Based Appraisal for Internal Process Improvement*
Basic use	Internal Process Improvement Contract Monitoring Acquisitions SCEs can be done throughout the enterprise by an external team	Internal Process Improvement CBA IPIs must have participation from each organization for it to be used; one organization may not assess a different organization without participation
Led By	SEI Certified Lead Evaluator	SEI Certified Lead Assessor
Basic participants	One SCE Lead Evaluator Two external evaluators Two internal evaluators or One SCE Lead Evaluator Four external evaluators This is tailorable, based on the type of SCE to be performed; the SEI has now mandated at least four people on a SCE team	One Lead Assessor Six internal participants Number of team members is tailorable; however, IPI teams are generally larger than SCE teams
Training	Each participant *must* receive SEI authorized CMM and SCE training prior to the evaluation This training is required only once; it does not have to be repeated for each SCE, unless a new member is added to the team; then only that team member needs to receive the training	Each participant usually receives IPI training each time an assessment is performed as part of team training led by the Lead Assessor The CMM course need not be the SEI authorized course; any Lead Assessor must receive the SEI authorized CMM course
Approximate cost	$30,000 – $75,000	$50,000 – $200,000

and findings of strengths, weaknesses, and improvement activities using the CMMI. What are these results used for? The results are used to award contracts and to baseline processes for process improvement. Results are based on how the organization satisfies the goals for each process area. Several projects, several process areas, and several maturity levels (and possibly several capability levels) are investigated. So, the steps in the SCAMPI are basically:

- Documentation is gathered and reviewed.
- Interviews are conducted.
- Deficiencies are discovered and documented.
- Findings are presented.

And the primary components of a SCAMPI are:

- Planning and preparing for the appraisal
- Collecting and consolidating data, both before and during the appraisal
- Making judgments
- Determining ratings
- Reporting results

There are three types of appraisals: Class A (SCAMPI), B, and C. Each class is distinguished by its degree of rigor. SCAMPI is discussed in greater detail in Chapter 11.

Appendix B

Myths and Legends of the CMMI®

These myths and legends have been gathered from the marketing of the CMMI, user perceptions, organizational implementations of the model, appraisals, public statements made during conferences, and conflicting statements in the CMMI itself. The authors of this book do not make any claims as to these arguments. We believe readers should be able to make up their own minds.

1. CMM® Maturity Level 2 is the same as CMMI Maturity Level 2.

Because several of the process areas are named the same, uninitiated users feel that the two models are not significantly different. We disagree. For example, Requirements Management under the CMM only included requirements as they related to building your software. So while you may have had some systemwide requirements, the only responsibility you had toward them was to use them as the basis for initially deriving software-related requirements. You did not have to ensure that the higher-level requirements had been met. Now, Requirements Management under the CMMI includes *all* requirements — from the systems engineering people, the hardware people, the software people, and any other requirements that need to be met. Thus, the scope has been greatly expanded. In addition, a few more process areas have been added. For example, Measurement and Analysis is now its own process area, and includes not only metrics to collect, but describes different activities recommended/ required to be instituted. Most smaller organizations and less-mature organizations have indicated that this is a good process area but far too difficult to implement at Level 2. So with the increased scope of the model including the various disciplines (systems engineering, supplier sourcing, etc.), plus the additional process areas, the two models and the two levels are dissimilar.

2. The process areas and practices for Levels 4 and 5 do not significantly raise the bar, as higher maturity organizations helped devise this model.

Reports from appraisals done by the Ministry of Defence in Australia have specifically reported that the CMMI has made achieving Levels 4 and 5 much more difficult. Whereas in the previous CMM for Software, the recommendation was to "keep it simple," now the implementation of these areas requires much more training and quantitative measurement techniques to be instituted in the organization. Responses heard at industry conferences have also mentioned that the CMMI focuses too heavily on sophisticated measurement techniques.

3. Transitioning from the CMM to the CMMI will be a trivial effort.

Not if you read and understand points 1 and 2 above. There are also more procedures and training to be done, due to the additional process areas included in the model, and more people and groups to get involved. A presentation at the 2002 European SEPG Conference in Amsterdam described one organization's attempt to transition from the Systems Engineering Maturity Model, which they had been using for two to three years, to the CMMI. They described their struggle as "significant."

4. The continuous representation allows you to select fewer process areas to institutionalize.

Well, sort of. Yes, you can de-select process areas. But it does not really save an organization much in time, effort, and cost because the process areas are so interrelated and interdependent that you will soon discover that you must back up and include more and more process areas (or at least several of the practices contained within the process areas) to be successful. For example, in the continuous representation, how can you attempt Validation, or Verification, or practically any other process area, without also tackling to some extent Project Planning, Project Monitoring and Control, and Product and Process Quality Assurance? Do you not need to plan, track, and ensure the quality of your product or process? And the generic goals and generic practices seem to enforce that you do so. So where do you go for guidance in structuring this effort? To those process areas that directly relate to them. So, those of you thinking of selecting the continuous representation so that you can select only a few process areas for improvement may be disappointed.

5. There are fewer procedures to write in the CMMI than in the CMM.

Ha ha! Big laugh there. The CMM specifically called out the term "according to a documented procedure." However, those of you who have done process improvement have noticed that, just because the CMM did not specifically call out the use of a procedure, one was often required to enlighten staff as to *how* to perform a function, and *how* to perform that function consistently within a project or across many projects. The phrase "according to a documented procedure" is rarely, if ever, used in the CMMI. However, if you read what constitutes a "plan" in the CMMI, you will find that it includes a process description. So, just because the CMMI does not specifically reference the term "procedures," it does not mean that there do not need to be any. We also have found that most of the procedures an organization writes relate to how to implement the practices and subpractices within the process areas. Well, just looking at the CMMI demonstrates that there are an awful lot of process areas and practices included. So you better get cracking on those procedures.

6. CMMI is not prescriptive.

The CMMI consists of many process areas. Those process areas are so interrelated as to make them mandatory. While tailoring of the model is discussed in the body of the CMMI (with tailoring meaning "tailoring out" a process or practice), the resulting instructions or information describing tailoring options tend to disparage the tailoring out of anything. We feel that the process areas listed and their accompanying practices basically attempt to provide the steps that *must* be taken to achieve a level, or to be successful in improving your organization's process capability.

Where the model is not prescriptive is in the details describing the practices. This omission is unfortunate, as that is the area where more guidance is necessary but cannot really be found. Appraisal teams have reported that during SCAMPIs, it was difficult to not ask "Yes/No" questions when trying to ascertain whether a practice had been implemented and how it had been implemented. And when more guidance was needed to understand the practice, there was none.

7. CMMI is based on the best practices and lessons learned reported from usage of the CMM.

At the 2002 SEPG Conference in Phoenix, Arizona, this question was specifically asked of three of the authors of the original CMM for Software. Their presentation was about what they would have included in the CMM, based on what they now know many years later, having assessed or assisted in many implementations in many organizations. The question posed was based on their discussion: were any of these lessons learned included in the CMMI? Their response was a moment of silence and then a reference to Organizational Innovation and Deployment (OID at Level 5). Although the CMMI purports to include the improvements devised under CMM version 2.0, that statement was also heatedly discussed during the same conference in a later presentation. (Buttons were handed out at this presentation that said, "Free version 2.0.") As a contributor to CMM version 2.0, one of the authors of this book does not see much of a resemblance.

8. CMMI was the result of overwhelming demand across the industry.

While there were some requests that we personally knew about (from DoD aerospace contractors), most organizations were busy using the CMM for Software, with a lesser number of organizations implementing the Systems Engineering Maturity Model. However, some organizations wishing to expand the sphere of influence of the CMM for Software to a more enterprisewide application simply took the word "software" out of the CMM, and used the CMM across their enterprise. After all, the CMM was touted as being based on project management principles that could be expanded to include almost any type of project. Several presentations from organizations at the 2002 European SEPG Conference in Amsterdam described their efforts tailoring the CMM for more than software tasks, and these organizations seemed to have been quite effective in this deployment. While there may have been a DoD mandate for the generation of this model and the integration of all existing models, we know of no large outpouring of grief that an integrated model had not been created.

And is the CMMI really one integrated model? Well, if you can select the disciplines, and you can divide it up into systems engineering, software engineering, IPPD, and supplier sourcing, then — no. While the areas are interrelated, they are not really integrated into one seamless model.

9. CMMI supports organizational business objectives.

One of the exercises in the official CMMI class is to count the number of times the words "business objectives" appear in the model. So, apparently the thinking is that by simply repeating the words over and over, then it must be so. (The answer, by the way, is over 40 times.) We think it depends on what your organization's business objectives actually are. Are they to save money? Well, maybe the CMMI will help and maybe not. Do you have the resources and funds to dedicate to process improvement using the CMMI? Do you have problems in your organization that can benefit from providing structure and documenting your processes? Maybe — maybe not. It all depends on your organization. And no, the CMMI — like the CMM — is *not* for every organization. We cannot find statistics that detail the number of organizations that begin this journey and then drop out. We can only find data on organizations that have achieved a level rating and been awarded contracts. How many of you have worked in organizations that needed to achieve Level 3 for contract awards, and once it was achieved, those organizations dropped out of the program? We know of several organizations like that. We also know of many organizations that drop out during the road to Level 2. There are many reasons, from not having the budget to not having enough people, to not having the right people, to being driven by time-to-market, to not being able to support the time it takes to institute this path. Also, it takes a somewhat mature organization to actually have achievable business objectives that can be used to map to the CMMI. Most organizations simply say that their business objective is Level 3 for contract awards so they can make money.

10. CMMI leads to consistent assessment results and ratings.

The SCAMPI method using the CMMI has the same problems as the previous assessment methods using the CMM — that is, the make-up of the team members and their individual experiences will flavor their interpretations of the model and their interpretations of the implementation of the model in the assessed organization. As discussed previously, SCAMPI teams are having trouble interpreting the practices. They refer to the explanations in the practices in the model and come up lacking. So, most teams have reported simply using their own experiences to interpret the meaning of the practices. While we do not want a book that mandates how to improve our organization, we still need more information on what the details mean. Without this guidance, we see no guarantee that this model supports more consistent results and ratings than the previous model. In fact, with the lack of explanations and examples, we see this model leading to even more inconsistent results.

Appendix C

Implementation/ Operations Plan Template

The following template can be used to structure your process improvement efforts. See Chapter 15 for more information.

1.0 Set Up
    1.1   SCAMPI Results
    1.2   Areas of Focus
    1.3   EPG Structure
    1.4   Process Action Team (PAT) Structure
    1.5   Configuration Control Boards
    1.6   Quality Assurance
    1.7   Schedule
    1.8   Tools
    1.9   Risks
    1.10 Reviews and Approvals

2.0 Design Phase
    2.1   Generate PAT Charter
    2.2   Review, modify, and approve charter
    2.3   Generate Action Plan
    2.4   Review, modify, and approve plan
    2.5   Assign work per Action Plan
    2.6   Do the work (policies, procedures, standards)

2.7 Develop metrics and measurement techniques

2.8 Develop required training material

2.9 Track status

2.10 Review/recommend tools

2.11 Facilitate, review, and monitor work

2.12 Update Action Plans

2.13 Attend meetings/support EPG

3.0 Pilot Phase

3.1 Select pilot projects

3.2 Document success criteria and measurement techniques

3.3 Orient and train project members in CMMI concepts

3.4 Orient and train members in processes and procedures

3.5 Perform the pilots

3.6 Monitor the pilots

3.7 Analyze results from the pilots

3.8 Measure success

3.9 Provide lessons learned

3.10 Update procedures and OSSP as needed

4.0 Implementation Phase

4.1 Select one or more true projects

4.2 Document success criteria and measurement techniques

4.3 Orient and train project members in CMMI® concepts

4.4 Orient and train members in procedures

4.5 Assist in implementation as needed

4.6 Monitor and measure success

4.7 Provide lessons learned

4.8 Update procedures and OSSP as needed

4.9 Implement across more projects as needed

4.10 Sign off completion of PATs

5.0. Control and Monitoring

Appendix D

Sample Action Plan Template

This template can be used to help you write measurable action plans. See Chapter 15 for more information.

Executive Overview

1. Objective/Scope
   1.1 Problem Statement
   1.2 Vision After Success
   1.3 Goal Statement
2. Entry Criteria
   2.1 Management Sponsor(s)
3. Major Inputs
   3.1 Relevant Assessment Information (Results/Deficiencies)
   3.2 Relevant Existing Work
       (Projects/Tasks/Pilots/PA Improvements and Results)
4. Summary of Approach
   4.1 Steps/Tasks for PA (Based on Practices)
   4.2 Short-Term Scenario (Schedule for Implementation)
5. Major Outputs
6. Exit Criteria

Detailed Plan

7. Programmatic Issues
   7.1 Constraints/Limitations
   7.2 Assumptions/Dependencies
   7.3 Risks
   7.4 Alternatives
8. Schedule
   8.1 Steps
   8.2 Process Improvement Project (PERT/GANTT)
9. Required Resources
   9.1 People (Who/How much of their time)
   9.2 Training
   9.3 Computer/Technological Resources
   9.4 Other

Management of Plan

10. Reviews
    10.1 Peer Reviews
    10.2 Management Reviews
    10.3 Other Reviews
    10.4 Measurement Criteria
11. "Roll Out"/Implementation/Training Plan

Appendix E

Sample CMMI® Compliance Matrix

The following table can be used to plan and track completion of artifacts and implementation associated with CMMI® process area practices and goals. See Chapter 15 for more information.

No.	Practice or Activity	Associated Procedure/Document	Assigned To	Date Due	Date Reviewed	Status
	Process Area: RM					
	Process Area: GG2 Institutionalize a Managed Process					
1	GP2.1 (CO1): Establish an organizational policy	Policy			03/02/02	Approved
2	GP2.2 (AB1): Plan the process	Plan Process description Schedule Estimates			03/02/02	Complete
3	GP2.3 (AB2): Provide resources	See Plan				Complete
4	GP2.4 (AB3): Assign responsibility	See Plan				Complete
5	GP2.5 (AB4): Train people	See Plan and training materials				In progress
6	GP2.6 (DI1): Manage configurations	TBD				In progress
7	GP2.7 (DI2): Identify and involve relevant stakeholders	See Implementation Plan				Complete
8	GP2.8 (DI3): Monitor and control the process	TBD				Deferred
9	GP2.9 (VE1): Objectively evaluate adherence	Procedure PI5 Procedure PI7				Complete
10	GP2.10 (VE2): Review status with higher-level management	Procedure PI6				Complete

Process Area: SG1: Manage Requirements

11	SP1.1: Obtain an understanding of requirements	Procedure RM1		EPG review
12	SP1.2: Obtain commitment to requirements	Procedure RM2		EPG review
13	SP1.3: Manage requirements changes	Procedure RM3, RM4 Procedure CM4		Pending
14	SP1.4: Maintain bidirectional traceability of requirements	Procedure RM4		Rejected
15	SP1.5: Identify inconsistencies between project work and requirements	Procedure RM5		Pending

Appendix F

Sample CMM®
Compliance Matrix

The following table can be used to plan and track completion of artifacts and implementation associated with CMM® process area practices and goals. See Chapter 15 for more information.

No.	Process Area	CMM Reference	Document	Assigned To	Date Due/Reviewed	Status
1	Infrastructure		SPI Plan			
2	Infrastructure		Implementation Plan			
3	Infrastructure		Organization's Standard Software Process (OSSP)			
4	Infrastructure		SEPG Charter			
5	Infrastructure		SEPG Presentation Template			
6	Infrastructure		Procedure Template			
7	Infrastructure		Training Packet Guidelines for Pilots			
8	Requirements Management		RM Charter			
9	Requirements Management		RM Action Plan			
10	Requirements Management		RM WBS			
11	Requirements Management		RM Schedule			
12	Requirements Management	CO1, AB1, AB3, AB4	Policy for managing system requirements allocated to software: includes establishing responsibility, providing adequate resources and required RM training			
13	Requirements Management	AB2, AC1	Procedure for Requirements Specification and Review			

14	Requirements Management	AB2, AC2	Procedure for completing Requirements Traceability Matrix (RTM); includes use as basis for SDP and work products						
15	Requirements Management	AC3	Procedure for SRS and RTM changes						
16	Requirements Management	ME1	Procedure for RM metrics						
17	Requirements Management	VE1, VE2	Procedure for Project and Senior Management reviews						
18	Software Project Planning		SPP Charter						
19	Software Project Planning		SPP Action Plan						
20	Software Project Planning		SPP WBS						
21	Software Project Planning		SPP Schedule						
22	Software Project Planning		SPP Process Overview Document						
23	Software Project Planning	Com-1	Software PM designated in Policy for SDP and commitments						
24	Software Project Planning	Com-2	Policy for planning a software project						
25	Software Project Planning	Abil-1	Statement of Work for each software project						

No.	Process Area	CMM Reference	Document	Assigned To	Date Due/ Reviewed	Status
26	Software Project Planning	Act-6	Procedure for developing a Software Development Plan			
27	Software Project Planning	Act-7	Software Development Plan for each software project (*Note:* may be contained in several "documents" of different names)			
28	Software Project Planning	Act-9	Procedure for estimating size of software work products			
29	Software Project Planning	Act-10	Procedure for estimating effort and cost for the software project			
30	Software Project Planning	Act-11	Procedure for estimating critical computer resources			
31	Software Project Planning	Act-12	Procedure for deriving software project schedule			
32	Software Project Planning	Act-13	Risk identification and assessment document for each software project			
33	Software Project Planning	Act-14	Plans for software facilities and tools for each software project			
34	Software Project Planning	Act-15	Estimates and basis for estimates data is recorded for each software project			
35	Software Project Planning	ME1	Measurements are made to determine status of software planning activities (rationale for measurements and how to collect and analyze them)			

| 36 | Software Project Planning | VE1 VE2 | The activities of SW project planning are reviewed with Senior Management and Project Management — procedures for both | | |
| 37 | Software Project Planning | VE3 | SQA audit of PP Activities — procedures for quality reviews — may be found in SQA KPA | | |

Appendix G

Checklist for the Staged Representation of the CMMI®

This checklist displays the specific goals and specific practices for each process area. For process improvement efforts, this checklist can be used to document whether procedures have been written for a practice, what stage the documentation is in, and who is responsible. For appraisals, the appraisal team can use this checklist to determine whether the practices have been institutionalized in order to achieve the goals for each process area. Feel free to add columns or rows to insert comments, tasks, status indicators, subpractices, artifacts, or anything else you feel will help structure and track your efforts.

The process areas are arranged by Maturity Levels 2 through 5. We list the Specific Goals and Specific Practices for each process area first. Rather than list the Generic Goals and Generic Practices for each process area immediately after that process area, we list all of the Generic Goals and their associated Generic Practices at the end of this appendix. Remember: generic goals and generic practices must be satisfied for each process area for each level, as well as the specific goals and specific practices for that process area. The differences in the wording of the practices between the staged representation and the continuous representation are also displayed.

See the appropriate chapters for more information, especially the planning and tracking chapters.

Maturity Level 2

Requirements Management

The purpose of Requirements Management is to manage the requirements of the project's products and product components, and to identify inconsistencies between those requirements and the project's plans and work products.

Specific Practices by Specific Goal:

SG1 Manage Requirements
Requirements are managed and inconsistencies with project plans and work products are identified.
SP1.1 Obtain an Understanding of Requirements
Develop an understanding with the requirements providers on the meaning of the requirements.
SP1.2 Obtain Commitment to Requirements
Obtain commitment to the requirements from the project participants.
SP1.3 Manage Requirements Changes
Manage changes to the requirements as they evolve during the project.
SP1.4 Maintain Bidirectional Traceability of Requirements
Maintain bidirectional traceability among the requirements and the project plans and work products.
SP1.5 Identify Inconsistencies between Project Work and Requirements
Identify inconsistencies between the project plans and work products and the requirements.

Project Planning

The purpose of Project Planning is to establish and maintain plans that define project activities.

Specific Practices by Specific Goal:

SG1 Establish Estimates
Estimates of project planning parameters are established and maintained.

SP1.1   Estimate the Scope of the Project
Establish a top-level work breakdown structure (WBS) to estimate the scope of the project.

SP1.2   Establish Estimates of Work Product and Task Attributes
Establish and maintain estimates of the attributes of the work products and tasks.

SP1.3   Define Project Life Cycle
Define the project life-cycle phases upon which to scope the planning effort.

SP1.4   Determine Estimates of Effort and Cost
Estimate the project effort and cost for the work products and tasks based on estimation rationale.

SG2   Develop a Project Plan
A project plan is established and maintained as the basis for managing the project.

SP2.1   Establish the Budget and Schedule
Establish and maintain the project's budget and schedule.

SP2.2   Identify Project Risks
Identify and analyze project risks.

SP2.3   Plan for Data Management
Plan for the management of project data.

SP2.4   Plan for Project Resources
Plan for necessary resources to perform the project.

SP2.5   Plan for Needed Knowledge and Skills
Plan for knowledge and skills needed to perform the project.

SP2.6   Plan Stakeholder Involvement
Plan the involvement of identified stakeholders.

SP2.7   Establish the Project Plan
Establish and maintain the overall project plan content.

SG3   Obtain Commitment to the Plan
Commitments to the project plan are established and maintained.

SP3.1   Review Plans that Affect the Project
Review all plans that affect the project to understand project commitments.

SP3.2   Reconcile Work and Resource Levels
Reconcile the project plan to reflect available and estimated resources.

SP3.3   Obtain Plan Commitment
Obtain commitment from relevant stakeholders responsible for performing and supporting plan execution.

Project Monitoring and Control

The purpose of Project Monitoring and Control is to provide an understanding of the project's progress so that appropriate corrective actions can be taken when the project's performance deviates significantly from the plan.

Specific Practices by Specific Goal:

SG1   Monitor Project against Plan
       Actual performance and progress of the project are monitored against the project plan.
       SP1.1   Monitor Project Planning Parameters
                Monitor the actual values of the project planning parameters against the project plan.
       SP1.2   Monitor Commitments
                Monitor commitments against those identified in the project plan.
       SP1.3   Monitor Project Risks
                Monitor risks against those identified in the project plan.
       SP1.4   Monitor Data Management
                Monitor the management of project data against the project plan.
       SP1.5   Monitor Stakeholder Involvement
                Monitor stakeholder involvement against the project plan.
       SP1.6   Conduct Progress Reviews
                Periodically review the project's progress, performance, and issues.
       SP1.7   Conduct Milestone Reviews
                Review the accomplishments and results of the project at selected project milestones.

SG2   Manage Corrective Action to Closure
       Corrective actions are managed to closure when the project's performance or results deviate significantly from the plan.
       SP2.1   Analyze Issues
                Collect and analyze the issues and determine the corrective actions necessary to address the issues.
       SP2.2   Take Corrective Action
                Take corrective action on identified issues.
       SP2.3   Manage Corrective Action
                Manage corrective actions to closure.

Supplier Agreement Management

The purpose of Supplier Agreement Management is to manage the acquisition of products from suppliers for which there exists a formal agreement.

Specific Practices by Specific Goal:

SG1 Establish Supplier Agreements
Agreements with the suppliers are established and maintained.
SP1.1 Determine Acquisition Type
Determine the type of acquisition for each product or product component to be acquired.
SP1.2 Select Suppliers
Select suppliers based on an evaluation of their ability to meet the specified requirements and established criteria.
SP1.3 Establish Supplier Agreements
Establish and maintain formal agreements with the supplier.

SG2 Satisfy Supplier Agreements
Agreements with the suppliers are satisfied by both the project and the supplier.
SP2.1 Review COTS Products
Review candidate COTS products to ensure they satisfy the specified requirements that are covered under a supplier agreement.
SP2.2 Execute the Supplier Agreement
Perform activities with the supplier as specified in the supplier agreement.
SP2.3 Accept the Acquired Product
Ensure that the supplier agreement is satisfied before accepting the acquired product.
SP2.4 Transition Products
Transition the acquired products from the supplier to the project.

Measurement and Analysis

The purpose of Measurement and Analysis is to develop and sustain a measurement capability that is used to support management information needs.

Specific Practices by Specific Goal:

SG1 Align Measurement and Analysis Activities
Measurement objectives and activities are aligned with identified information needs and objectives.

SP1.1 Establish Measurement Objectives
Establish and maintain measurement objectives that are derived from identified information needs and objectives.

SP1.2 Specify Measures
Specify measures to address the measurement objectives.

SP1.3 Specify Data Collection and Storage Procedures
Specify how measurement data will be obtained and stored.

SP1.4 Specify Analysis Procedures
Specify how measurement data will be analyzed and reported.

SG2 Provide Measurement Results
Measurement results that address identified information needs and objectives are provided.

SP2.1 Collect Measurement Data
Obtain specified measurement data.

SP2.2 Analyze Measurement Data
Analyze and interpret measurement data.

SP2.3 Store Data and Results
Manage and store measurement data, measurement specifications, and analysis results.

SP2.4 Communicate Results
Report results of measurement and analysis activities to all relevant stakeholders.

Process and Product Quality Assurance

The purpose of Process and Product Quality Assurance is to provide staff and management with objective insight into processes and associated work products.

Specific Practices by Specific Goal:

SG1 Objectively Evaluate Processes and Work Products
Adherence of the performed process and associated work products and services to applicable process descriptions, standards, and procedures is objectively evaluated.

SP1.1 Objectively Evaluate Processes
Objectively evaluate the designated performed processes against the applicable process descriptions, standards, and procedures.

SP1.2 Objectively Evaluate Work Products and Services
Objectively evaluate the designated work products and services against the applicable process descriptions, standards, and procedures.

SG2 Provide Objective Insight
Noncompliance issues are objectively tracked and communicated, and resolution is ensured.

SP2.1 Communicate and Ensure Resolution of Noncompliance Issues
Communicate quality issues and ensure resolution of noncompliance issues with the staff and managers.

SP2.2 Establish Records
Establish and maintain records of the quality assurance activities.

Configuration Management

The purpose of Configuration Management is to establish and maintain the integrity of work products using configuration identification, configuration control, configuration status accounting, and configuration audits.

Specific Practices by Specific Goal:

SG1 Establish Baselines
Baselines of identified work products are established.

SP1.1 Identify Configuration Items
Identify the configuration items, components, and related work products that will be placed under configuration management.

SP1.2 Establish a Configuration Management System
Establish and maintain a configuration management and change management system for controlling work products.

SP1.3 Create or Release Baselines
Create or release baselines for internal use and for delivery to the customer.

SG2 Track and Control Changes
Changes to the work products under configuration management are tracked and controlled.

SP2.1   Track Change Requests
         Track change requests for the configuration items.
SP2.2   Control Configuration Items
         Control changes to the configuration items.

SG3   Establish Integrity
       Integrity of baselines is established and maintained.
       SP3.1   Establish Configuration Management Records
                Establish and maintain records describing configuration items.
       SP3.2   Perform Configuration Audits
                Perform configuration audits to maintain integrity of the configuration baselines.

Requirements Development

The purpose of Requirements Development is to produce and analyze customer, product, and product-component requirements.

Specific Practices by Specific Goal:

SG1   Develop Customer Requirements
       Stakeholder needs, expectations, constraints, and interfaces are collected and translated into customer requirements.
       SP1.1   Elicit Needs
                Elicit stakeholder needs, expectations, constraints, and interfaces for all phases of the product life cycle.

> The following specific practice appears in the continuous representation as SP1.1-1, but is subsumed in the staged representation by SP1.1, Elicit Needs. The specific practice is presented here in gray only as informative material.
>
> SP1.1-1 Collect Stakeholder Needs
>   Identify and collect stakeholder needs, expectations, constraints, and interfaces for all phases of the product life cycle.

       SP1.2   Develop the Customer Requirements
                Transform stakeholder needs, expectations, constraints, and interfaces into customer requirements.

SG2   Develop Product Requirements
Customer requirements are refined and elaborated to develop product and product-component requirements.

SP2.1   Establish Product and Product-Component Requirements
Establish and maintain product and product-component requirements, which are based on the customer requirements.

SP2.2   Allocate Product-Component Requirements
Allocate the requirements for each product component.

SP2.3   Identify Interface Requirements
Identify interface requirements.

SG3   Analyze and Validate Requirements
The requirements are analyzed and validated, and a definition of required functionality is developed.

SP3.1   Establish Operational Concepts and Scenarios
Establish and maintain operational concepts and associated scenarios.

SP3.2   Establish a Definition of Required Functionality
Establish and maintain a definition of required functionality.

SP3.3   Analyze Requirements
Analyze requirements to ensure that they are necessary and sufficient.

SP3.4   Analyze Requirements to Achieve Balance
Analyze requirements to balance stakeholder needs and constraints.

SP3.5   Validate Requirements with Comprehensive Methods
Validate requirements to ensure the resulting product will perform as intended in the user's environment using multiple techniques as appropriate.

The following specific practice appears in the continuous representation as SP3.5-1, but is subsumed in the staged representation by SP3.5, Validate Requirements with Comprehensive Methods. The specific practice is presented here in gray only as informative material.

SP3.5-1 Validate Requirements
Validate requirements to ensure the resulting product will perform appropriately in its intended-use environment.

Technical Solution

The purpose of Technical Solution is to design, develop, and implement solutions to requirements. Solutions, designs, and implementations encompass products, product components, and product-related life-cycle processes either singly or in combinations, as appropriate.

Specific Practices by Specific Goal:

SG1   Select Product-Component Solutions
       Product or product-component solutions are selected from alternative solutions.
       SP1.1   Develop Detailed Alternative Solutions and Selection Criteria
                Develop detailed alternative solutions and selection criteria.

> The following specific practice appears in the continuous representation as SP1.1-1, but is subsumed in the staged representation by SP1.1, Develop Detailed Alternative Solutions and Selection Criteria. The specific practice is presented here in gray only as informative material.
>
> SP1.1-1 Develop Alternative Solutions and Selection Criteria
> Develop alternative solutions and selection criteria.

       SP1.2   Evolve Operational Concepts and Scenarios
                Evolve the operational concept, scenarios, and environments to describe the conditions, operating modes, and operating states specific to each product component.
       SP1.3   Select Product-Component Solutions
                Select the product-component solutions that best satisfy the criteria established.

SG2   Develop the Design
       Product or product-component designs are developed.
       SP2.1   Design the Product or Product Component
                Develop a design for the product or product component.
       SP2.2   Establish a Technical Data Package
                Establish and maintain a technical data package.
       SP2.3   Design Interfaces Using Criteria
                Design comprehensive product-component interfaces in terms of established and maintained criteria.

The following specific practice appears in the continuous representation as SP2.3-1, but is subsumed in the staged representation by SP2.3, Design Interfaces Using Criteria. The specific practice is presented here in gray only as informative material.

SP2.3-1 Establish Interface Descriptions
Establish and maintain the solution for product-component interfaces.

SP2.4 Perform Make, Buy, or Reuse Analyses
Evaluate whether the product components should be developed, purchased, or reused based on established criteria.

SG3 Implement the Product Design
Product components and associated support documentation are implemented from their designs.
SP3.1 Implement the Design
Implement the designs of the product components.
SP3.2 Develop Product Support Documentation
Develop and maintain the end-use documentation.

Product Integration

The purpose of Product Integration is to assemble the product from the product components, ensure that the product, as integrated, functions properly, and deliver the product.

Specific Practices by Specific Goal:

SG1 Prepare for Product Integration
Preparation for product integration is conducted.
SP1.1 Determine Integration Sequence
Determine the product-component integration sequence.
SP1.2 Establish the Product Integration Environment
Establish and maintain the environment needed to support the integration of the product components.
SP1.3 Establish Product Integration Procedures and Criteria
Establish and maintain procedures and criteria for integration of the product components.

SG2   Ensure Interface Compatibility
The product-component interfaces, both internal and external, are compatible.
> SP2.1   Review Interface Descriptions for Completeness
> Review interface descriptions for coverage and completeness.
>
> SP2.2   Manage Interfaces
> Manage internal and external interface definitions, designs, and changes for products and product components.

SG3   Assemble Product Components and Deliver the Product
Verified product components are assembled and the integrated, verified, and validated product is delivered.
> SP3.1   Confirm Readiness of Product Components for Integration
> Confirm, prior to assembly, that each product component required to assemble the product has been properly identified, functions according to its description, and that the product-component interfaces comply with the interface descriptions.
>
> SP3.2   Assemble Product Components
> Assemble product components according to the product integration sequence and available procedures.
>
> SP3.3   Evaluate Assembled Product Components
> Evaluate assembled product components for interface compatibility.
>
> SP3.4   Package and Deliver the Product or Product Component
> Package the assembled product or product component and deliver it to the appropriate customer.

Verification

The purpose of Verification is to ensure that selected work products meet their specified requirements.

Specific Practices by Specific Goal:

SG1   Prepare for Verification
Preparation for verification is conducted.
> SP1.1   Select Work Products for Verification
> Select the work products to be verified and the verification methods that will be used for each.

SP1.2   Establish the Verification Environment
Establish and maintain the environment needed to support verification.

SP1.3   Establish Verification Procedures and Criteria
Establish and maintain verification procedures and criteria for the selected work products.

SG2   Perform Peer Reviews
Peer reviews are performed on selected work products.
SP2.1   Prepare for Peer Reviews
Prepare for peer reviews of selected work products.
SP2.2   Conduct Peer Reviews
Conduct peer reviews on selected work products and identify issues resulting from the peer review.
SP2.3   Analyze Peer Review Data
Analyze data about preparation, conduct, and results of the peer reviews.

SG3   Verify Selected Work Products
Selected work products are verified against their specified requirements.
SP3.1   Perform Verification
Perform verification on the selected work products.
SP3.2   Analyze Verification Results and Identify Corrective Action
Analyze the results of all verification activities and identify corrective action.

Validation

The purpose of Validation is to demonstrate that a product or product component fulfills its intended use when placed in its intended environment.

Specific Practices by Specific Goal:

SG1   Prepare for Validation
Preparation for validation is conducted.
SP1.1   Select Products for Validation
Select products and product components to be validated and the validation methods that will be used for each.

SP1.2   Establish the Validation Environment
         Establish and maintain the environment needed to support
         validation.
SP1.3   Establish Validation Procedures and Criteria
         Establish and maintain procedures and criteria for valida-
         tion.

SG2   Validate Product or Product Components
       The product or product components are validated to ensure that
       they are suitable for use in their intended operating environment.
SP2.1   Perform Validation
         Perform validation on the selected products and product
         components.
SP2.2   Analyze Validation Results
         Analyze the results of the validation activities and identify
         issues.

Organizational Process Focus

The purpose of Organizational Process Focus is to plan and implement
organizational process improvement based on a thorough understanding
of the current strengths and weaknesses of the organization's processes
and process assets.

Specific Practices by Specific Goal:

SG1   Determine Process-Improvement Opportunities
       Strengths, weaknesses, and improvement opportunities for the
       organization's processes are identified periodically and as needed.
SP1.1   Establish Organizational Process Needs
         Establish and maintain the description of the process needs
         and objectives for the organization.
SP1.2   Appraise the Organization's Processes
         Appraise the processes of the organization periodically
         and as needed to maintain an understanding of their
         strengths and weaknesses.
SP1.3   Identify the Organization's Process Improvements
         Identify improvements to the organization's processes and
         process assets.

SG2   Plan and Implement Process-Improvement Activities
Improvements are planned and implemented, organizational process assets are deployed, and process-related experiences are incorporated into the organizational process assets.

    SP2.1   Establish Process Action Plans
Establish and maintain process action plans to address improvements to the organization's processes and process assets.

    SP2.2   Implement Process Action Plans
Implement process action plans across the organization.

    SP2.3   Deploy Organizational Process Assets
Deploy organizational process assets across the organization.

    SP2.4   Incorporate Process-Related Experiences into the Organizational Process Assets
Incorporate process-related work products, measures, and improvement information derived from planning and performing the process into the organizational process assets.

Organizational Process Definition

The purpose of Organizational Process Definition is to establish and maintain a usable set of organizational process assets.

Specific Practices by Specific Goal:

SG1   Establish Organizational Process Assets
A set of organizational process assets is established and maintained.

    SP1.1   Establish Standard Processes
Establish and maintain the organization's set of standard processes.

    SP1.2   Establish Life-Cycle Model Descriptions
Establish and maintain descriptions of the life-cycle models approved for use in the organization.

    SP1.3   Establish Tailoring Criteria and Guidelines
Establish and maintain the tailoring criteria and guidelines for the organization's set of standard processes.

    SP1.4   Establish the Organization's Measurement Repository
Establish and maintain the organization's measurement repository.

SP1.5   Establish the Organization's Process Asset Library
         Establish and maintain the organization's process asset
         library.

Organizational Training

The purpose of Organizational Training is to develop the skills and knowledge of people so they can perform their roles effectively and efficiently.

Specific Practices by Specific Goal:

SG1   Establish an Organizational Training Capability
       A training capability that supports the organization's management
       and technical roles is established and maintained.
       SP1.1   Establish the Strategic Training Needs
                Establish and maintain the strategic training needs of the
                organization.
       SP1.2   Determine Which Training Needs Are the Responsibility
                of the Organization
                Determine which training needs are the responsibility of
                the organization and which will be left to the individual
                project or support group.
       SP1.3   Establish an Organizational Training Tactical Plan
                Establish and maintain an organizational training tactical
                plan.
       SP1.4   Establish Training Capability
                Establish and maintain training capability to address orga-
                nizational training needs.

SG2   Provide Necessary Training
       Training necessary for individuals to perform their roles effectively
       is provided.
       SP2.1   Deliver Training
                Deliver the training following the organizational training
                tactical plan.
       SP2.2   Establish Training Records
                Establish and maintain records of the organizational training.
       SP2.3   Assess Training Effectiveness
                Assess the effectiveness of the organization's training pro-
                gram.

Integrated Project Management for IPPD

The purpose of Integrated Project Management is to establish and manage the project and the involvement of the relevant stakeholders according to an integrated and defined process that is tailored from the organization's set of standard processes.

For Integrated Product and Process Development, Integrated Project Management also covers the establishment of a shared vision for the project and a team structure for integrated teams that will carry out the objectives of the project.

Specific Practices by Specific Goal:

SG1   Use the Project's Defined Process
      The project is conducted using a defined process that is tailored from the organization's set of standard processes.

      SP1.1   Establish the Project's Defined Process
          Establish and maintain the project's defined process.

      SP1.2   Use Organizational Process Assets for Planning Project Activities
          Use the organizational process assets and measurement repository for estimating and planning the project's activities.

      SP1.3   Integrate Plans
          Integrate the project plan and the other plans that affect the project to describe the project's defined process.

      SP1.4   Manage the Project Using the Integrated Plans
          Manage the project using the project plan, the other plans that affect the project, and the project's defined process.

      SP1.5   Contribute to the Organizational Process Assets
          Contribute work products, measures, and documented experiences to the organizational process assets.

SG2   Coordinate and Collaborate with Relevant Stakeholders
      Coordination and collaboration of the project with relevant stakeholders is conducted.

      SP2.1   Manage Stakeholder Involvement
          Manage the involvement of the relevant stakeholders in the project.

      SP2.2   Manage Dependencies
          Participate with relevant stakeholders to identify, negotiate, and track critical dependencies.

      SP2.3   Resolve Coordination Issues
          Resolve issues with relevant stakeholders.

SG3   Use the Project's Shared Vision for IPPD
       The project is conducted using the project's shared vision.
       SP3.1   Define Project's Shared-Vision Context
                Identify expectations, constraints, interfaces, and opera-
                tional conditions applicable to the project's shared vision.
       SP3.2   Establish the Project's Shared Vision
                Establish and maintain a shared vision for the project.

SG4   Organize Integrated Teams for IPPD
       The integrated teams needed to execute the project are identified,
       defined, structured, and tasked.
       SP4.1   Determine Integrated Team Structure for the Project
                Determine the integrated team structure that will best meet
                the project objectives and constraints.
       SP4.2   Develop a Preliminary Distribution of Requirements to
                Integrated Teams
                Develop a preliminary distribution of requirements,
                responsibilities, authorities, tasks, and interfaces to teams
                in the selected integrated team structure.
       SP4.3   Establish Integrated Teams
                Establish and maintain teams in the integrated team structure.

Risk Management

The purpose of Risk Management is to identify potential problems before
they occur, so that risk-handling activities may be planned and invoked
as needed across the life of the product or project to mitigate adverse
impacts on achieving objectives.

Specific Practices by Specific Goal:

SG1   Prepare for Risk Management
       Preparation for risk management is conducted.
       SP1.1   Determine Risk Sources and Categories
                Determine risk sources and categories.
       SP1.2   Define Risk Parameters
                Define the parameters used to analyze and categorize risks,
                and the parameters used to control the risk management
                effort.
       SP1.3   Establish a Risk Management Strategy
                Establish and maintain the strategy to be used for risk
                management.

SG2   Identify and Analyze Risks
Risks are identified and analyzed to determine their relative importance.
SP2.1   Identify Risks
Identify and document the risks.
SP2.2   Evaluate, Categorize, and Prioritize Risks
Evaluate and categorize each identified risk using the defined risk categories and parameters, and determine its relative priority.

SG3   Mitigate Risks
Risks are handled and mitigated, where appropriate, to reduce adverse impacts on achieving objectives.
SP3.1   Develop Risk Mitigation Plans
Develop a risk mitigation plan for the most important risks to the project, as defined by the risk management strategy.
SP3.2   Implement Risk Mitigation Plans
Monitor the status of each risk periodically and implement the risk mitigation plan as appropriate.

Integrated Teaming

The purpose of Integrated Teaming is to form and sustain an integrated team for the development of work products.

Specific Practices by Specific Goal:

SG1   Establish Team Composition
A team composition that provides the knowledge and skills required to deliver the team's product is established and maintained.
SP1.1   Identify Team Tasks
Identify and define the team's specific internal tasks to generate the team's expected output.
SP1.2   Identify Needed Knowledge and Skills
Identify the knowledge, skills, and functional expertise needed to perform team tasks.
SP1.3   Assign Appropriate Team Members
Assign the appropriate personnel to be team members based on required knowledge and skills.

SG2   Govern Team Operation
Operation of the integrated team is governed according to established principles.

    SP2.1   Establish a Shared Vision
Establish and maintain a shared vision for the integrated team that is aligned with any overarching or higher-level vision.

    SP2.2   Establish a Team Charter
Establish and maintain a team charter based on the integrated team's shared vision and overall team objectives.

    SP2.3   Define Roles and Responsibilities
Clearly define and maintain each team member's roles and responsibilities.

    SP2.4   Establish Operating Procedures
Establish and maintain integrated team operating procedures.

    SP2.5   Collaborate among Interfacing Teams
Establish and maintain collaboration among interfacing teams.

Integrated Supplier Management

The purpose of Integrated Supplier Management is to proactively identify sources of products that may be used to satisfy the project's requirements and to manage selected suppliers while maintaining a cooperative project-supplier relationship.

Specific Practices by Specific Goal:

SG1   Analyze and Select Sources of Products
Potential sources of products that best fit the needs of the project are identified, analyzed, and selected.

    SP1.1   Analyze Potential Sources of Products
Identify and analyze potential sources of products that can be used to satisfy the project's requirements.

    SP1.2   Evaluate and Determine Sources of Products
Use a formal evaluation process to determine which sources of custom-made and off-the-shelf products to use.

SG2   Coordinate Work with Suppliers
Work is coordinated with suppliers to ensure the supplier agreement is executed appropriately.

SP2.1　Monitor Selected Supplier Processes
　　　　Monitor and analyze selected processes used by the supplier.

SP2.2　Evaluate Selected Supplier Work Products
　　　　For custom-made products, evaluate selected supplier work products.

SP2.3　Revise the Supplier Agreement or Relationship
　　　　Revise the supplier agreement or relationship, as appropriate, to reflect changes in conditions.

Decision Analysis and Resolution

The purpose of Decision Analysis and Resolution is to analyze possible decisions using a formal evaluation process that evaluates identified alternatives against established criteria.

Specific Practices by Specific Goal:

SG1　Evaluate Alternatives
　　　Decisions are based on an evaluation of alternatives using established criteria.

SP1.1　Establish Guidelines for Decision Analysis
　　　　Establish and maintain guidelines to determine which issues are subject to a formal evaluation process.

SP1.2　Establish Evaluation Criteria
　　　　Establish and maintain the criteria for evaluating alternatives, and the relative ranking of these criteria.

SP1.3　Identify Alternative Solutions
　　　　Identify alternative solutions to address issues.

SP1.4　Select Evaluation Methods
　　　　Select the evaluation methods.

SP1.5　Evaluate Alternatives
　　　　Evaluate alternative solutions using the established criteria and methods.

SP1.6　Select Solutions
　　　　Select solutions from the alternatives based on the evaluation criteria.

Organizational Environment for Integration

The purpose of Organizational Environment for Integration is to provide an Integrated Product and Process Development (IPPD) infrastructure and manage people for integration.

Specific Practices by Specific Goal:

SG1 Provide IPPD Infrastructure
An infrastructure that maximizes the productivity of people and affects the collaboration necessary for integration is provided.

SP1.1 Establish the Organization's Shared Vision
Establish and maintain a shared vision for the organization.

SP1.2 Establish an Integrated Work Environment
Establish and maintain an integrated work environment that supports IPPD by enabling collaboration and concurrent development.

SP1.3 Identify IPPD-Unique Skill Requirements
Identify the unique skills needed to support the IPPD environment.

SG2 Manage People for Integration
People are managed to nurture the integrative and collaborative behaviors of an IPPD environment.

SP2.1 Establish Leadership Mechanisms
Establish and maintain leadership mechanisms to enable timely collaboration.

SP2.2 Establish Incentives for Integration
Establish and maintain incentives for adopting and demonstrating integrative and collaborative behaviors at all levels of the organization.

SP2.3 Establish Mechanisms to Balance Team and Home Organization Responsibilities
Establish and maintain organizational guidelines to balance team and home organization responsibilities.

Maturity Level 4

Organizational Process Performance

The purpose of Organizational Process Performance is to establish and maintain a quantitative understanding of the performance of the organization's set of standard processes in support of quality and process-performance objectives, and to provide the process performance data, baselines, and models to quantitatively manage the organization's projects.

Specific Practices by Specific Goal:

SG1   Establish Performance Baselines and Models
Baselines and models that characterize the expected process performance of the organization's set of standard processes are established and maintained.

SP1.1   Select Processes
Select the processes or process elements in the organization's set of standard processes that are to be included in the organization's process performance analyses.

SP1.2   Establish Process Performance Measures
Establish and maintain definitions of the measures that are to be included in the organization's process performance analyses.

SP1.3   Establish Quality and Process-Performance Objectives
Establish and maintain quantitative objectives for quality and process performance for the organization.

SP1.4   Establish Process Performance Baselines
Establish and maintain the organization's process performance baselines.

SP1.5   Establish Process Performance Models
Establish and maintain the process performance models for the organization's set of standard processes.

Quantitative Project Management

The purpose of the Quantitative Project Management process area is to quantitatively manage the project's defined process to achieve the project's established quality and process-performance objectives.

Specific Practices by Specific Goal:

SG1   Quantitatively Manage the Project
The project is quantitatively managed using quality and process-performance objectives.

SP1.1   Establish the Project's Objectives
Establish and maintain the project's quality and process-performance objectives.

SP1.2   Compose the Defined Process
Select the subprocesses that compose the project's defined process, based on historical stability and capability data.

SP1.3 Select the Subprocesses that Will Be Statistically Managed
Select the subprocesses of the project's defined process that will be statistically managed.

SP1.4 Manage Project Performance
Monitor the project to determine whether the project's objectives for quality and process performance will be satisfied, and identify corrective action as appropriate.

SG2 Statistically Manage Subprocess Performance
The performance of selected subprocesses within the project's defined process is statistically managed.

SP2.1 Select Measures and Analytic Techniques
Select the measures and analytic techniques to be used in statistically managing the selected subprocesses.

SP2.2 Apply Statistical Methods to Understand Variation
Establish and maintain an understanding of the variation of the selected subprocesses using the selected measures and analytic techniques.

SP2.3 Monitor Performance of the Selected Subprocesses
Monitor the performance of the selected subprocesses to determine their capability to satisfy their quality and process-performance objectives, and identify corrective action as necessary.

SP2.4 Record Statistical Management Data
Record statistical and quality management data in the organization's measurement repository.

Maturity Level 5

Organizational Innovation and Deployment

The purpose of Organizational Innovation and Deployment is to select and deploy incremental and innovative improvements that measurably improve the organization's processes and technologies. The improvements support the organization's quality and process-performance objectives as derived from the organization's business objectives.

Specific Practices by Specific Goal:

SG1 Select Improvements
Process and technology improvements that contribute to meeting quality and process-performance objectives are selected.

SP1.1 Collect and Analyze Improvement Proposals
Collect and analyze process- and technology-improvement proposals.

SP1.2 Identify and Analyze Innovations
Identify and analyze innovative improvements that could increase the organization's quality and process performance.

SP1.3 Pilot Improvements
Pilot process and technology improvements to select which ones to implement.

SP1.4 Select Improvements for Deployment
Select process- and technology-improvement proposals for deployment across the organization.

SG2 Deploy Improvements
Measurable improvements to the organization's processes and technologies are continually and systematically deployed.

SP2.1 Plan the Deployment
Establish and maintain the plans for deploying the selected process and technology improvements.

SP2.2 Manage the Deployment
Manage the deployment of the selected process and technology improvements.

SP2.3 Measure Improvement Effects
Measure the effects of the deployed process and technology improvements.

Causal Analysis and Resolution

The purpose of Causal Analysis and Resolution is to identify causes of defects and other problems and take action to prevent them from occurring in the future.

Specific Practices by Specific Goal:

SG1 Determine Causes of Defects
Root causes of defects and other problems are systematically determined.

SP1.1 Select Defect Data for Analysis
Select the defects and other problems for analysis.

SP1.2 Analyze Causes
Perform causal analysis of selected defects and other problems and propose actions to address them.

SG2   Address Causes of Defects

      Root causes of defects and other problems are systematically addressed to prevent their future occurrence.

    SP2.1   Implement the Action Proposals

        Implement the selected action proposals that were developed in causal analysis.

    SP2.2   Evaluate the Effect of Changes

        Evaluate the effect of changes on process performance.

    SP2.3   Record Data

        Record causal analysis and resolution data for use across the project and organization.

Generic Practices by Generic Goal

GG2   Institutionalize a Managed Process

                       The process is institutionalized as a managed process.

Commitment to Perform

GP2.1   (CO1)   Establish an Organizational Policy

                Establish and maintain an organizational policy for planning and performing the (process area name) process.

Ability to Perform

GP2.2   (AB1)   Plan the Process

                Establish and maintain the plan for performing the (process area name) process.

GP2.3   (AB2)   Provide Resources

                Provide adequate resources for performing the (process area name) process, developing the work products, and providing the services of the (process area name) process.

GP2.4   (AB3)   Assign Responsibility

                Assign responsibility and authority for performing the process, developing the work products, and providing the services of the (process area name) process.

GP2.5   (AB4)   Train People

                Train the people performing or supporting the (process area name) process as needed.

Directing Implementation

| GP2.6 | (DI1) | Manage Configurations |
| | | Place designated work products of the (process area name) process under appropriate levels of configuration management. |

| GP2.7 | (DI2) | Identify and Involve Relevant Stakeholders |
| | | Identify and involve the relevant stakeholders of the (process area name) process as planned. |

| GP2.8 | (DI3) | Monitor and Control the Process |
| | | Monitor and control the (process area name) process against the plan for performing the process and take appropriate corrective action. |

Verifying Implementation

| GP2.9 | (VE1) | Objectively Evaluate Adherence |
| | | Objectively evaluate adherence of the (process area name) process against its process description, standards, and procedures, and address noncompliance. |

| GP2.10 | (VE2) | Review Status with Higher-Level Management |
| | | Review the activities, status, and results of the (process area name) process with higher-level management and resolve issues. |

Generic Practices by Generic Goal

| GG3 | | Institutionalize a Defined Process |
| | | The process is institutionalized as a defined process. |

Ability to Perform

| GP3.1 | (AB1) | Establish a Defined Process |
| | | Establish and maintain the description of a defined (process area name) process. |

Directing Implementation

| GP3.2 | (DI4) | Collect Improvement Information |
| | | Collect work products, measures, measurement results, and improvement information derived from planning and performing the (process area name) process to support the future use and improvement of the organization's processes and process assets. |

Appendix H

Checklist for the Continuous Representation of the CMMI®

This checklist displays the specific goals and specific practices for each process area. For process improvement efforts, this checklist can be used to document if procedures have been written for a practice, what stage the documentation is in, and who is responsible. For appraisals, the appraisal team can use this checklist to determine if the practices have been institutionalized in order to achieve the goals for each process area. Feel free to add columns or rows to insert comments, tasks, status indicators, subpractices, artifacts, or anything else you feel will help structure and track your efforts.

The process areas are arranged by category, to include:

- Process Management
- Project Management
- Engineering
- Support

We list the Specific Goals and Specific Practices for each process area first. Rather than list the generic goals and generic practices for each process area immediately after that process area, we list all the generic goals (GGs) and their associated generic practices (GPs) at the end of this appendix. Remember: generic goals and generic practices must be satisfied for each process area for each level, as well as the specific goals and specific practices for that process area. In the continuous representation, if you are trying to achieve a Capability Level 3 for a particular process area, then all of the generic goals and generic practices related to Capability Level 3 must be satisfied for that process area, as well as the specific goals and specific practices of that process area. The differences in the wording of the practices between the continuous representation and the staged representation are also displayed.

See the appropriate chapters for more information, especially the planning and tracking chapter (Chapter 15).

Process Management

Organizational Process Focus

The purpose of Organizational Process Focus is to plan and implement organizational process improvement, based on a thorough understanding of the current strengths and weaknesses of the organization's processes and process assets.

Specific Practices by Specific Goal:

SG1 Determine Process-Improvement Opportunities
Strengths, weaknesses, and improvement opportunities for the organization's processes are identified periodically and as needed.
SP1.1-1 Establish Organizational Process Needs
Establish and maintain the description of the process needs and objectives for the organization.
SP1.2-1 Appraise the Organization's Processes
Appraise the processes of the organization periodically and as needed to maintain an understanding of their strengths and weaknesses.
SP1.3-1 Identify the Organization's Process Improvements
Identify improvements to the organization's processes and process assets.

SG2 Plan and Implement Process-Improvement Activities
Improvements are planned and implemented, organizational process assets are deployed, and process-related experiences are incorporated into the organizational process assets.
SP2.1-1 Establish Process Action Plans
Establish and maintain process action plans to address improvements to the organization's processes and process assets.

SP2.2-1   Implement Process Action Plans
Implement process action plans across the organization.

SP2.3-1   Deploy Organizational Process Assets
Deploy organizational process assets across the organization.

SP2.4-1   Incorporate Process-Related Experiences into the Organizational Process Assets
Incorporate process-related work products, measures, and improvement information derived from planning and performing the process into the organizational process assets.

Organizational Process Definition

The purpose of Organizational Process Definition is to establish and maintain a usable set of organizational process assets.

Specific Practices by Specific Goal:

SG1   Establish Organizational Process Assets
A set of organizational process assets is established and maintained.

SP1.1-1   Establish Standard Processes
Establish and maintain the organization's set of standard processes.

SP1.2-1   Establish Life-Cycle Model Descriptions
Establish and maintain descriptions of the life-cycle models approved for use in the organization.

SP1.3-1   Establish Tailoring Criteria and Guidelines
Establish and maintain the tailoring criteria and guidelines for the organization's set of standard processes.

SP1.4-1   Establish the Organization's Measurement Repository
Establish and maintain the organization's measurement repository.

SP1.5-1   Establish the Organization's Process Asset Library
Establish and maintain the organization's process asset library.

Organizational Training

The purpose of Organizational Training is to develop the skills and knowledge of people so they can perform their roles effectively and efficiently.

Specific Practices by Specific Goal:

SG1   Establish an Organizational Training Capability
A training capability that supports the organization's management and technical roles is established and maintained.

    SP1.1-1   Establish the Strategic Training Needs
Establish and maintain the strategic training needs of the organization.

    SP1.2-1   Determine Which Training Needs Are the Responsibility of the Organization
Determine which training needs are the responsibility of the organization and which will be left to the individual project or support group.

    SP1.3-1   Establish an Organizational Training Tactical Plan
Establish and maintain an organizational training tactical plan.

    SP1.4-1   Establish Training Capability
Establish and maintain training capability to address organizational training needs.

SG2   Provide Necessary Training
Training necessary for individuals to perform their roles effectively is provided.

    SP2.1-1   Deliver Training
Deliver the training following the organizational training tactical plan.

    SP2.2-1   Establish Training Records
Establish and maintain records of the organizational training.

    SP2.3-1   Assess Training Effectiveness
Assess the effectiveness of the organization's training program.

Organizational Process Performance

The purpose of Organizational Process Performance is to establish and maintain a quantitative understanding of the performance of the organization's set of standard processes in support of quality and process-performance objectives, and to provide the process performance data, baselines, and models to quantitatively manage the organization's projects.

Specific Practices by Specific Goal:

SG1 Establish Performance Baselines and Models
Baselines and models that characterize the expected process performance of the organization's set of standard processes are established and maintained.

SP1.1-1 Select Processes
Select the processes or process elements in the organization's set of standard processes that are to be included in the organization's process performance analyses.

SP1.2-1 Establish Process Performance Measures
Establish and maintain definitions of the measures that are to be included in the organization's process performance analyses.

SP1.3-1 Establish Quality and Process Performance Objectives
Establish and maintain quantitative objectives for quality and process performance for the organization.

SP1.4-1 Establish Process Performance Baselines
Establish and maintain the organization's process performance baselines.

SP1.5-1 Establish Process Performance Models
Establish and maintain the process performance models for the organization's set of standard processes.

Organizational Innovation and Deployment

The purpose of Organizational Innovation and Deployment is to select and deploy incremental and innovative improvements that measurably improve the organization's processes and technologies. The improvements support the organization's quality and process-performance objectives as derived from the organization's business objectives.

Specific Practices by Specific Goal:

SG1 Select Improvements
Process and technology improvements that contribute to meeting quality and process-performance objectives are selected.

SP1.1-1 Collect and Analyze Improvement Proposals
Collect and analyze process- and technology-improvement proposals.

SP1.2-1 Identify and Analyze Innovations
Identify and analyze innovative improvements that could increase the organization's quality and process performance.

SP1.3-1 Pilot Improvements
Pilot process and technology improvements to select which ones to implement.

SP1.4-1 Select Improvements for Deployment
Select process- and technology-improvement proposals for deployment across the organization.

SG2 Deploy Improvements
Measurable improvements to the organization's processes and technologies are continually and systematically deployed.

SP2.1-1 Plan the Deployment
Establish and maintain the plans for deploying the selected process and technology improvements.

SP2.2-1 Manage the Deployment
Manage the deployment of the selected process and technology improvements.

SP2.3-1 Measure Improvement Effects
Measure the effects of the deployed process and technology improvements.

Project Management

Project Planning

The purpose of Project Planning is to establish and maintain plans that define project activities.

Specific Practices by Specific Goal:

SG1 Establish Estimates
Estimates of project planning parameters are established and maintained.

SP1.1-1 Estimate the Scope of the Project
Establish a top-level work breakdown structure (WBS) to estimate the scope of the project.

SP1.2-1 Establish Estimates of Work Product and Task Attributes
Establish and maintain estimates of the attributes of the work products and tasks.

SP1.3-1 Define Project Life Cycle
Define the project life-cycle phases upon which to scope the planning effort.

SP1.4-1 Determine Estimates of Effort and Cost
Estimate the project effort and cost for the work products and tasks based on estimation rationale.

SG2 Develop a Project Plan
A project plan is established and maintained as the basis for managing the project.

SP2.1-1 Establish the Budget and Schedule
Establish and maintain the project's budget and schedule.

SP2.2-1 Identify Project Risks
Identify and analyze project risks.

SP2.3-1 Plan for Data Management
Plan for the management of project data.

SP2.4-1 Plan for Project Resources
Plan for necessary resources to perform the project.

SP2.5-1 Plan for Needed Knowledge and Skills
Plan for knowledge and skills needed to perform the project.

SP2.6-1 Plan Stakeholder Involvement
Plan the involvement of identified stakeholders.

SP2.7-1 Establish the Project Plan
Establish and maintain the overall project plan content.

SG3 Obtain Commitment to the Plan
Commitments to the project plan are established and maintained.

SP3.1-1 Review Plans that Affect the Project
Review all plans that affect the project to understand project commitments.

SP3.2-1 Reconcile Work and Resource Levels
Reconcile the project plan to reflect available and estimated resources.

SP3.3-1 Obtain Plan Commitment/Obtain commitment from relevant stakeholders responsible for performing and supporting plan execution.

Project Monitoring and Control

The purpose of Project Monitoring and Control is to provide an understanding of the project's progress so that appropriate corrective actions can be taken when the project's performance deviates significantly from the plan.

Specific Practices by Specific Goal:

SG1   Monitor Project against Plan
Actual performance and progress of the project are monitored against the project plan.
    SP1.1-1   Monitor Project Planning Parameters
        Monitor the actual values of the project planning parameters against the project plan.
    SP1.2-1   Monitor Commitments
        Monitor commitments against those identified in the project plan.
    SP1.3-1   Monitor Project Risks
        Monitor risks against those identified in the project plan.
    SP1.4-1   Monitor Data Management
        Monitor the management of project data against the project plan.
    SP1.5-1   Monitor Stakeholder Involvement
        Monitor stakeholder involvement against the project plan.
    SP1.6-1   Conduct Progress Reviews
        Periodically review the project's progress, performance, and issues.
    SP1.7-1   Conduct Milestone Reviews
        Review the accomplishments and results of the project at selected project milestones.

SG2   Manage Corrective Action to Closure
Corrective actions are managed to closure when the project's performance or results deviate significantly from the plan.
    SP2.1-1   Analyze Issues
        Collect and analyze the issues and determine the corrective actions necessary to address the issues.
    SP2.2-1   Take Corrective Action
        Take corrective action on identified issues.
    SP2.3-1   Manage Corrective Action
        Manage corrective actions to closure.

Supplier Agreement Management

The purpose of Supplier Agreement Management is to manage the acquisition of products from suppliers for which there exists a formal agreement.

Specific Practices by Specific Goal:

SG1   Establish Supplier Agreements
       Agreements with the suppliers are established and maintained.
       SP1.1-1   Determine Acquisition Type
                  Determine the type of acquisition for each product or
                  product component to be acquired.
       SP1.2-1   Select Suppliers
                  Select suppliers based on an evaluation of their ability
                  to meet the specified requirements and established cri-
                  teria.
       SP1.3-1   Establish Supplier Agreements
                  Establish and maintain formal agreements with the sup-
                  plier.

SG2   Satisfy Supplier Agreements
       Agreements with the suppliers are satisfied by both the project and
       the supplier.
       SP2.1-1   Review COTS Products
                  Review candidate COTS products to ensure they satisfy
                  the specified requirements that are covered under a
                  supplier agreement.
       SP2.2-1   Execute the Supplier Agreement
                  Perform activities with the supplier as specified in the
                  supplier agreement.
       SP2.3-1   Accept the Acquired Product
                  Ensure that the supplier agreement is satisfied before
                  accepting the acquired product.
       SP2.4-1   Transition Products
                  Transition the acquired products from the supplier to the
                  project.

Integrated Project Management for IPPD

The purpose of Integrated Project Management is to establish and manage
the project and the involvement of the relevant stakeholders according to
an integrated and defined process that is tailored from the organization's
set of standard processes.

For Integrated Product and Process Development, Integrated Project
Management also covers the establishment of a shared vision for the
project and a team structure for integrated teams that will carry out the
objectives of the project.

Specific Practices by Specific Goal:

SG1   Use the Project's Defined Process
       The project is conducted using a defined process that is tailored
       from the organization's set of standard processes.

       SP1.1-1   Establish the Project's Defined Process
                  Establish and maintain the project's defined process.

       SP1.2-1   Use Organizational Process Assets for Planning Project
                  Activities
                  Use the organizational process assets and measurement
                  repository for estimating and planning the project's activ-
                  ities.

       SP1.3-1   Integrate Plans
                  Integrate the project plan and the other plans that affect
                  the project to describe the project's defined process.

       SP1.4-1   Manage the Project Using the Integrated Plans
                  Manage the project using the project plan, the other plans
                  that affect the project, and the project's defined process.

       SP1.5-1   Contribute to the Organizational Process Assets
                  Contribute work products, measures, and documented
                  experiences to the organizational process assets.

SG2   Coordinate and Collaborate with Relevant Stakeholders
       Coordination and collaboration of the project with relevant stake-
       holders is conducted.

       SP2.1-1   Manage Stakeholder Involvement
                  Manage the involvement of the relevant stakeholders in
                  the project.

       SP2.2-1   Manage Dependencies
                  Participate with relevant stakeholders to identify, nego-
                  tiate, and track critical dependencies.

       SP2.3-1   Resolve Coordination Issues
                  Resolve issues with relevant stakeholders.

SG3   Use the Project's Shared Vision for IPPD
       The project is conducted using the project's shared vision.

       SP3.1-1   Define Project's Shared-Vision Context
                  Identify expectations, constraints, interfaces, and opera-
                  tional conditions applicable to the project's shared vision.

       SP3.2-1   Establish the Project's Shared Vision
                  Establish and maintain a shared vision for the project.

SG4 Organize Integrated Teams for IPPD
The integrated teams needed to execute the project are identified, defined, structured, and tasked.
SP4.1-1 Determine Integrated Team Structure for the Project
Determine the integrated team structure that will best meet the project objectives and constraints.
SP4.2-1 Develop a Preliminary Distribution of Requirements to Integrated Teams
Develop a preliminary distribution of requirements, responsibilities, authorities, tasks, and interfaces to teams in the selected integrated team structure.
SP4.3-1 Establish Integrated Teams
Establish and maintain teams in the integrated team structure.

Risk Management

The purpose of Risk Management is to identify potential problems before they occur, so that risk-handling activities may be planned and invoked as needed across the life of the product or project to mitigate adverse impacts on achieving objectives.

Specific Practices by Specific Goal:

SG1 Prepare for Risk Management
Preparation for risk management is conducted.
SP1.1-1 Determine Risk Sources and Categories
Determine risk sources and categories.
SP1.2-1 Define Risk Parameters
Define the parameters used to analyze and categorize risks, and the parameters used to control the risk management effort.
SP1.3-1 Establish a Risk Management Strategy
Establish and maintain the strategy to be used for risk management.

SG2 Identify and Analyze Risks
Risks are identified and analyzed to determine their relative importance.
SP2.1-1 Identify Risks
Identify and document the risks.

SP2.2-1   Evaluate, Categorize, and Prioritize Risks
Evaluate and categorize each identified risk using the defined risk categories and parameters, and determine its relative priority.

SG3   Mitigate Risks
Risks are handled and mitigated, where appropriate, to reduce adverse impacts on achieving objectives.

SP3.1-1   Develop Risk Mitigation Plans
Develop a risk mitigation plan for the most important risks to the project, as defined by the risk management strategy.

SP3.2-1   Implement Risk Mitigation Plans
Monitor the status of each risk periodically and implement the risk mitigation plan as appropriate.

Integrated Teaming

The purpose of Integrated Teaming is to form and sustain an integrated team for the development of work products.

Specific Practices by Specific Goal:

SG1   Establish Team Composition
A team composition that provides the knowledge and skills required to deliver the team's product is established and maintained.

SP1.1-1   Identify Team Tasks
Identify and define the team's specific internal tasks to generate the team's expected output.

SP1.2-1   Identify Needed Knowledge and Skills
Identify the knowledge, skills, and functional expertise needed to perform team tasks.

SP1.3-1   Assign Appropriate Team Members
Assign the appropriate personnel to be team members based on required knowledge and skills.

SG2   Govern Team Operation
Operation of the integrated team is governed according to established principles.

SP2.1-1 Establish a Shared Vision
Establish and maintain a shared vision for the integrated team that is aligned with any overarching or higher-level vision.

SP2.2-1 Establish a Team Charter
Establish and maintain a team charter based on the integrated team's shared vision and overall team objectives.

SP2.3-1 Define Roles and Responsibilities
Clearly define and maintain each team member's roles and responsibilities.

SP2.4-1 Establish Operating Procedures
Establish and maintain integrated team operating procedures.

SP2.5-1 Collaborate among Interfacing Teams
Establish and maintain collaboration among interfacing teams.

Integrated Supplier Management

The purpose of Integrated Supplier Management is to proactively identify sources of products that may be used to satisfy the project's requirements and to manage selected suppliers while maintaining a cooperative project-supplier relationship.

Specific Practices by Specific Goal:

SG1 Analyze and Select Sources of Products
Potential sources of products that best fit the needs of the project are identified, analyzed, and selected.

SP1.1-1 Analyze Potential Sources of Products
Identify and analyze potential sources of products that can be used to satisfy the project's requirements.

SP1.2-1 Evaluate and Determine Sources of Products
Use a formal evaluation process to determine which sources of custom-made and off-the-shelf products to use.

SG2 Coordinate Work with Suppliers
Work is coordinated with suppliers to ensure the supplier agreement is executed appropriately.

SP2.1-1   Monitor Selected Supplier Processes
Monitor and analyze selected processes used by the supplier.

SP2.2-1   Evaluate Selected Supplier Work Products
For custom-made products, evaluate selected supplier work products.

SP2.3-1   Revise the Supplier Agreement or Relationship
Revise the supplier agreement or relationship, as appropriate, to reflect changes in conditions.

Quantitative Project Management

The purpose of the Quantitative Project Management process area is to quantitatively manage the project's defined process to achieve the project's established quality and process-performance objectives.

Specific Practices by Specific Goal:

SG1   Quantitatively Manage the Project
The project is quantitatively managed using quality and process-performance objectives.

SP1.1-1   Establish the Project's Objectives
Establish and maintain the project's quality and process-performance objectives.

SP1.2-1   Compose the Defined Process
Select the subprocesses that compose the project's defined process based on historical stability and capability data.

SP1.3-1   Select the Subprocesses that Will Be Statistically Managed
Select the subprocesses of the project's defined process that will be statistically managed.

SP1.4-1   Manage Project Performance
Monitor the project to determine whether the project's objectives for quality and process performance will be satisfied, and identify corrective action as appropriate.

SG2   Statistically Manage Subprocess Performance
The performance of selected subprocesses within the project's defined process is statistically managed.

SP2.1-1   Select Measures and Analytic Techniques
Select the measures and analytic techniques to be used in statistically managing the selected subprocesses.

SP2.2-1   Apply Statistical Methods to Understand Variation
Establish and maintain an understanding of the variation of the selected subprocesses using the selected measures and analytic techniques.

SP2.3-1   Monitor Performance of the Selected Subprocesses
Monitor the performance of the selected subprocesses to determine their capability to satisfy their quality and process-performance objectives, and identify corrective action as necessary.

SP2.4-1   Record Statistical Management Data
Record statistical and quality management data in the organization's measurement repository.

Engineering

Requirements Management

The purpose of Requirements Management is to manage the requirements of the project's products and product components, and to identify inconsistencies between those requirements and the project's plans and work products.

Specific Practices by Specific Goal:

SG1   Manage Requirements
Requirements are managed, and inconsistencies with project plans and work products are identified.

SP1.1-1   Obtain an Understanding of Requirements
Develop an understanding with the requirements providers on the meaning of the requirements.

SP1.2-2   Obtain Commitment to Requirements
Obtain commitment to the requirements from the project participants.

SP1.3-1   Manage Requirements Changes
Manage changes to the requirements as they evolve during the project.

SP1.4-2   Maintain Bidirectional Traceability of Requirements
Maintain bidirectional traceability among the requirements and the project plans and work products.

SP1.5-1   Identify Inconsistencies between Project Work and Requirements
Identify inconsistencies between the project plans and work products and the requirements.

Requirements Development

The purpose of Requirements Development is to produce and analyze customer, product, and product-component requirements.

Specific Practices by Specific Goal:

SG1   Develop Customer Requirements
      Stakeholder needs, expectations, constraints, and interfaces are collected and translated into customer requirements.
      SP1.1-1   Collect Stakeholder Needs
                Identify and collect stakeholder needs, expectations, constraints, and interfaces for all phases of the product life cycle.

> In the staged representation, this specific practice is only included as informative material and appears after the Elicit Needs specific practice.

      SP1.1-2   Elicit Needs
                Elicit stakeholder needs, expectations, constraints, and interfaces for all phases of the product life cycle.

> In the staged representation, this specific practice takes the place of the Collect Stakeholder Needs specific practice.

      SP1.2-1   Develop the Customer Requirements
                Transform stakeholder needs, expectations, constraints, and interfaces into customer requirements.

SG2   Develop Product Requirements
      Customer requirements are refined and elaborated to develop product and product-component requirements.
      SP2.1-1   Establish Product and Product-Component Requirements
                Establish and maintain product and product-component requirements, which are based on the customer requirements.
      SP2.2-1   Allocate Product-Component Requirements
                Allocate the requirements for each product component.
      SP2.3-1   Identify Interface Requirements
                Identify interface requirements.

SG3   Analyze and Validate Requirements
      The requirements are analyzed and validated, and a definition of required functionality is developed.

SP3.1-1 Establish Operational Concepts and Scenarios
Establish and maintain operational concepts and associated scenarios.

SP3.2-1 Establish a Definition of Required Functionality
Establish and maintain a definition of required functionality.

SP3.3-1 Analyze Requirements
Analyze requirements to ensure that they are necessary and sufficient.

SP3.4-3 Analyze Requirements to Achieve Balance
Analyze requirements to balance stakeholder needs and constraints.

SP3.5-1 Validate Requirements
Validate requirements to ensure that the resulting product will perform appropriately in its intended-use environment.

> In the staged representation, this specific practice is only included as informative material and appears after the Validate Requirements with Comprehensive Methods specific practice.

SP3.5-2 Validate Requirements with Comprehensive Methods
Validate requirements to ensure the resulting product will perform as intended in the user's environment using multiple techniques as appropriate.

> In the staged representation, this specific practice takes the place of the Validate Requirements specific practice.

Technical Solution

The purpose of Technical Solution is to design, develop, and implement solutions to requirements. Solutions, designs, and implementations encompass products, product components, and product-related life-cycle processes either singly or in combinations as appropriate.

Specific Practices by Specific Goal:

SG1 Select Product-Component Solutions
Product or product-component solutions are selected from alternative solutions.

SP1.1-1 Develop Alternative Solutions and Selection Criteria
Develop alternative solutions and selection criteria.

> In the staged representation, this specific practice is only included as informative material and appears after the Develop Detailed Alternative Solutions and Selection Criteria specific practice.

SP1.1-2 Develop Detailed Alternative Solutions and Selection Criteria

Develop detailed alternative solutions and selection criteria.

> In the staged representation, this specific practice takes the place of the Develop Alternative Solutions and Selection Criteria specific practice.

SP1.2-2 Evolve Operational Concepts and Scenarios

Evolve the operational concept, scenarios, and environments to describe the conditions, operating modes, and operating states specific to each product component.

SP1.3-1 Select Product-Component Solutions

Select the product-component solutions that best satisfy the criteria established.

SG2 Develop the Design

Product or product-component designs are developed.

SP2.1-1 Design the Product or Product Component

Develop a design for the product or product component.

SP2.2-3 Establish a Technical Data Package

Establish and maintain a technical data package.

SP2.3-1 Establish Interface Descriptions

Establish and maintain the solution for product-component interfaces.

> In the staged representation, this specific practice is only included as informative material and appears after the design interfaces using criteria specific practice.

SP2.3-3 Design Interfaces Using Criteria

Design comprehensive product-component interfaces in terms of established and maintained criteria.

> In the staged representation, this specific practice takes the place of the Establish Interface Descriptions specific practice.

SP2.4-3 Perform Make, Buy, or Reuse Analyses

Evaluate whether the product components should be developed, purchased, or reused based on established criteria.

SG3   Implement the Product Design
       Product components, and associated support documentation are
       implemented from their designs.
       SP3.1-1   Implement the Design
                  Implement the designs of the product components.
       SP3.2-1   Develop Product Support Documentation
                  Develop and maintain the end-use documentation.

Product Integration

The purpose of Product Integration is to assemble the product from the
product components, ensure that the product, as integrated, functions
properly, and deliver the product.

Specific Practices by Specific Goal:

SG1   Prepare for Product Integration
       Preparation for product integration is conducted.
       SP1.1-1   Determine Integration Sequence
                  Determine the product-component integration sequence.
       SP1.2-2   Establish the Product Integration Environment
                  Establish and maintain the environment needed to sup-
                  port the integration of the product components.
       SP1.3-3   Establish Product Integration Procedures and Criteria
                  Establish and maintain procedures and criteria for inte-
                  gration of the product components.

SG2   Ensure Interface Compatibility
       The product-component interfaces, both internal and external, are
       compatible.
       SP2.1-1   Review Interface Descriptions for Completeness
                  Review interface descriptions for coverage and complete-
                  ness.
       SP2.2-1   Manage Interfaces
                  Manage internal and external interface definitions,
                  designs, and changes for products and product compo-
                  nents.

SG3   Assemble Product Components and Deliver the Product
       Verified product components are assembled and the integrated,
       verified, and validated product is delivered.

SP3.1-1 Confirm Readiness of Product Components for Integration

Confirm, prior to assembly, that each product component required to assemble the product has been properly identified, functions according to its description, and that the product-component interfaces comply with the interface descriptions.

SP3.2-1 Assemble Product Components

Assemble product components according to the product integration sequence and available procedures.

SP3.3-1 Evaluate Assembled Product Components

Evaluate assembled product components for interface compatibility.

SP3.4-1 Package and Deliver the Product or Product Component

Package the assembled product or product component and deliver it to the appropriate customer.

Verification

The purpose of Verification is to ensure that selected work products meet their specified requirements.

Specific Practices by Specific Goal:

SG1 Prepare for Verification

Preparation for verification is conducted.

SP1.1-1 Select Work Products for Verification

Select the work products to be verified and the verification methods that will be used for each.

SP1.2-2 Establish the Verification Environment

Establish and maintain the environment needed to support verification.

SP1.3-3 Establish Verification Procedures and Criteria

Establish and maintain verification procedures and criteria for the selected work products.

SG2 Perform Peer Reviews

Peer reviews are performed on selected work products.

SP2.1-1 Prepare for Peer Reviews

Prepare for peer reviews of selected work products.

SP2.2-1 Conduct Peer Reviews

Conduct peer reviews on selected work products and identify issues resulting from the peer review.

SP2.3-2 Analyze Peer Review Data
Analyze data about preparation, conduct, and results of the peer reviews.

SG3 Verify Selected Work Products
Selected work products are verified against their specified requirements.

SP3.1-1 Perform Verification
Perform verification on the selected work products.

SP3.2-2 Analyze Verification Results and Identify Corrective Action
Analyze the results of all verification activities and identify corrective action.

Validation

The purpose of Validation is to demonstrate that a product or product component fulfills its intended use when placed in its intended environment.

Specific Practices by Specific Goal:

SG1 Prepare for Validation
Preparation for validation is conducted.

SP1.1-1 Select Products for Validation
Select products and product components to be validated and the validation methods that will be used for each.

SP1.2-2 Establish the Validation Environment
Establish and maintain the environment needed to support validation.

SP1.3-3 Establish Validation Procedures and Criteria
Establish and maintain procedures and criteria for validation.

SG2 Validate Product or Product Components
The product or product components are validated to ensure that they are suitable for use in their intended operating environment.

SP2.1-1 Perform Validation
Perform validation on the selected products and product components.

SP2.2-1 Analyze Validation Results
Analyze the results of the validation activities and identify issues.

Support

Configuration Management

The purpose of Configuration Management is to establish and maintain the integrity of work products using configuration identification, configuration control, configuration status accounting, and configuration audits.

Specific Practices by Specific Goal:

SG1 Establish Baselines
Baselines of identified work products are established.
SP1.1-1 Identify Configuration Items
Identify the configuration items, components, and related work products that will be placed under configuration management.
SP1.2-1 Establish a Configuration Management System
Establish and maintain a configuration management and change management system for controlling work products.
SP1.3-1 Create or Release Baselines
Create or release baselines for internal use and for delivery to the customer.

SG2 Track and Control Changes
Changes to the work products under configuration management are tracked and controlled.
SP2.1-1 Track Change Requests
Track change requests for the configuration items.
SP2.2-1 Control Configuration Items
Control changes to the configuration items.

SG3 Establish Integrity
Integrity of baselines is established and maintained.
SP3.1-1 Establish Configuration Management Records
Establish and maintain records describing configuration items.
SP3.2-1 Perform Configuration Audits

Perform configuration audits to maintain integrity of the configuration baselines.

Process and Product Quality Assurance

The purpose of Process and Product Quality Assurance is to provide staff and management with objective insight into processes and associated work products.

Specific Practices by Specific Goal:

SG1   Objectively Evaluate Processes and Work Products
        Adherence of the performed process and associated work products and services to applicable process descriptions, standards, and procedures is objectively evaluated.
        SP1.1-1   Objectively Evaluate Processes
                    Objectively evaluate the designated performed processes against the applicable process descriptions, standards, and procedures.
        SP1.2-1   Objectively Evaluate Work Products and Services
                    Objectively evaluate the designated work products and services against the applicable process descriptions, standards, and procedures.

SG2   Provide Objective Insight
        Noncompliance issues are objectively tracked and communicated, and resolution is ensured.
        SP2.1-1   Communicate and Ensure Resolution of Noncompliance Issues
                    Communicate quality issues and ensure resolution of noncompliance issues with the staff and managers.
        SP2.2-1   Establish Records
                    Establish and maintain records of the quality assurance activities.

Measurement and Analysis

The purpose of Measurement and Analysis is to develop and sustain a measurement capability that is used to support management information needs.

Specific Practices by Specific Goal:

SG1   Align Measurement and Analysis Activities
Measurement objectives and activities are aligned with identified information needs and objectives.
SP1.1-1   Establish Measurement Objectives
Establish and maintain measurement objectives that are derived from identified information needs and objectives.
SP1.2-1   Specify Measures
Specify measures to address the measurement objectives.
SP1.3-1   Specify Data Collection and Storage Procedures
Specify how measurement data will be obtained and stored.
SP1.4-1   Specify Analysis Procedures
Specify how measurement data will be analyzed and reported.

SG2   Provide Measurement Results
Measurement results that address identified information needs and objectives are provided.
SP2.1-1   Collect Measurement Data
Obtain specified measurement data.
SP2.2-1   Analyze Measurement Data
Analyze and interpret measurement data.
SP2.3-1   Store Data and Results
Manage and store measurement data, measurement specifications, and analysis results.
SP2.4-1   Communicate Results
Report results of measurement and analysis activities to all relevant stakeholders.

Decision Analysis and Resolution

The purpose of Decision Analysis and Resolution is to analyze possible decisions using a formal evaluation process that evaluates identified alternatives against established criteria.

Specific Practices by Specific Goal:

SG1   Evaluate Alternatives
Decisions are based on an evaluation of alternatives using established criteria.

SP1.1-1 Establish Guidelines for Decision Analysis
Establish and maintain guidelines to determine which issues are subject to a formal evaluation process.

SP1.2-1 Establish Evaluation Criteria
Establish and maintain the criteria for evaluating alternatives, and the relative ranking of these criteria.

SP1.3-1 Identify Alternative Solutions
Identify alternative solutions to address issues.

SP1.4-1 Select Evaluation Methods
Select the evaluation methods.

SP1.5-1 Evaluate Alternatives
Evaluate alternative solutions using the established criteria and methods.

SP1.6-1 Select Solutions
Select solutions from the alternatives based on the evaluation criteria.

Organizational Environment for Integration

The purpose of Organizational Environment for Integration is to provide an Integrated Product and Process Development (IPPD) infrastructure and manage people for integration.

Specific Practices by Specific Goal:

SG1 Provide IPPD Infrastructure
An infrastructure that maximizes the productivity of people and affects the collaboration necessary for integration is provided.

SP1.1-1 Establish the Organization's Shared Vision
Establish and maintain a shared vision for the organization.

SP1.2-1 Establish an Integrated Work Environment
Establish and maintain an integrated work environment that supports IPPD by enabling collaboration and concurrent development.

SP1.3-1 Identify IPPD-Unique Skill Requirements
Identify the unique skills needed to support the IPPD environment.

SG2 Manage People for Integration
People are managed to nurture the integrative and collaborative behaviors of an IPPD environment.

SP2.1-1 Establish Leadership Mechanisms
Establish and maintain leadership mechanisms to enable timely collaboration.

SP2.2-1 Establish Incentives for Integration
Establish and maintain incentives for adopting and demonstrating integrative and collaborative behaviors at all levels of the organization.

SP2.3-1 Establish Mechanisms to Balance Team and Home Organization Responsibilities
Establish and maintain organizational guidelines to balance team and home organization responsibilities.

Causal Analysis and Resolution

The purpose of Causal Analysis and Resolution is to identify causes of defects and other problems and take action to prevent them from occurring in the future.

Specific Practices by Specific Goal:

SG1 Determine Causes of Defects
Root causes of defects and other problems are systematically determined.

SP1.1-1 Select Defect Data for Analysis
Select the defects and other problems for analysis.

SP1.2-1 Analyze Causes
Perform causal analysis of selected defects and other problems and propose actions to address them.

SG2 Address Causes of Defects
Root causes of defects and other problems are systematically addressed to prevent their future occurrence.

SP2.1-1 Implement the Action Proposals
Implement the selected action proposals that were developed in causal analysis.

SP2.2-1 Evaluate the Effect of Changes
Evaluate the effect of changes on process performance.

SP2.3-1 Record Data
Record causal analysis and resolution data for use across the project and organization.

Generic Goals and Generic Practices

GG1 Achieve Specific Goals
The process supports and enables achievement of the specific goals of the process area by transforming identifiable input work products to produce identifiable output work products.
GP1.1 Perform Base Practices
Perform the base practices of the process area to develop work products and provide services to achieve the specific goals of the process area.

GG2 Institutionalize a Managed Process
The process is institutionalized as a managed process.
GP2.1 Establish an Organizational Policy
Establish and maintain an organizational policy for planning and performing the process.
GP2.2 Plan the Process
Establish and maintain the plan for performing the process.
GP2.3 Provide Resources
Provide adequate resources for performing the process, developing the work products, and providing the services of the process.
GP2.4 Assign Responsibility
Assign responsibility and authority for performing the process, developing the work products, and providing the services of the process.
GP2.5 Train People
Train the people performing or supporting the process as needed.
GP2.6 Manage Configurations
Place designated work products of the process under appropriate levels of configuration management.
GP2.7 Identify and Involve Relevant Stakeholders
Identify and involve the relevant stakeholders as planned.
GP2.8 Monitor and Control the Process
Monitor and control the process against the plan for performing the process and take appropriate corrective action.
GP2.9 Objectively Evaluate Adherence
Objectively evaluate adherence of the process against its process description, standards, and procedures, and address noncompliance.

GP2.10   Review Status with Higher-Level Management
Review the activities, status, and results of the process with higher-level management and resolve issues.

GG3   Institutionalize a Defined Process
The process is institutionalized as a defined process.
GP3.1   Establish a Defined Process
Establish and maintain the description of a defined process.
GP3.2   Collect Improvement Information
Collect work products, measures, measurement results, and improvement information derived from planning and performing the process to support the future use and improvement of the organization's processes and process assets.

GG4   Institutionalize a Quantitatively Managed Process
The process is institutionalized as a quantitatively managed process.
GP4.1   Establish Quantitative Objectives for the Process
Establish and maintain quantitative objectives for the process that address quality and process performance based on customer needs and business objectives.
GP4.2   Stabilize Subprocess Performance
Stabilize the performance of one or more subprocesses to determine the ability of the process to achieve the established quantitative quality and process-performance objectives.

GG5   Institutionalize an Optimizing Process
The process is institutionalized as an optimizing process.
GP5.1   Ensure Continuous Process Improvement
Ensure continuous improvement of the process in fulfilling the relevant business objectives of the organization.
GP5.2   Correct Root Causes of Problems
Identify and correct the root causes of defects and other problems in the process.

Appendix I

Process Example (Short Version)

The following is an example process template that, although textual, is written very to-the-point. For more information, see Chapter 16.

Requirements Management Process

Action	Responsibility
Obtain work request from the customer	SM, PM
Review work request	PM
Create initial budget/estimates/schedule	PM
Initial planning	PM, project team
High-level requirements	PM, project team, customer
Risk identification and documentation	PM
Requirements spec draft	PM, project team
Technical review	PM, project team, QA
Customer review	Customer
Refine requirements	PM, project team, customer
Create requirements traceability matrix (RTM)	PM, project team
Review requirements and RTM	PM, customer, project team, QA

Requirements Management Process (continued)

Action	Responsibility
Review/update risks	PM
Update estimates and schedules	PM
Review requirements and schedules and estimates	PM, project team, QA, customer
Requirements spec final	PM, analysts
Approvals and sign-offs	Customer, QA, PM, SM, EPG
Baseline requirements spec	PM, CCB, EPG
Assess, track, and incorporate changes	PM, CCB, QA, EPG, customer, project team

Appendix J

Process Example (Long Version)

The following is an example process template that is very textually based. For more information, see Chapter 16.

Requirements Management (RM) Process

Table of Contents

Appendix K

Sample Procedure Template

The following template contains information that should be included in your procedures. See Chapter 16 for more information.

Procedure Template

Document Number:	Date:
	Revision Number:

Description:
This procedure involves… The activity's primary aim is to...

Entry Criteria/Inputs:	Exit Criteria/Outputs:

Roles:
Role Name: What does s/he do?

Assets:

Standards, reference material, deliverables, previous process descriptions…

Summary of Tasks (List major tasks/process steps):
Task 1
Task 2
Task 3
Task 4

PROCEDURE STEPS
Task 1
       Detail Step 1
       Detail Step 2
       Detail Step 3
       Detail Step 4
Task 2
       Detail Step 1
       Detail Step 2
       Detail Step 3
       Detail Step 4

Continue…

Appendix L

Sample Policy

The following information can be used to structure your policies. See Chapter 16 for more information.

Requirements Management (RM) Policy

1.0 Purpose

The purpose of Requirements Management (RM) is to manage the requirements of the project's products and product components and to identify inconsistencies between those requirements and the project's plans and work products.

2.0 Scope

This policy applies to software projects within the xxx Division of the xxx organization. The term "project," as used in this policy, includes system and software engineering, maintenance, conversion, enhancements, and procurement projects.

3.0 Responsibilities

The project manager shall ensure that the RM process is followed. Each project will follow a process that ensures that requirements will be documented, managed, and traced.

4.0 Verification

RM activities will be reviewed with higher-level management, and the process will be objectively evaluated for adherence by the Quality Assurance (QA) staff.

5.0 Sign-offs

The following shall review and approve this policy:

- Associate Director
- Quality Assurance
- EPG Chairman

Appendix M

Sample PAT Charter

The following information can be used to build your PAT charters. See Chapter 16 for more information, including a fully developed EPG Charter.

PAT Charter Template

Customer:

Sponsor:

Start: **End:**

Purpose of the PAT:

Linkage to Business Objectives:
(from strategic or business plan if we have it)

Scope:

Deliverables:

PAT Members:

Name	% of Time	Role
1.		
2.		
3.		
4.		

PAT Authority:

Assumptions:

Ground Rules:
Attendance

Decisions

Behaviors

Sign-offs:

Appendix N

Checklists for Pilot Projects

This appendix consists of checklists for pilots. The checklists presented include:

- Pilot Life-Cycle Phases
- Steps in the Pilot Process
- Checklist for Planning and Conducting Pilots
- Checklist for Evaluating the Effectiveness of the Pilot

These checklists are formatted according to pilot project phases. These checklists can be applied against almost any pilot — those that are process-improvement based as well as those that are not. An example of a non-process improvement pilot may be when an organization switches over from a non-automated system to an automated one. In that case, maybe only a few offices within a department may pilot the system, or only portions of the new system may be tried. Process improvement pilots can work the same way, except that we focus on piloting processes, not developed systems.

These checklists were made for pilots that follow a "quasi-experimental design," not those that follow an "experimental design." Most of you in software or systems engineering will not really care. Those of you who are social scientists conducting blind and double-blind studies might take offense at some of the items left out of these checklists. For example, we do not impale ourselves over the integrity of raw data, and we do not draw intermediate and final conclusions that can be traced back to the raw data. We also do not assign accountability. For more information on quasi versus experimental design, we suggest that you contact Charlie Weber, one of the original authors of the CMM for Software. It is one of his favorite subjects.

These checklists might also be considered to help structure several activities that reside in the CMMI process area Organizational Innovation and Deployment.

As a reminder, the phases of process improvement are:

- *Set Up:* Set up the EPG and infrastructure. Baseline and plan. Get funding and commitment.
- *Design:* Write policies, procedures, identify/write standards.
- *Pilot:* Train participants and try out the procedures in a few areas. Update the procedures as necessary.
- *Implement:* Follow the procedures on all projects.

The pilot life-cycle phases are somewhat similar to those of process improvement. They are the:

- Set Up Phase
- Design Phase
- Conduct Phase
- Evaluate Phase
- Implement Phase

Steps in the pilot process are to:

- Select pilot projects.
- Document success criteria and measurement techniques.
- Orient and train project members in process improvement concepts.
- Orient pilot participants in the purpose, strategy, and plan for the pilot.
- Orient and train members in procedures that will be piloted.
- Orient and train members in their roles and responsibilities.
- Conduct the pilots.
- Monitor and measure results.
- Provide lessons learned.
- Refine the procedures and processes based on pilot results.
- Plan for roll-out.
- Update the projects' processes and organizational processes, as needed.
- Train/re-train, re-plan, re-pilot, as needed.

Checklist for Planning and Conducting Pilots

Set Up:

1. Define the problem that is to be addressed.
2. Generate alternatives, if possible.
3. If alternatives exist, examine alternative solutions to the problem for technical feasibility and cost/benefit.
4. Choose at least one alternative solution for piloting.
5. Identify the key points to be measured.
6. Define the methods and techniques that will be used to draw conclusions about pilot results (e.g., committee of senior managers, EPG, survey of the pilot project members, definition of success/failure, supporting data to be collected), including technical, operational, and financial capability.

Design:

7. Document the processes and procedures to be used on the pilot.
8. Define the pilot evaluation criteria. Include quality factors.
9. Define the methods, processes, roles, personnel, timing, report formats, and data collection activities needed to perform the evaluation.
10. Identify all affected parties whose input and ideas are beneficial to the pilot. Do not include "squeaky wheels" at this point.
11. Define ways of gathering and tracking cost and benefit data.
12. Derive a schedule and plan for the pilot. Include milestones for the pilot and associated deliverables.

Conduct:

13. Conduct the pilot according to the plan generated during the Design phase:
    - Execute the processes.
    - Contact all affected parties.
    - Collect the necessary data.
    - Achieve the milestones and deliverables.
14. If the design could not be followed, log and explain all deviations.
15. Record all issues that occurred during the conduct of the pilot, important thoughts about those issues, and how the issues were resolved.
16. Save all data and intermediate and final results for evaluation and lessons learned.

Evaluate:

17. Conduct the evaluation according to the Plan.
18. Use the evaluation methods and techniques:
    - Investigate results.
    - Analyze data.
    - Achieve the milestones and deliverables.
19. If the evaluation plan could not be followed, log and explain all deviations.
20. Record all issues encountered during the evaluation, important thoughts about those issues, and how the issue was resolved.
21. Save all data and intermediate and final results for lessons learned.
22. Draw conclusions about the workability and effectiveness of the approach that was the subject of the pilot, based on pilot results.
23. Conduct a cost-benefit analysis as part of the final decision to implement the results of this pilot.
24. Gather all of the lessons learned, refine them, and document them for future use and applicability on other pilots.
25. Make recommendations regarding future use.
26. Analyze the pilot itself, in regard to how it was conducted and for ways of improving future pilots.

Implement:

27. Base implementation decisions on pilot evaluation results and recommendations, and not on personal or political biases.
28. Base implementation decisions on any ongoing alternatives analyses, comparing pilot findings with information from updated alternatives.
29. Base implementation decisions on any other pilots that may occur in the organization.
30. Continue to gather data to determine the effectiveness of the pilot results when implemented in the organization (costs-benefits, schedule improvement, quality improvement, etc.).
31. Continue to collect, document, and analyze lessons learned.

Checklist for Evaluating the Effectiveness of the Pilot

Set Up

1. Was this the first-ever attempt to do a pilot? (Either the first attempt within the organization, or the first attempt planned and administered by this group of people.)

2. Was this the first attempt to pilot this particular issue/process/approach?
3. Was the pilot project of small enough scope that its results could be meaningful for future implementation decisions?
4. Have personal or political biases (visions of success or failure of the pilot) been injected into the pilot process or the pilot plan?
5. Have costs and benefits been addressed in planning?
6. Have alternative approaches been taken into consideration?
7. Has planning for re-piloting been addressed?

Design

8. Was an evaluation plan prepared?
9. Did the plan contain evaluation and measurement criteria?
10. Were key factors for evaluation identified?
11. Were all affected parties identified?
12. Were plans made to consider and include (as appropriate) the opinions and reactions of the affected parties pertaining to the results of the pilot?
13. Was provision made for collecting and analyzing cost-benefit information?
14. Was there an analysis identifying appropriate cost-benefit information?

Conduct

15. Was the primary focus of the pilot on evaluating the process/issue/approach addressed in the pilot, or was the motivation for the pilot biased in any way?
16. Were pilot results documented?
17. Were lessons learned recorded?
18. Is associated documentation adequate?
19. Were feedback mechanisms implemented to foster proper evaluation of the pilot?
20. Were all the affected parties' constituencies approached for their reactions?
21. Were these reactions documented and analyzed?
22. Was cost-benefit information collected and analyzed?

Evaluation

23. Was there a documented evaluation phase?
24. Was there a serious attempt to evaluate the pilot results?
25. Were the reactions of affected parties collected and analyzed?
26. Were recommendations resulting from the pilot based on lessons learned and not on personal/political biases?
27. Was there a formal decision-making process regarding the future use of the pilots in the organization?
28. Was there a formal decision-making process regarding the future use of the results of this pilot in the organization?
29. Were costs and benefits compared?
30. To what extent did the pilot work/not work?
31. Were cost and benefit data included as part of the decision-making process?
32. If the pilot did not work, are there any potentially beneficial results that can be drawn from this pilot?
33. Was there a plan for evaluation, and was it followed?
34. Were evaluation and measurement criteria identified?
35. Was a methodology or tracking system for data collection defined?
36. Were the tasks involved in that methodology carefully defined?
37. Were evaluation conclusions clearly stated and well supported?
38. Is sufficient evidence presented to support the conclusions drawn?
39. How confident are you in *all* of the results of the pilot?
40. Do we need to re-pilot?

Implement

41. Were evaluation results used in a decision to implement?
42. Were alternatives to the pilot concept explored during planning for implementation?
43. In the decision making regarding implementation, are costs and benefits addressed?
44. Is there a discussion in the decision making of potential savings, or of monetary impact of implementation/nonimplementation?
45. In the decision-making process, were costs and benefits, and other insights, gained during the conduct of the pilot, as well as possible alternatives, addressed?
46. Was implementation based on the original pilot methodology, or modifications to it?
47. Were cost-benefit and schedule considerations adjusted due to any such modifications?

48. Were accurate cost and benefit data kept during implementation and use?
49. Was a comparison made between estimated versus actual costs, benefits, schedule improvement, and quality?
50. What modifications to the product or process must be made to make this work?
51. What lessons learned can we draw?
52. Were the pilot tests true pilot efforts? (A true pilot will follow the phases of the pilot life cycle, especially concerning Set Up and Planning.)
53. Are the pilots concerned only with technical feasibility, or do they also examine the cost and schedule effectiveness of the proposed and alternate solutions? What, if any, cost and benefit measures were used?
54. Did pilot monitoring and control procedures follow the organization's standards and processes?
55, Did formal, documented evaluation processes exist for pilots? If so, did they yield valid results?
56. For pilots that led to system or process implementation, were the claimed/projected benefits actually realized?

Appendix O

List of Metrics

This appendix contains a list of metrics that your organization can consider using. For more information, review Chapter 17.

Level 2

Requirements Management

1. Requirements volatility (percentage of requirements changes)
2. Number of requirements by type or status (defined, reviewed, approved, and implemented)
3. Cumulative number of changes to the allocated requirements, including total number of changes proposed, open, approved, and incorporated into the system baseline
4. Number of changes requests per month, compared to the original number of requirements for the project
5. Number of time spent, effort spent, cost of implementing change requests
6. Number and size of change requests after the Requirements phase is finished
7. Cost of implementing a change request
8. Number of change requests versus the total number of change requests during the life of the project
9. Number of change requests accepted but not implemented
10. Number of requirements (changes and additions to the baseline)

Project Planning

11. Completion of milestones for the project planning activities compared to the plan (estimates versus actuals)
12. Work completed, effort expended, and funds expended in the project planning activities compared to the plan
13. Number of revisions to the project plans
14. Cost, schedule, and effort variance per plan revision
15. Re-planning effort due to change requests
16. Effort expended over time to manage the project compared to the plan
17. Frequency, causes, and magnitude of the re-planning effort

Project Monitoring and Control

18. Effort and other resources expended in performing monitoring and oversight activities
19. Change activity for the project plan, which includes changes to size estimates of the work products, cost estimates, resource estimates, and schedule
20. Number of open and closed corrective actions or action items
21. Project milestone dates (planned versus actual)
22. Number of project milestone dates made on time
23. Number and types of reviews performed
24. Schedule, budget, and size variance between planned versus actual reviews
25. Comparison of actuals versus estimates for all planning and tracking items

Measurement and Analysis

26. Number of projects using progress and performance measures
27. Number of measurement objectives addressed

Supplier Agreement Management

28. Cost of the COTS (commercial off-the-shelf) products
29. Cost and effort to incorporate the COTS products into the project
30. Number of changes made to the supplier requirements
31. Cost and schedule variance per supplier agreement

32. Costs of the activities for managing the contract compared to the plan
33. Actual delivery dates for contracted products compared to the plan
34. Actual dates of prime contractor deliveries to the subcontractor compared to the plan
35. Number of on-time deliveries from the vendor, compared with the contract
36. Number and severity of errors found after delivery
37. Number of exceptions to the contract to ensure schedule adherence
38. Number of quality audits compared to the plan
39. Number of senior management reviews to ensure adherence to budget and schedule versus the plan
40. Number of contract violations by supplier or vendor

Process and Product Quality Assurance (QA)

41. Completions of milestones for the QA activities compared to the plan
42. Work completed, effort expended in the QA activities compared to the plan
43. Numbers of product audits and activity reviews compared to the plan
44. Number of process audits and activities versus those planned
45. Number of defects per release or build
46. Amount of time/effort spent in rework
47. Amount of QA time/effort spent in each phase of the life cycle
48. Number of reviews and audits versus number of defects found
49. Total number of defects found in internal reviews and testing versus those found by the customer or end user after delivery
50. Number of defects found in each phase of the life cycle
51. Number of defects injected during each phase of the life cycle
52. Number of noncompliances written versus number resolved
53. Number of noncompliances elevated to senior management
54. Complexity of module or component (McCabe, McClure, and Halstead metrics)

Configuration Management (CM)

55. Number of change requests or change board requests processed per unit of time
56. Completions of milestones for the CM activities compared to the plan

57. Work completed, effort expended, and funds expended in the CM activities
58. Number of changes to configuration items
59. Number of configuration audits conducted
60. Number of fixes returned as "Not Yet Fixed"
61. Number of fixes returned as "Could Not Reproduce Error"
62. Number of violations of CM procedures (noncompliance found in audits)
63. Number of outstanding problem reports versus rate of repair
64. Number of times changes are overwritten by someone else (or number of times people have the wrong initial version or baseline)
65. Number of engineering change proposals proposed, approved, rejected, implemented
66. Number of changes by category to code source, and to supporting documentation
67. Number of changes by category, type, and severity
68. Source lines of code stored in libraries placed under configuration control

Level 3

Requirements Development

69. Cost, schedule, and effort expended for rework
70. Defect density of requirements specifications
71. Number of requirements approved for build (versus the total number of requirements)
72. Actual number of requirements documented (versus the total number of estimated requirements)
73. Staff hours (total and by Requirements Development activity)
74. Requirements status (percentage of defined specifications out of the total approved and proposed; number of requirements defined)
75. Estimates of total requirements, total requirements definition effort, requirements analysis effort, and schedule
76. Number and type of requirements changes

Technical Solution

77. Cost, schedule, and effort expended for rework
78. Number of requirements addressed in the product or product-component design

79. Size and complexity of the product, product components, interfaces, and documentation
80. Defect density of technical solutions work products (number of defects per page)
81. Number of requirements by status or type throughout the life of the project (e.g., number defined, approved, documented, implemented, tested, and signed-off by phase)
82. Problem reports by severity and length of time they are open
83. Number of requirements changed during implementation and test
84. Effort to analyze proposed changes for each proposed change and cumulative totals
85. Number of changes incorporated into the baseline by category (e.g., interface, security, system configuration, performance, and usability)
86. Size and cost to implement and test incorporated changes, including initial estimate and actual size and cost
87. Estimates and actuals of system size, reuse, effort, and schedule
88. The total estimated and actual staff hours needed to develop the system by job category and activity
89. Estimated dates and actuals for the start and end of each phase of the life cycle
90. Number of diagrams completed versus the estimated total diagrams
91. Number of design modules/units proposed
92. Number of design modules/units delivered
93. Estimates and actuals of total lines of code — new, modified, and reused
94. Estimates and actuals of total design and code modules and units
95. Estimates and actuals for total CPU hours used to date
96. The number of units coded and tested versus the number planned
97. Errors by category, phase discovered, phase injected, type, and severity
98. Estimates of total units, total effort, and schedule
99. System tests planned, executed, passed, failed
100. Test discrepancies reported, resolved, not resolved
101. Source code growth by percentage of planned versus actual

Product Integration

102. Product-component integration profile (e.g., product-component assemblies planned and performed, and number of exceptions found).

103. Integration evaluation problem report trends (e.g., number written and number closed)
104. Integration evaluation problem report aging (i.e., how long each problem report has been opened)

Verification

105. Verification profile (e.g., the number of verifications planned and performed, and the defects found; perhaps categorized by verification method or type)
106. Number of defects detected by defect category
107. Verification problem report trends (e.g., number written and number closed)
108. Verification problem report status (i.e., how long each problem report has been open)
109. Number of peer reviews performed compared to the plan
110. Overall effort expended on peer reviews compared to the plan
111. Number of work products reviewed compared to the plan

Validation

112. Number of validation activities completed (planned versus actual)
113. Validation problem reports trends (e.g., number written and number closed)
114. Validation problem report aging (i.e., how long each problem report has been open)

Organizational Process Focus

115. Number of process improvement proposals submitted, accepted, or implemented
116. CMMI maturity level or capability level
117. Work completed, effort expended, and funds expended in the organization's activities for process assessment, development, and improvement compared to the plans for these activities
118. Results of each process assessment, compared to the results and recommendations of previous assessments

Organizational Process Definition

119. Percentage of projects using the process architectures and process elements of the organization's set of standard processes
120. Defect density of each process element of the organization's set of standard processes
121. Number of on schedule milestones for process development and maintenance
122. Costs for the process definition activities

Organizational Training

123. Number of training courses delivered (e.g., planned versus actual)
124. Post-training evaluation ratings
125. Training program quality surveys
126. Actual attendance at each training course compared to the projected attendance
127. Progress in improving training courses compared to the organization's and projects' training plans
128. Number of training waivers approved over time

Integrated Project Management for IPPD

129. Number of changes to the project's defined process
130. Effort to tailor the organization's set of standard processes
131. Interface coordination issue trends (e.g., number identified and number closed)

Risk Management

132. Number of risks identified, managed, tracked, and controlled
133. Risk exposure and changes to the risk exposure for each assessed risk, and as a summary percentage of management reserve
134. Change activity for the risk mitigation plans (e.g., processes, schedules, funding)
135. Number of occurrences of unanticipated risks
136. Risk categorization volatility

137. Estimated versus actual risk mitigation effort
138. Estimated versus actual risk impact
139. The amount of effort and time spent on risk management activities versus the number of actual risks
140. The cost of risk management versus the cost of actual risks
141. For each identified risk, the realized adverse impact compared to the estimated impact

Integrated Teaming

142. Performance according to plans, commitments, and procedures for the integrated team, and deviations from expectations
143. Number of times team objectives were not achieved
144. Actual effort and other resources expended by one group to support another group or groups, and vice versa
145. Actual completion of specific tasks and milestones by one group to support the activities of other groups, and vice versa

Integrated Supplier Management

146. Effort expended to manage the evaluation of sources and selection of suppliers
147. Number of changes to the requirements in the supplier agreement
148. Number of documented commitments between the project and the supplier
149. Interface coordination issue trends (e.g., number identified and number closed)
150. Number of defects detected in supplied products (during integration and after delivery)

Decision Analysis and Resolution

151. Cost-to-benefit ratio of using formal evaluation processes

Organizational Environment for Integration

152. Parameters for key operating characteristics of the work environment

Level 4

Organizational Process Performance

153. Trends in the organization's process performance with respect to changes in work products and task attributes (e.g., size growth, effort, schedule, and quality)

Quantitative Project Management

154. Time between failures
155. Critical resource utilization
156. Number and severity of defects in the released product
157. Number and severity of customer complaints concerning the provided service
158. Number of defects removed by product verification activities (perhaps by type of verification, such as peer reviews and testing)
159. Defect escape rates
160. Number and density of defects by severity found during the first year following product delivery or start of service
161. Cycle time
162. Amount of rework time
163. Requirements volatility (i.e., number of requirements changes per phase)
164. Ratios of estimated to measured values of the planning parameters (e.g., size, cost, and schedule)
165. Coverage and efficiency of peer reviews (i.e., number/amount of products reviewed compared to total, number of defects found per hour)
166. Test coverage and efficiency (i.e., number/amount of products tested compared to total, number of defects found per hour)
167. Effectiveness of training (i.e., percent of planned training completed and test scores)
168. Reliability (i.e., mean time-to-failure usually measured during integration and systems test)
169. Percentage of the total defects inserted or found in the different phases of the project life cycle
170. Percentage of the total effort expended in the different phases of the project life cycle

171. Profile of subprocesses under statistical management (i.e., number planned to be under statistical management, number currently being statistically managed, and number that are statistically stable)
172. Number of special causes of variation identified
173. The cost over time for the quantitative process management activities compared to the plan
174. The accomplishment of schedule milestones for quantitative process management activities compared to the approved plan (i.e., establishing the process measurements to be used on the project, determining how the process data will be collected, and collecting the process data)
175. The cost of poor quality (e.g., amount of rework, re-reviews, and re-testing)
176. The costs for achieving quality goals (e.g., amount of initial reviews, audits, and testing)

Level 5

Organizational Innovation and Deployment

177. Change in quality after improvements (e.g., number of reduced defects)
178. Change in process performance after improvements (e.g., change in baselines)
179. The overall technology change activity, including number, type, and size of changes
180. The effect of implementing the technology change compared to the goals (i.e., actual cost saving to projected)
181. The number of process improvement proposals submitted and implemented for each process area
182. The number of process improvement proposals submitted by each project, group, and department
183. The number and types of awards and recognitions received by each of the projects, groups, and departments
184. The response time for handling process improvement proposals
185. Number of process improvement proposals accepted per reporting period
186. The overall change activity including number, type, and size of changes
187. The effect of implementing each process improvement compared to its defined goals

188. Overall performance of the organization's and project's processes, including effectiveness, quality, and productivity compared to their defined goals
189. Overall productivity and quality trends for each project
190. Process measurements that relate to the indicators of the customer's satisfaction (e.g., survey results, number of customer complains, and number of customer compliments)

Causal Analysis and Resolution

191. Defect data (problem reports, defects reported by the customer, defects reported by the user, defects found in peer reviews, defects found in testing, process capability problems, time and cost for identifying the defect and fixing it, estimated cost of not fixing the problem)
192. Number of root causes removed
193. Change in quality or process performance per instance of the causal analysis and resolution process (e.g., number of defects and change in baseline)
194. The costs of defect prevention activities (i.e., holding causal analysis meetings and implementing action items), cumulatively
195. The time and cost for identifying the defects and correcting them compared to the estimated cost of not correcting the defects
196. Profiles measuring the number of action items proposed, open, and completed
197. The number of defects injected in each stage, cumulatively, and over-releases of similar products
198. The number of defects

Appendix P

Measurement Plan Outline

This appendix contains an outline to use when generating a Measurement Plan. For more information, review Chapter 17.

    I. Introduction (Purpose, Scope)
   II. Organizational and Project Issues
  III. Overall Measurement Approach
  IV. Approach for Project Management Metrics
   V. Approach for Technical Metrics
  VI. Approach for Introducing Metrics into the Organization
 VII. How Metrics Will Be Collected and Used
VIII. Roles and Responsibilities
  IX. Communication/Feedback Plan
   X. List of Measurements

Appendix Q

References and Further Reading

Bate, R. et al., *A Systems Engineering Capability Maturity Model, Version 1.1,* Handbook SECMM-95–01, Pittsburgh, PA, Software Engineering Institute, Carnegie Mellon University, 1995.

Dunaway, D. and Masters, S., *CMM-Based Appraisal for Internal Process Improvement (CBA IPI): Method Description (CMU/SEI-96-TR-007),* Software Engineering Institute, Carnegie Mellon University, Pittsburgh, PA, April 1996; www.sei.cmu.edu/publications/documents/96.reports/96.tr.007.html.

Electronic Industries Alliance, *Systems Engineering Capability Model (EIA/IS-731),* Washington, D.C., 1998; http://geia.org/sstc/G47/731dwnld.htm.

Ferguson, J., Cooper, J., Falat, M., Fisher, M., Guido, A., Marciniak, J., Matejceck, J., and Webster, R., *Software Acquisition Capability Maturity Model Version 1.02 (CMU/SEI-96-TR-020),* Software Engineering Institute, Carnegie Mellon University, Pittsburgh, PA, December 1996; www.sei.cmu.edu/publications/documents/96.reports/96.tr.020.html.

Florac, W. and Carleton, A., *Measuring the Software Process,* Addison-Wesley, Reading, MA, 1999.

Johnson, K. and Dindo, J., *Expanding the Focus of Software Process Improvement to Include Systems Engineering,* Software Technology Support Center, Hill Air Force Base, Utah, Crosstalk, October 1998.

Kan, S., *Metrics and Models in Software Quality Engineering,* Addison-Wesley, Reading, MA, 1995.

Konrad, M. and Shrum, S., *Architectural and Functional Comparison of the CMMI Model Representation,* Software Engineering Institute, Carnegie Mellon University, Pittsburgh, PA, *(Draft),* December 1999.

Kulpa, M., *Ten Things Your Mother Never Told You About the Capability Maturity Model,* Crosstalk, Software Technology Support Center, Hill Air Force Base, Utah, September 1998.

McGarry, J., Card, D., Jones, C., Layman, B., Clark, E., Dean, J., and Hall, F., *Practical Software Measurement,* Addison-Wesley, Reading, MA, 2002.

Paulk, M.C., Curtis, B., Chrissis, M.B., and Weber, C.V., *Capability Maturity Model: Guidelines for Improving the Software Process,* Addison-Wesley, Reading, MA, 1994.

Software Engineering Institute, *Appraisal Requirements for CMMI®, Version 1.1 (ARC, V1.1),* CMU/SEI-2001-TR-034, Carnegie Mellon University, Pittsburgh, PA, December 2001.

Software Engineering Institute, *Capability Maturity Model – Integration (CMMI) for Systems Engineering (SE)/Software Engineering (SW)/Integrated Product and Process Development (IPPD), Version 1.1,* Carnegie Mellon University, Pittsburgh, PA, March 2002.

Software Engineering Institute, *Capability Maturity Model (CMM) for Software, Version 1.1,* Carnegie Mellon University, Pittsburgh, PA, 1994.

Software Engineering Institute, *IDEAL^sm: A Users Guide to Software Process Improvement,* CMU/SEI-96-HB-001, Carnegie Mellon University, Pittsburgh, PA, February 1996.

Software Engineering Institute, *Software Acquisition Capability Maturity Model (SA-CMM) Version 1.02* (CMU/SEI-99-TR-002, ESC-TR-99–002), Software Engineering Institute, Carnegie Mellon University, Pittsburgh, PA, April 1999; www.sei.cmu.edu/publications/documents/99.reports/99tr002/99tr002abstract.html.

Software Engineering Institute, *Software Capability Evaluation V3.0 Implementation Guide for Supplier Selection Version 3.0* (CMU/SEI-95-TR-012, ESC-TR-95–012), Carnegie Mellon University, Pittsburgh, PA, April 1996.

Software Engineering Institute, *Software CMM, Version 2 (Draft C),* Oct. 22, 1997, Carnegie Mellon University, Pittsburgh, PA; www.sei.cmu.edu/activities/cmm/draft-c/c.html.

Software Engineering Institute, *Standard CMMI® Appraisal Method for Process Improvement (SCAMPI^m), Version 1.1: Method Definition Document,* CMU/SEI-2001-HB-001, Carnegie Mellon University, Pittsburgh PA, December 2001.

Software Engineering Institute, *The Systems Engineering Capability Maturity Model, Version 1.1,* Carnegie Mellon University, Pittsburgh, PA, November 1995.

Webpages:

www.agiledigm.com AgileDigm Home Page
www.sei.cmu.edu Software Engineering Institute
www.stsc.af.mil/crosstalk *Crosstalk Magazine*
www.crcpress.com CRC Press

Index